T0345184

EMERGING METHODS, TECHNOLOGIES, AND PROCESS MANAGEMENT IN SOFTWARE ENGINEERING

EMERGING METHODS, TECHNOLOGIES, AND PROCESS MANAGEMENT IN SOFTWARE ENGINEERING

EDITED BY

Andrea De Lucia
Filomena Ferrucci
Genny Tortora
Maurizio Tucci

A JOHN WILEY & SONS, INC., PUBLICATION

Published by John Wiley & Sons, Inc., Hoboken, New Jersey.
Published simultaneously in Canada.

For general information on our other products and services, please contact our Customer Care Department within the United States at (877) 762-2974, outside the United States at (317) 572-3993 or fax (317) 572-4002.

Wiley also publishes its books in a variety of electronic formats. Some content that appears in print, however, may not be available in electronic format.

Library of Congress Cataloging-in-Publication Data

Emerging methods, technologies and process management in software engineering / edited by Andrea De Lucia ... [et al.].
     p. cm.
  Includes index.
  ISBN 978-0-470-08571-4 (cloth)
1. Software engineering—Management. I. De Lucia, Andrea.
  QA76.758.E49 2008
  005.1068′4—dc22

                                          2007032135

Printed in the United States of America
10 9 8 7 6 5 4 3 2 1

CONTENTS

PREFACE

*"Employ your time in improving yourself by
other men's writings, so that you shall gain
easily what others have labored hard for."*

—Socrates

Software dramatically impacts our everyday lives and continuously pervades our modern society. Indeed, incessant innovations in information and communication technologies provide new opportunities and quickly increase the spectrum of possible applications. These innovations pose new technical and practical challenges to software engineers who have to identify solutions to better exploit new technologies and develop new kinds of software applications. At the same time, software engineers need to maintain and evolve existing software systems to make them compliant with requirement changes and to exploit fully the opportunities provided by new technologies. As a result of software evolution, the size and complexity of software systems have been growing significantly, thus making software development and maintenance more and more challenging and requiring enhanced means.

Software engineering is then a very dynamic discipline that must continuously evolve by searching for new methods, tools, and methodologies to make software development and maintenance more reliable and efficient. Critical trade-offs related to cost, quality, and flexibility must be taken into account. For that reason, today software engineering is one of the most exciting, stimulating, and profitable research areas with significant practical impacts on software industry.

This book addresses some of the latest findings in the field of software engineering. Its chapters originate from tutorial lectures given by internationally recognized research leaders at the first three sessions of the International Summer School on Software Engineering, organized at the University of Salerno, Italy.

The book is not meant to cover all software engineering topics but rather to present a good range of current research in software engineering dealing with some very relevant and emerging topics for the scientific community. The book is intended for graduate and postgraduate students who want to approach the field as well as academic and industrial researchers working in different areas of software engineering.

This volume is organized in four parts: Software Architectures, Emerging Methods, Technologies for Software Evolution, and Process Management.

Software architecture design is a crucial activity for the development of software systems. It focuses on establishing the overall structure of a software system by identifying major system components and their communications. It provides useful abstractions that help to master system complexity. In recent years, software architectures have been evolving from being predefined, monolithic, and centralized to being increasingly decentralized, distributed, and dynamically composed federations of components. Chapter 1 surveys this evolution from the interesting perspective of evolution of software composition mechanisms, i.e., the way the whole system is constructed by binding components together. The chapter shows how binding mechanisms have been evolving from static to highly dynamic schemes based on discovery, negotiation, and optimization. The chapter includes a short list of important challenges that should be part of the future agenda of software engineering research.

Chapter 2 focuses on software product families that have achieved broad adoption in the software and embedded systems industry. Many companies do not develop software from scratch but rather focus on the commonalities between different products and capture those in a product-line architecture and an associated set of reusable assets. This chapter addresses several challenges posed by the increasing spectrum of successful product lines and introduces new concepts for a compositional approach to software product lines.

Chapter 3 focuses on design patterns or template solutions that developers have refined over time to solve a range of recurring design problems, and addresses the difficult-to-understand object-oriented pattern-based development by offering a practical presentation through a case study. A sequence of increasingly complex non-functional requirements for an interactive game is provided, and design patterns such as Observer, Adapter, Strategy, and Abstract Factory are introduced to provide the solution to these requirements.

Part II covers some emerging methods such as software agents, service-oriented computing, testing of object-oriented systems, formal methods, and Web development. Chapter 4 discusses the impact of Agent Oriented Software Engineering (AOSE) in service-oriented computing. An agent system is a way of thinking about systems composed of active entities, agents, and their collective behavior. The agent metaphor is especially effective for building software for complex networked systems, where no global control is possible. In particular, the authors consider some key ideas of the Service-Oriented Architecture (SOA) in the context of the agents technologies for the coordination and composition of Web and Grid services.

Chapter 5 addresses the software quality issue and focuses on emerging methods for testing object-oriented systems. Testing is a crucial activity to ensure adequate software dependability. Although the object-oriented paradigm allows avoidance of some problems typical of procedural development, it introduces new problems that classic testing methods are not able to address. In this chapter, the authors present the most recent research solutions proposed to test object-oriented systems which cope with problems deriving from some features of object-oriented systems such as state-dependent behavior, encapsulation, inheritance, and polymorphism.

Chapter 6 reports on the EU-funded project DEGAS (Design Environments for Global Applications) that aims to combine the use of UML for design of global applications with formal methods for their analysis and verification. These emerging systems consist of computing devices connected through computer networks. Statically analyzing and verifying security of the communication protocols used in such distributed systems is an important issue. The project exploits an approach based on process calculi to formally specify and verify security behavioral models of systems which complements analyses of structural aspects typically carried out on UML models. The chapter highlights some relevant aspects of UML currently representing the standard visual notation for specifying, constructing, and documenting the artifacts of a software system. A framework is presented that supports the designer in specifying in the UML models the protocols which are to be analyzed for authentication breaches.

Chapter 7 reviews the current and future trends in Web application development and examines them from a software engineering point of view. The Web definitely is one of the most important innovations of the last decade which deeply impacts our lives. The explosive advances in information and communication technologies have determined (and at the same time have been determined by) the rapid evolution of the Web. Just one decade has been enough to transform the Web from a repository of pages used mainly for accessing static information to a powerful platform for application development and deployment. Indeed, new Web technologies, languages, and methodologies make it possible to create dynamic applications that provide a new model of cooperation and collaboration among large numbers of users. Chapter 7 focuses in particular on advances in browser technology, Web server and network infrastructures, and application level and software engineering trends.

Part III covers technologies for software evolution. The dynamic nature of software is one of its most significant characteristics but also one of the most important sources of its complexity. Indeed, software needs to continuously evolve to meet the ever-changing requirements of the real world and to incorporate novel technologies. Chapter 8 addresses the issues introduced by service-oriented architectures that represent the last major technology paradigm change determining a radical break with previous technologies. This chapter outlines different strategies for supplying Web services to a service-oriented architecture and focuses on how to recover Web services from existing applications. Several research issues that deserve to be investigated in this context highlight this chapter.

Chapter 9 addresses the problem of analyzing the evolution of software systems to gain information about the reasons and effects of particular changes and to get a clear picture about the problems concerning specific features. This is a critical issue for dealing with increasing complexity and architectural deterioration and requires effective techniques to convey the relevant information present in a huge amount of data. The chapter presents some visualization techniques that enable the analysis of different evolutionary aspects of software systems.

Part IV focuses on process management, another key subject in software engineering. Indeed, it is widely recognized that the quality of a software system is heavily influenced by the quality of the process used to develop and maintain it. Process management is the use of skills, knowledge, tools, and techniques to define, measure, control, and improve processes to realize high quality software systems in a cost-effective way. In this context, empirical investigations can have an important role in transferring software engineering research results to industrial software processes and to transform experience in knowledge. Chapter 10 introduces essential concepts that are available in literature, then describes the steps that scientific research carries out starting from observation to theory and how empirical investigations support development processes in software engineering.

Chapter 11 closes the book by presenting the foundations of Agile Methods, a family of development techniques introduced in the 1990s and designed to address some problems of modern software development, such as delivering products on time, on budget, and with high quality and customer satisfaction, including the most popular eXtreme Programming (XP) introduced by Kent Beck. For specific contexts and specific problems, these methods represent a suitable alternative to the traditional software development approaches, supporting the realization of the right product without wasting time and effort. The authors analyse the key concepts of agile development and difficulties for their effective implementation, focusing in particular on XP.

We express our gratitude to the many people who supported the publication of this volume with their time and energy. First of all, we thank all the authors for their valuable contribution. We also gratefully acknowledge the Scientific Committee Members for their work and for promoting the International School on Software Engineering. Thanks are due to our department (Dipartimento di Matematica e Informatica, Università di Salerno) for the assistance we received day after day. We are also grateful to Fausto Fasano, Rocco Oliveto, Sergio Di Martino, Rita Francense, Giuseppe Scanniello, Monica Sebillo, Vincenzo Deufemia, Carmine Gravino, and Michele Risi who were of great help in organizing the different editions of the school. Finally, we want to thank Wiley for providing us the opportunity to publish this volume and all the staff involved, in particular Assistant Editor Cassie Craig and Production Editors Lisa Van Horn of Wiley and Paul Beaney and Pravina Patel of Techset Composition.

We hope you enjoy reading the book and find it relevant and useful for your work. We also wish that the tackled topics will encourage your research in software engineering and your participation in the International School on Software Engineering.

ANDREA DE LUCIA
FILOMENA FERRUCCI
GENNY TORTORA
MAURIZIO TUCCI

December 2007

PART I

SOFTWARE ARCHITECTURES

1

EVOLUTION OF SOFTWARE COMPOSITION MECHANISMS: A SURVEY

Carlo Ghezzi and Filippo Pacifici

1.1. INTRODUCTION

In engineering, developing a system always implies designing its structure, by providing a proper decomposition into separate parts and relationships among them. This approach allows engineers to address the complexity of a system by applying a divide-and-conquer approach—that is, by recursively focusing on limited subsystems and on the interaction between them.

In this setting, it is possible to identify two phases: the definition of the behavior of single parts and the composition of parts. Composition is the way the whole system is constructed by binding components together. In this phase, engineers focus on how the relations among parts are established, rather than on the specific internal structure or behavior of the components.

Software systems evolved from small and monolithic systems to increasingly large and distributed systems. Accordingly, composition gained greater importance because soon software engineers realized that software development could not be considered as a one-person, monolithic task. Instead, software systems had to be described as complex structures, obtained through careful application of specific composition mechanisms.

Software composition can be analyzed along two directions: process and product architecture. From a process viewpoint, composition has to do with the way software

Emerging Methods, Technologies, and Process Management in Software Engineering. Edited by De Lucia, Ferrucci, Tortora, and Tucci
Copyright © 2008 John Wiley & Sons, Inc.

development is structured in terms of work units and organizations. From a product architecture viewpoint, it refers to the way products are structured in terms of components and their connections.

This chapter focuses on the evolution of software composition principles and mechanisms over the past decades. The evolution has been consistently in the direction of increasing flexibility: from static to dynamic and from centralized to decentralized software compositions. For example, at the code level, there has been an evolution from monolithic program structures to functional and then object-oriented program decompositions. At a more abstract and higher level, software architectures evolved from tightly coupled and structured composites, as in the case of multi-tier architectures, to decentralized, peer-to-peer composites. In a similar way, software processes evolved from fixed, sequential, and monolithic to agile, iterative, and decentralized workflows (9).

This chapter surveys several concepts from software engineering and puts them in a historical perspective. It can be considered as a tutorial on software composition.

This chapter is organized as follows. Section 1.2 provides some basic foundational concepts for software composition. Sections 1.3 and 1.4 set the stage by discussing when the problem of software composition originated and how it was initially tackled. Section 1.5 focuses on some milestone contributions to concepts, methods, and techniques supporting design of evolvable software. Section 1.6 is about the current stage. It argues that our main challenge is to write evolvable software that lives in an open world. It identifies where the main challenges are and outlines some possible research directions.

1.2. BASIC CONCEPTS

The concept of *binding* (21) is a recurring key to understanding software composition at the code and architecture level. Binding is the establishment of a relationship among elements that form a *structure*. *Binding time* is the time at which such a relationship is established. For example, these concepts may be used to describe the semantic properties of programming languages, which may differ in the policy adopted to bind variables to their type, subclasses to their superclasses, function invocations to function definitions, or executable code to virtual machines. At an architectural level, a server may be bound to several clients. Typical binding times are: *design time, translation time, deployment time*, and *run time*. A design-time binding is, for example, an association that links a class in a UML class diagram to its parent class. A translation-time binding is established when the source description is processed.[1] For example, there are languages that bind variables to their type and function calls to function definitions at translation time. Object-oriented languages perform the binding at run time. Likewise, there are cases where the binding between a certain executable program unit and the node of distributed system on which it is

---

[1]We use this term instead of the most common, but more restricted, term "compile-time" to also include other languages processing aspects like link/load and preprocessing.

executed is set at deployment time; in other cases, it is set at run time to support system reconfiguration.

Another important orthogonal concept is *binding stability*. A binding is *static* if it cannot vary after being established; otherwise, it is *dynamic*. In most cases, design-time, translation-time, and deployment-time bindings are static and run-time bindings are dynamic, although there are exceptions. The key difference is thus between pre-run-time binding and run-time binding: Run-time binding adds much flexibility to the system with respect to pre-run-time binding because of the change policies it can be based upon. In the case of dynamic binding, one may further distinguish between *explicit* and *automatic* binding. In the former case, for example, the user asks the system to change a binding and specifies the new component that has to be bound, while in the second case the system has some autonomy in deciding when the binding has to be changed and is provided with mechanisms to find the new element to be bound. In practice, there is a spectrum of possible solutions that stay in between fully dynamic run-time binding and static pre-run-time binding.

These concepts may also be applied at process level, to describe or specify how software development is organized. For example, one may bind people to specific roles (such as *tester*) in an almost static way, or this can change as process development proceeds. Similarly, a development phase (such as *detail design* may be required to be completed before the next phase (*coding*) can be started. In this case, the binding between a phase and the next is established through a predefined, sequential control flow. Alternatively, one may organize the two phases as finer-grain concurrent steps.

Binding characterization is useful to understand the evolution of the software, both in the way engineers develop software and in the way they structure the architecture of applications. This evolution brought software systems from static, centralized, and monolithic structures, where bindings were defined at design time and frozen during the whole system life cycle, to modular, dynamic, and decentralized designs and design process, where bindings define loosely coupled structures, can change without stopping the system, and can cross interorganizational borders.

It is worthwhile to try to identify the ultimate sources and driving forces of this evolution. Advances in software technology are of course an endogenous force. Indeed, modern languages and design methods provide support for dynamic bindings and continuous change. However, the demand for dynamism and evolution mainly originates in the environment in which software systems live. The boundaries between the software system and the external environment are subject to continuous change. We have used the term *open-world software* to describe this concept (7). In the early days of software development, a closed-world assumption was made. It assumed that the requirements specifying the border between environment and systems to develop were sufficiently stable and they could be fully elicited in advance, before starting design and development. As we will illustrate in the rest of this chapter, this assumption proved to be wrong. Software increasingly lives in an open world, where the boundaries with the real world change continuously, even as the software is executing. This demands change management policies that can support dynamic evolution through run-time bindings.

1.3. EARLY DAYS

Up to the 1960s,[2] software development was mainly a single-person task; the problem to be solved was well understood, and often the developer was also the expected user of the resulting application. Thus, often there was no distinction between developers and users. The problems to solve were mainly of a mathematical nature, and the programmers had the needed mathematical background to understand the problem being solved. Programs were relatively simple, compared to today's standards, and were developed by using low-level languages, without any tool support. As for process, engineers did not follow any systematic development model, but rather proceeded through continuous *code and fix*—that is, an iteration of the activities of writing code and fixing it to eliminate errors.

Soon this approach proved to be inadequate, due to (a) the growing complexity of software systems and (b) the need for applying computing not only to scientific problems but also to other domains, like business administration and process control, where problems were less understood.

At the beginning of the 1970s, after software engineering was recognized as a crucial scientific topic (8, 31), the *waterfall development process* was developed (38) as a reference process model for software engineers. It was an attempt to bring discipline and predictability to software development. It specified a sequential, phased workflow where a requirements elicitation phase is followed by a design phase, followed by a coding phase, and finally by a validation phase. The proposed process model was fixed and static: The decomposition into phases and the binding between one phase and the next were precisely defined. The conditions for exiting a phase and entering the next were also precisely formulated, with the goal of making any rework on previously completed phases unnecessary, and even forbidden. The underlying motivation was that rework—that is, later changes in the software—was perceived as detrimental to quality, responsible for high development costs, and responsible for late time to market. This led to investing efforts in the elicitation, specification, and analysis of the needed requirements, which had to be frozen before development of the entire application could start.

This approach made very strong implicit assumptions about the world in which the software was going to be embedded. This world was assumed to be static; that is, the system's requirements were assumed not to change. The problem was just to elicit the requirements right, so that they could be fully specified prior to development. Completely and precisely specified requirements would ensure that that no need for software changes would arise during development and after delivery.

Another assumption was that the organizations in which the software had to be used had a monolithic structure. Companies were isolated entities with centralized operations and management. Communication and coordination among different companies were limited and not crucial for their business. Centralized solutions were therefore natural in this setting.

---

[2]For a short history of software engineering, the reader can refer to reference 22.

Based on these assumptions and on the software technology available at the time, engineers developed monolithic software systems to be run on mainframes. Even though the size of the application required several people to share the development effort, little attention was put on the modular structure of the application. Separately developed functions were in any case bound together at translation time, and no features were available to support change in the running application. To make a change, the system had to be put in offline mode, the source code had to be modified, each module had to be recompiled, rebound, and redeployed. Because little or no attention was put on the modular structure, changes were difficult to make and their effect was often unpredictable.

1.4. ACHIEVING FLEXIBILITY

The need to accommodate change and software evolution asked for more flexible approaches. It became clear that in most practical circumstances, system requirements cannot be fully gathered upfront, because sometimes customers do not know in advance what they actually require. If they do, requirements are then likely to change, maybe before an application that satisfies their initial specification has been developed completely. This of course questions the implicit assumptions on which the waterfall model is based. Moreover, software architectures turned out to be difficult to modify, because the tight coupling among the various parts made it impossible to isolate the effect of changes to restricted portions of the application. Seemingly minor changes could have a global effect that disrupted the integrity of the whole system.

Finally, the evolution of business organizations also asked for more flexibility. The structure of monolithic and centralized organizations evolved toward more dynamic aggregates of autonomous and decentralized units. Software development processes also changed, because off-the-shelf components and frameworks became progressively available. Software development became distributed and decentralized over different organizations: component developers and system integrators.

In the sequel we discuss the major steps and the landmark contributions on the road that led to increasing levels of flexibility.

1.4.1. Design for Change

A first conceptual contribution toward supporting evolution of software systems was the principle of *design for change* and the definition of techniques supporting it. Parnas (35–37) suggested that software designers should pay much attention in the requirements phase to understand the future changes a system is likely to undergo. If changes can be anticipated, design should try to achieve a structure where the effect of change is isolated within restricted parts of the system. Examples of possible changes to be taken into account are: changes in the algorithms that are used for a specific task; changes in data representation; and changes in the specific devices used by a program, such as sensors or actuators, with which the system interacts.

Parnas elaborated a design technique, called *information hiding*, through which an application is decomposed into modules, where the major sources of anticipated requirements changes are encapsulated and hidden as module secrets and unaccessible to other modules. A clear separation between *module interface* and *module implementation* decouples the stable design decisions concerning the use of a module by other modules from the changeable parts that are hidden inside it. Module clients are unaffected by changes as long as changes do not affect the interface. This great design principle enables separation of concerns, a key principle that supports multi-person design, and software evolution.

Information hiding allows the design of a large system to be decomposed in a series of modules, each of which has an interface separated from the implementation. If the binding between interface and implementation is established statically at translation time, interfaces can be statically checked for consistency both against their implementation and against their use from client modules. Static checks prevent faults from remaining undetected in running systems.

The concepts of information hiding and interface versus implementation were incorporated in programming languages and supported separate development and separate compilation of units in large systems (39). As an example, let us consider the Ada programming language, which was designed in the late 1970s. Ada modules (21), called *packages*, support information hiding and separate compilation of interfaces and implementations. Once an interface is defined and compiled, both its implementation and its client modules' implementation can be compiled. In general, a unit can be compiled if all the modules it depends on have already been compiled. This allows the compiler to perform static type checking among the various units (see Fig. 1.1).

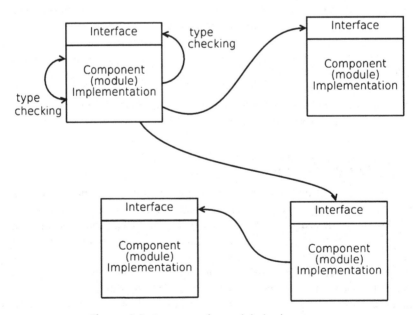

Figure 1.1. Structure of a modularized program.

There are many examples of languages that provide, at least in part, similar features. For example, in C programs it is possible, though not mandatory, to separate the declarations of function prototypes from the implementation and to place them in different files (from the implementation). In this way it is possible to define the interface exported by a module, though it is not possible to specify exactly which functions a module imports from another one.

Although changes are conceptually facilitated if they can be isolated within module implementations, the resulting implementation structure is fixed. All bindings are resolved prior to run time and cannot change dynamically. To make a change, the entire application has to be moved back to design time, changes are made and checked by the translation process, and then the system is restarted in the new configuration.

1.4.2. Object-Oriented Languages

The direct way information hiding was embedded into modular languages provided only a limited support to software evolution and flexible composition of software systems. Object-oriented design techniques and programming languages provided a further major step in this direction. Object orientation aims at providing improved support to modularization and incremental development; it also supports dynamic change.

According to object-oriented design, a software system is decomposed into *classes*, which encapsulate data and operations and define new abstract data types, whose operations are exported through the class interface. A major contribution of object-oriented languages is that the binding between an operation requested by a client module and the implementation provided by a server module can change dynamically at run time. This is a fundamental feature to support software evolution in a flexible manner. Moreover, most object-oriented languages provide it in a way that retains the safety of static type checking (21).

As an example, consider an application, in the field of logistics, that tracks containers. The operations available on a container allow its users to load an item into the container, to get the list of contained items, and to associate the container with a carrier. The carrier may be a train or a truck where the container is loaded for transportation, or it may be the parking area where the container is temporarily stored. The container provides an operation to get its geographical position, which is implemented by asking its carrier to provide it. A parking area has a fixed position, while the truck and the train have their own way of providing the position dynamically. Consider an evolution of the system where containers are equipped with a GPS antenna that can be used to provide their position. This can be implemented as a change in the implementation of the get_position( ) operation, which now uses the data provided by the GPS instead of asking its carrier. A client that uses a container would be unaffected by this new way of implementing the operation: An invocation of get_position( ) would be automatically redirected to the redefined operation (Fig. 1.2).

In general, given a class that defines an abstract data type, it is possible to define changes by means of a *subclass*. A subclass is statically bound to the originating class (its *parent class*) through the *inheritance* relation. A subclass, in turn, may have

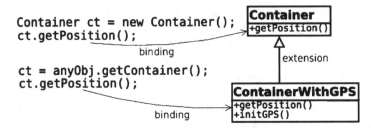

Figure 1.2. At run time we can't be sure on what version of a method will be called.

subclasses; this generates a hierarchy of classes. A subclass may add new features to its parent class (such as new operations) and/or redefine existing operations. Adding new operations does not affect preexisting clients of the class, because clients may continue to ignore them. Redefining an operation is also guaranteed not to affect clients if certain constraints are enforced by the programming language, as in the case of Java. The key composition features that support evolution are *polymorphism* and *dynamic binding*. With polymorphism, it is possible to define variables that may refer to different classes; that is, the binding between a variable and the class of the object it refers to is set at run time. These variables (called polymorphic variables) are defined as a reference to a class, and they can refer to objects of any of its subclasses. In other words, the *static type* of a variable is defined by the class it refers to in the variable's declaration. Its *dynamic type* is determined by the class of the object it currently refers to. The dynamic type can be defined by any subclass of the class that defines the static type. With dynamic binding, the operation invoked on an object is determined by the class that defines its dynamic type.

    The flexibility ensured by dynamic binding may raise type safety problems: Since the invoked operation cannot be determined at compile time, how can one be sure that it will be correctly called at run time? Most object-oriented languages, including Java, retain the benefits of type safety in the context of dynamic binding by restricting the way a method may be redefined in a subclass. Because type checking is performed at compile time by considering the static type of a variable, a possible solution consists of constraining a redefinition not to change the interface of the method being redefined.[3] Software composition can thus be type checked statically even if bindings among objects may change dynamically at run time.

1.4.3. Components and Distribution

Off-the-shelf components (41) became progressively available to software developers. This asked for changes in the methods used to design applications: The traditional dominant design approaches based on top-down decomposition were at least partly replaced by bottom-up integration. With the advent of off-the-shelf components, process development became decentralized, since different organizations at different times are in

---

[3]References 11 and 27 provide a thorough analysis of these issues and give general criteria for type safety.

charge of different parts of a system. This has clear advantages in terms of efficiency of the development process, which can proceed at a higher speed, since large portions of the solution are supported by reusable components. Decentralized responsibilities also imply less control over the whole system, because no single organization is in charge of it. For example, the evolution of components to incorporate new features or replace existing features is not under control of the system integrator.

Components are often part of a system that is distributed over different machines. Indeed, distribution has been another major step in the evolution of software composition. With distribution, the binding between a component and the virtual machine that executes it becomes an important design decision. The requirement to distribute an application over different nodes of a network often comes from the need to reflect a distributed organization for which the application is developed. Often, however, the binding of functions to nodes can be ignored during system development and can be delayed to deployment time.

In a distributed system, the binding among components is performed by the *middleware* (18). Java RMI (28) is a well-known example of a middleware that supports client–server architectures by means of remote method invocations (Fig. 1.3). A Java object can be accessed by a remote machine as if it were executed on the same machine. The client invokes methods as if it was invoking them on a local object. The RMI middleware realizes the binding by marshaling the request and then sending it via TCP/IP. Then the server unmarshals the request, executes the method, and sends back the result in the same way. CORBA (33) is another middleware that supports distributed components written in different programming languages.

Different binding policies may be adopted to support distribution. One possibility is to perform a static deployment-time binding between a component and a virtual machine. Alternatively, one may think of dynamically binding a component to a virtual machine at run time. This is the case of dynamic system reconfiguration,

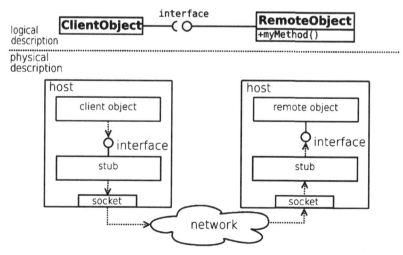

Figure 1.3. Distinction between logical and physical description with Java RMI.

whose purpose is to try to achieve better tuning of the reliability and performance of a distributed application by rebinding components to network nodes at run time.

1.5. SOFTWARE COMPOSITION IN THE OPEN WORLD

As we discussed, software development evolved toward flexible and decentralized approaches to support continuous requirements evolution. This was achieved by trying to anticipate change as far as possible, as well as by shielding large portions of an existing application from certain kinds of changes occurring in other parts. This approach continues to be a key design principle that software engineers should master. However, the speed of evolution is now reaching unprecedented levels: The boundary between the systems to develop and the real world they interact with changes continuously. In some cases, changes cannot be anticipated; they occur as the system is executing, and the running system must be able to react to them in some meaningful manner. Earlier we called this an *open-world scenario.*

Open world scenarios occur in emerging application areas, like ambient intelligence (17) and pervasive computing (40). In these frameworks, computational nodes are mobile and the physical topology of the system changes dynamically. The logical structure (i.e., software composition) is also required to change to support location-aware services. For example, if a person equipped with a PDA or a phone moves around in a building and issues a command to print a document, the binding should be dynamically redirected to the driver of the physically closest printer.

Location-aware binding is just a case of the more abstract concept of *context-aware binding.* In the case of ambient intelligence, context information may be provided by sensors. As an example, an outdoor light sensor may indicate daylight; a request for more light in a room may be bound to a software module that sends signals to an actuator that opens the shutters. Conversely, outdoor dark conditions would cause binding the request to switching the electric light on. Other examples of context-aware binding may take into account the current status of the user who interacts with the environment.

New enterprise-level applications are also subject to continuously changing requirements. Emerging enterprise models are based on the notion of networked organizations that dynamically federate their behaviors to achieve their business goals. Goal-oriented federated organizations may be supported by dynamic software compositions at the information system level. In this case, the composition of the distributed software is made out of elements owned and run by different organizations. Each individual organization exposes fragments of its information system that offer services of possible use for others; and, in turn, it may exploit the services offered by others. The binding between a requested and a provided service may change dynamically.

Moving toward these scenarios requires both new software composition mechanisms and new levels of autonomy in the behavior of the systems, which should be able to self-adapt to changes by reorganizing their internal structure. This implies that composition mechanisms should be self-healing; and, more generally, they should be based on monitoring and optimizing the overall quality of service, which may vary over time due to changes in the environment.

The rest of this section describes some examples of composition mechanisms that aim at a high degree of decoupling and dynamism to cope with open-world requirements.

1.5.1. Global Coordination Spaces

A middleware can provide a Global Coordination Space (GCS, Fig. 1.4), through which components may interact with one another and coordinate their behaviors in a highly decoupled manner. The GCS acts as a *mediator*. Each component participating in the architecture may produce data of possible interest for other components. However, components do not interact directly to coordinate and exchange the data. Coordination and data exchange are mediated by the GCS. Thus, data producers have no explicit knowledge of the target consumers, nor have they any direct binding with one another. The mediator acts as an intermediary between producers and consumers of the data.

There are two main kinds of architectures based on GCSs: publish–subscribe architectures and tuple–space architectures. Both of them allow the system to be very dynamic since components can come and go without requiring any system reconfiguration and without requiring changes that affect the components that are already part of the architecture. Communication here is intrinsically asynchronous since producers send their data to the mediator and continue to execute without waiting for the target consumers to handle them.

Publish–Subscribe Systems. Publish–Subscribe (PS) systems (19) support a GCS where components may publish *events*, which are delivered to all the components that registered an interest in them through a *subscription*. The middleware thus provides facilities for components to register their interest in certain events, via a subscription, and to be notified when events of interest for the component are generated. The GCS, here an event *dispatcher*, is a logically global facility, but of course it may be implemented as a fully distributed middleware infrastructure. Many examples of PS middlewares have been described in the literature (13, 14, 16, 25). Some of them are industrial products, others are research prototypes providing advanced features. Some have a centralized

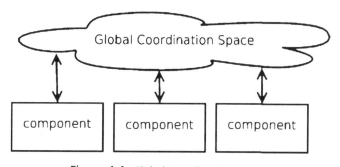

Figure 1.4. Global Coordination Spaces.

dispatcher; others have a distributed dispatcher. They may also differ both in the functionality they provide and in the quality of service they support. Regarding functionality, they may differ in the kinds of events they may generate and in the way subscriptions may be specified. For example, it is possible to distinguish between *content-based* and *subject-based* (or topic-based) PS systems. In the former case, an event is an object with certain attributes on which subscriptions may predicate. For example, an event may signal the availability of a new flight connecting two cities (Milano and Chicago) starting from a certain date (e.g., December, 1) and at a certain fare (e.g., 400 EUROs). A subscription may state an interest in flight information about flights from, say, Madrid to Dublin at a low fare (below 70 EUROs). In a topic-based PS system, instead, events are indivisible entities. For example, an event would be generated by an airline (say, for example, Alitalia) when a new flight announcement is published. Thus, for example, we might have "Alitalia" or "Continental" or "United" events. The events in this case do not carry a value.

Tuple–Space Systems.   Tuple–Space (TS) systems support coordination via persistent store: The GCS provides features to store and retrieve persistent data. This coordination style was pioneered by Linda (12). Linda supports persistent data in the form of *tuples*. Tuples may be written into the tuple space; they can also be read (nondestructively) and deleted. Read and delete operations specify a tuple via a template. The template is used to select a tuple via pattern matching. If the match procedure identifies more than one tuple, one is chosen nondeterministically. If none match, the component that issued the read or the delete remains suspended until a matching tuple is inserted in the tuple space.

Many variations of the original Linda approach have been implemented by TS-based middleware, such as Javaspaces (20). There are also implementations, such as Lime (29), that fit the requirements of mobile distributed systems even more closely.

PS and TS systems have similar goals. Both aim at providing flexible support to distributed and dynamic software architectures. PS middleware is more lightweight: Persistence may be added as a service, but it is not directly supported as a native feature.

1.5.2. Service-Oriented Architectures

GCSs support decoupling and dynamism by removing any direct binding between sources and targets of a message. Service-Oriented Architectures (SOAs) (34) reach similar goals by providing facilities that allow components to register their availability and the functions they perform, and support discovery of the components that can perform the requested functions. Once it has been discovered, a component can be used remotely through direct binding. In principle, registration, discovery, and binding can be performed dynamically at run time.

SOAs are composed mainly of three types of components (Fig. 1.5): *service consumer*, *service provider*, and *service broker*. The service provider provides a service. The service is described through a specification (which we may assume to consist roughly of its interface description). The provider advertises the presence of the service to the

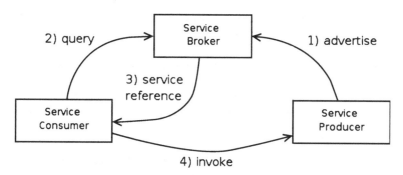

Figure 1.5. Service-oriented architecture.

broker, which maintains a link to the service and stores its interface. The consumer who needs a service must submit a request to a broker, providing a specification of the requested service. By querying the broker for a service, it gets back a link to a provider. From this point on, the consumer uses the operations offered by the provider by communicating with it directly.

SOAs provide a nice solution in the cases where complex interactions are needed between loosely coupled elements and where the requirements are subject to changes, thus requiring fast and continuous system reorganizations. Earlier we mentioned the example of ubiquitous mobile applications, where the discovery phase may be performed dynamically to identify the available local facilities to bind to, as the physical location changes during execution. We also mentioned the case of information systems for networked enterprises—that is, dynamic enterprise federations that are formed to respond to changing business opportunities. In this case, each organization participating in the federation exports certain functionalities, which grant a controlled access to internal application. In turn, it may use services offered by others and possibly choose among the different providers that provide similar services, based on some explicit notion of requested and offered quality of service.

Many middleware solutions exist which implement support for SOAs—for example, JINI network technology (43) or OSGI (3). At the enterprise level, *Web services* (4), and the rich set of standard solutions that accompany them, are emerging as a very promising approach, not only in the research area but also among practitioners. IBM (43) defines a Web service as

> ... a new breed of Web application. They are self-contained, self-describing, modular applications that can be published, located, and invoked across the Web. Web services perform functions, which can be anything from simple requests to complicated business processes. ... Once a Web service is deployed, other applications (and other Web services) can discover and invoke the deployed service ....

Web service (WS) technology offers a big advantage over other service-oriented technologies in that it aims at making interoperation between different platforms easy. This is particularly useful in an open-world environment, where it is impossible to force all the actors to adopt a specific technology to develop their systems. WS technology consists of a set of standards that specify the communication protocols and the interfaces exported by services, without imposing constraints on the internal implementation of the services. Conversely, other solutions, like Jini, are based on Java both for the communication and for the implementation of services. Interoperability allows a seamless integration of the web service solutions developed by different enterprises.

Communication among Web services is based on the Simple Object Access Protocol [SOAP (10)], which describes the syntax of messages that can be exchanged in the form of function calls. It is an XML-based protocol and interaction is usually performed over the http protocol, thus allowing a less intrusive intervention in information systems to export services. After discovery, once the binding between a service consumer and a service provider is established, communication is achieved by sending a message through the SOAP protocol.

Services can be seen as an evolution of off-the-shelf components. Both implement functions of possible use and value for others; both go in the direction decentralized developments, since the organization in charge of developing the off-the-shelf component or the service is, in general, different from the organization that uses them. In both cases, this has obvious advantages (reduced development time, possible enhanced reliability), but also possible disadvantages (dependency on other parties for future evolutions) over complete in-house developments. The main difference between services and off-the-shelf components is that the latter become part of the application and are executed in the application's domain. Services, on the other hand, are owned and run by the provider. Another difference concerns the composition mechanisms. In the case of services, the choice of possible targets for a binding and the establishment of the binding can be performed dynamically at run time.

The most striking difference, however, is in the degree of control and trust. Off-the-shelf components cannot change after they become part of the application, unless they are explicitly replaced by the owner of the application. On the other hand, services are owned by the providers, who control their evolution. Thus services can change unexpectedly for the users.

Although web services are becoming a real practical approach to evolvable system architectures, many problems are still to be solved before they can be applied in open environments or in the case where systems have to meet stringent dependability requirements. The next section outlines the main challenges that must be met by architectures supporting dynamic software compositions in general, and in particular by SOAs.

1.6. CHALLENGES AND FUTURE WORK

We discussed a number of existing and promising approaches supporting software composition in the open world. As we observed, as solutions become more dynamic and decentralized, many problems have to be solved to reach the necessary degree of dependability that is required in practice. In this section, we try to identify where the main problems are and possible research directions. Some of these are new problems; many have always been with us and are just getting more difficult in the new setting.

Challenge 1: Understand the External World. Requirements have always been a crucial problem for software engineers (32, 42). Eliciting and specifying them in continuous change conditions is even harder. In the case of pervasive systems, it is often required that solutions are highly adaptable. For example, support to elderly or physically impaired people in their homes requires developing solutions that can be adapted and personalized to the specific needs of their expected users. At the business level, the requirements of federated enterprises need to be properly captured to support their interoperation. It is important to identify what should be exposed as service for others and what should be kept and protected as proprietary. Easy and dynamic integration is then necessary to capture business opportunities quickly. Although this is a research topic in business organization, software engineers should be aware of these trends. They should be able to capture the requirements of dynamic organizations and shape architectural solutions accordingly.

Challenge 2: Software Process Support. Business organizations are increasingly agile in the way they respond to business opportunities. Software development must also proceed in an agile fashion, to provide fast solutions to achieve competitive advantages and reduced time to market. It is still an open issue as to how agile development methods can comply with the high dependability standards that may be required by the applications. Problems become even harder because development teams are increasingly distributed and autonomous (1, 9, 24). How can standardized practices be enforced? What are the key drivers of productivity? How can process quality be defined and measured?

Challenge 3: Service Specification. The continuous evolution toward services that can be developed and then published for use by other parties makes it necessary to provide a specification for the service that possible users may understand. Software specification has been and still is an active research area. The need for precise module specifications that client modules could use dates back to reference 35. The problem, however, is crucial in the case of services, because of the sharp separation between provider and user and because specifications need to be a stronger and enforceable contractual document. Being a contract, the specification must provide a precise statement that goes beyond a purely syntactic interface definition and even beyond a mere definition of functionality. It must also state the quality of service (QoS) assured by the service. Specifications should be searchable. They should be stated in terms of shared ontologies (2). Finally, they should be composable; that is, it should be possible to derive the specification of a composition of services whose specifications are known.

Challenge 4: Programming and Composition. We described different paradigms for dynamic service composition, such as PS, TS, and SOAs. Coordination among components range from *orchestrated* compositions, where a workflow coordinates the invocation of services, once they have been discovered and bound, to *choreographed* compositions, like in a PS or TS style, where services must comply with a common protocol of exchanged messages and proceed in a peer-to-peer fashion (26, 30). How can different composition mechanisms be integrated in programming language? How can such language support a full range of flexible binding mechanisms, from static and pre-run time to fully dynamic? How can binding policies include negotiation and even rebinding strategies in case of deviations from a stated target for service quality? How can self-healing or even self-organizing behaviors arise through proper compositions?

Challenge 5: Trust and Verification. Services are developed and run in their own domains. Service users have no control over them; they do not have access to their internals. If services can only be bound at translation or at deployment time, and no change occurs afterwards, then applications can undergo traditional verification and validation procedure. But in the case of dynamic binding, and because service implementations may change in an unannounced manner, traditional approaches fail. Verification and validation must extend to run time. Continuous service monitoring (6) must ensure that deviations from the expected QoS is detected, and proper reactions are put in place. In general, one must be able to find ways to make the service world as dependable and secure as required by the requirements. Building sufficiently dependable and secure systems out of low-trust services is a major challenge.

Challenge 6: Consistency. In a closed-world environment, a correct application is always in a consistent state with the environment. In an open-world setting, environment changes trigger changes in the software and generate inconsistencies. Inconsistency management has been recognized as problematic by many researchers in the past (5, 15, 23). It is necessary to deal with it in the case of dynamically evolvable systems.

This is just a short list of important challenges that should be part of the future agenda of software engineering research, By no means should the list be viewed as exhaustive. It just focuses on some of the problems our group is currently working on. Progress in these and other related areas is needed to continue to improve the quality of software applications in the new emerging domains.

ACKNOWLEDGMENTS

This work has been influenced by the experience gained in the National project ART DECO and the EU funded project SeCSE.

Elisabetta Di Nitto and Luciano Baresi helped develop our view of software composition.

REFERENCES

1. Flexible and distributed software processes: Old petunias in new bowls?
2. Owl specification. http://www.w3.org/TR/owl-ref/.
3. OSGI Alliance. *OSGI Service Platform: Release 3, March 2003*. IOS Press, Amsterdam, 2003.

4. G. Alonso, H. Kuno, F. Casati, and V. Machiraju. *Web Services: Concepts, Architectures and Applications.* Springer, Berlin, 2004.

5. R. Balzer. Tolerating inconsistency. In *Proceedings of the 13th International Conference on Software Engineering*, pages 158–165, 1991.

6. L. Baresi, C. Ghezzi, and S. Guinea. Smart monitors for composed services. In *Proceedings of the 2nd International Conference on Service Oriented Computing*, pages 193–202, 2004.

7. L. Baresi, E. Di Nitto, and C. Ghezzi. Toward open-world software: Issue and challenges. *IEEE Computer* **39**(10):36–43, 2006.

8. F. L. Bauer, L. Bolliet, and H. J. Helms. Report on a Conference Sponsored by the NATO Science Committee. In *NATO Software Engineering Conference 1968*, page 8.

9. B. W. Boehm and R. Turner. *Balancing Agility and Discipline: A Guide for the Perplexed.* Addison-Wesley, Reading, MA, 2004.

10. D. Box, D. Ehnebuske, G. Kakivaya, A. Layman, N. Mendelsohn, HF Nielsen, S. Thatte, and D. Winer. Simple Object Access Protocol (SOAP) 1.1.

11. L. Cardelli and P. Wegner. On understanding types, data abstraction, and polymorphism. *ACM Computing Surveys (CSUR)* **17**(4):471–523, 1985.

12. N. Carriero and D. Gelernter. Linda in context. *Communications of the ACM* **32**(4):444–458, 1989.

13. A. Carzaniga, D. S. Rosenblum, and A. L. Wolf. Achieving scalability and expressiveness in an Internet-scale event notification service. In *Proceedings of the Nineteenth Annual ACM Symposium on Principles of Distributed Computing*, pages 219–227, 2000.

14. G. Cugola, E. Di Nitto, and A. Fuggetta. The JEDI event-based infrastructure and its application to the development of the OPSS WFMS. *IEEE Transactions on Software Engineering* **27**(9):827–850, 2001.

15. G. Cugola, E. Di Nitto, A. Fuggetta, and C. Ghezzi. A framework for formalizing inconsistencies and deviations in human-centered systems. *ACM Transactions on Software Engineering and Methodology* **5**(3):191–230, 1996.

16. G. Cugola and G. P. Picco. REDS: A Reconfigurable Dispatching System. Technical report, Politecnico di Milano, 2005.

17. K. Ducatel, M. Bogdanowicz, F. Scapolo, J. Leijten, and J. C. Burgelma. Scenarios for ambient intelligence in 2010 (ISTAG 2001 Final Report). *IPTS, Seville*, 2000.

18. W. Emmerich *Engineering Distributed Objects.* John Wiley & Sons, New York, 2000.

19. P. T. H. Eugster, P. A. Felber, R. Guerraoui, and A. M. Kermarrec. The many faces of publish/subscribe. *ACM Computing Surveys* **35**(2):114–131, 2003.

20. E. Freeman, K. Arnold, and S. Hupfer. *JavaSpaces Principles, Patterns, and Practice.* Addison-Wesley Longman Ltd., Essex, UK, 1999.

21. C. Ghezzi and M. Jazayeri. *Programming Language Concepts.* John Wiley & Sons, New York, 1997.

22. C. Ghezzi, M. Jazayeri, and D. Mandrioli. *Fundamentals of Software Engineering.* Prentice-Hall, Englewood Cliffs, NJ, 2003.

23. C. Ghezzi and B. A. Nuseibeh. Special issue on managing inconsistency in software development. *IEEE Transactions on Software Engineering* **24**(11):906–907, 1998.

24. J. D. Herbsleb and D. Moitra. Global software development. *Software, IEEE* **18**(2):16–20, 2001.

25. Tibco Inc. TIB/Rendezvous White Paper, 1999.

26. N. Kavantzas, D. Burdett, and G. Ritzinger. WSCDL: Web Service Choreography Description Language, 2004.

27. B. H. Liskov and J. M. Wing. A behavioral notion of subtyping. *ACM Transactions on Programming Languages and Systems (TOPLAS)* **16**(6):1811–1841, 1994.

28. Sun Microsystems. Java Remote Method Invocation Specification, 2002.

29. A. L. Murphy, G. P. Picco, and G. C. Roman. Lime: A Middleware for Physical and Logical Mobility. In *Proceedings of the 21st International Conference on Distributed Computing Systems*, pages 524–533, 2001.

30. N. Busi, R. Gorrieri, C. Guidi, R. Lucchi, and G. Zavattaro. Choreography and orchestration conformance for system design. In *Proceedings of 8th International Conference on Coordination Models and Languages (COORDINATION06) LCNS 4038*, pages 63–81, 2006.

31. P. Naur, B. Randell, and J. N. Buxton. *Software Engineering: Concepts and Techniques: Proceedings of the NATO Conferences.* Petrocelli/Charter, New York, 1976.

32. B. Nuseibeh and S. Easterbrook. Requirements engineering: A roadmap. In *Proceedings of the Conference on The Future of Software Engineering*, pages 35–46, 2000.

33. R. Orfali and D. Harkey. *Client/Server Programming with Java and CORBA.* John Wiley & Sons, New York, 1998.

34. M. Papazoglou and D. Georgakopoulos. Service-oriented computing: Introduction. *Communications of ACM* **46**(10):24–28, 2003.

35. D. L. Parnas. On the criteria to be used in decomposing systems into modules. *Communications of the ACM* **15**(12):1053–1058, 1972.

36. D. L. Parnas. On the design and development of program families. *IEEE Transactions on Software Engineering* **2**(1):1–9, 1976.

37. D. L. Parnas. Designing software for ease of extension and contraction. In *Proceedings of the 3rd International Conference on Software Engineering*, pages 264–277, 1978.

38. W. W. Royce. Managing the Development of Large Software Systems. In *Proceedings of IEEE WESCON*, pages 1–9, 1970.

39. B. G. Ryder, M. L. Soffa, and M. Burnett. The impact of software engineering research on modern programming languages. *ACM Transactions on Software Engineering and Methodology (TOSEM)* **14**(4):431–477, 2005.

40. M. Satyanarayanan. Pervasive computing: Vision and challenges. *Personal Communications, IEEE [see also IEEE Wireless Communications]* **8**(4):10–17, 2001.

41. C. Szyperski. *Component Oriented Programming.* Springer, Berlin, 1998.

42. A. van Lamsweerde. Requirements Engineering in the Year 00: A Research Perspective. In *Proceedings of the 22nd International Conference on Software Engineering*, pages 5–19, 2000.

43. J. Waldo. Jini architecture for network-centric computing. *Communications of the ACM* **42**(7):76–82, 1999.

2

COMPOSITIONALITY IN SOFTWARE PRODUCT LINES

Christian Prehofer, Jilles van Gurp, and Jan Bosch

2.1. INTRODUCTION

Software product lines or platforms have received much attention in research, but especially in industry. Many companies have moved away from developing software from scratch for each product and instead focus on the commonalities between the different products and capturing those in a product line architecture and an associated set of reusable assets. This development is, especially in the embedded systems industry, a logical development since software is an increasingly large part of products and often defines the competitive advantage. When moving from a marginal to a major part of products, the required effort for software development also becomes a major issue, and industry searches for ways to increase reuse of existing software to minimize product-specific development and to increase the quality of software. A number of authors have reported on industrial experiences with product line architectures. Early work goes back to the late 1990s (2, 7, 12), and the field has since then developed in new directions to extend the applicability of the concept.

This chapter addresses several challenges posed by the increasing range of successful product lines and develops new concepts for a compositional approach to software product lines (5, 13, 14). Furthermore, the implications of this approach to

Emerging Methods, Technologies, and Process Management in Software Engineering. Edited by
De Lucia, Ferrucci, Tortora, and Tucci

the different aspects of software development are discussed, including process and organizational questions.

Although the concept of software platforms is easy to understand in theory, in practice there are significant challenges. As discussed in reference 3, the platform model is supposed to capture the most generic and consequently the least differentiating functionality. However, the product specific functionality frequently does not respect the boundary between the platform and the software on top of it. Innovations in embedded systems can originate from mechanics, hardware, or software. Both mechanical and hardware innovations typically have an impact on the software stack. However, due to the fact that the interface to hardware is placed in device drivers at the very bottom of the stack and the affected applications and their user interface are located at the very top of the stack, changes to mechanics and hardware typically have a cross-cutting effect that causes changes in many places both below and above the platform boundary.

A second source of cross-cutting changes is software-specific. New products often enable new use cases that put new demands on the software that cannot be captured in a single component or application, but rather have architectural impact. Examples include adding security, a more advanced user interface framework, or a web-services framework. Such demands result in cross-cutting changes that affect many places in the software, again both above and below the platform boundary.

Software product families have, in many cases, been very successful for the companies that have applied them. Due to their success, however, during recent years one can identify a development where companies are stretching their product families significantly beyond their initial scope. This occurs either because the company desires to ship a broader range of products due to, among others, convergence, or because the proven success of the product family causes earlier unrelated products to be placed under the same family. This easily causes a situation where the software product family becomes a victim of its own success. With the increasing scope and diversity of the products that are to be supported, the original integration-oriented platform approach increasingly results in several serious problems in the technical, process, organizational, and, consequently, the business dimension.

The "conventional," integration-oriented platform approach in software product lines typically splits R&D into a platform organization that delivers a platform as a large, integrated, and tested software system with an API that can be used by the product teams to derive their products from. In addition, there often is top-down, hierarchical governance by the central platform organization including the central management of requirements and roadmap, complete control of features, variability and product derivations, and integration and testing for product platform and derivations.

A specific refinement of the integration-oriented platform approach is the hierarchical platform approach (5), where a platform is used and extra functionality is added on top without modifying the base. This is, however, only suitable if the base is well-defined and sufficient for fast product creation. Second, it does not limit the sharing of code between different, derived products beyond the borderline of the base platform.

Despite the success of the integration-oriented platform approach, in this chapter we argue that the approach suffers from limitations when the scope of the product line starts to increase. An intuitive reaction adopted by some companies is to adopt a hierarchical platform approach. However, as discussed in reference 5, this approach fails to be sufficiently scalable for large systems with many product derivations, especially when there is a wide range of products with unpredicted variations and, in the case of product derivations, requiring to modify and reengineer significant parts of the system.

A main reason to question the traditional platform approach is that we have seen the organization into platform and product units to create a number of drawbacks regarding integration. First, because integration and testing are done both at the platform and at the product level, this can lead to an extremely high cost of integration if the scope of a software product line widens. This strong dependence on repeated integration also leads to lack of predictability and inefficiency. Second, the broad scope of the platform functionality impedes flexibility and time to market for new features. Third, this easily leads to a lack of flexibility and unacceptably long development cycles because of the brittleness of platform caused by its inability to go beyond initial scope. Finally, software developed in a product unit cannot properly be reused by other units before it has been included into a release of the platform unit. Because the platform unit has typically longer release cycles, such reuse of software is difficult to achieve in such an approach. In other words, we need to enable horizontal sharing between products in addition to vertical sharing between the platform and products.

Another significant fact is the growing significance of open-source and off-the-shelf components in software product lines. This presents several challenges to the traditional approaches to software product lines because it requires a more open approach that does not assume full control of features, roadmaps, and tools.

Because software development is now a key competence and differentiating factor in many areas such as embedded devices, there is a strong need for a new approach. We argue that we need a fundamental paradigm shift in the way that we engineer software product lines if we are to achieve a significant improvement in productivity and time to market.

This chapter details a more flexible and more open approach, called the *compositional product family approach*, which addresses the above issues. The main idea of the compositional approach to software product lines is that the software platform of the product line is not a fully integrated software solution, but a set of components, architecture guidelines, and principles as well as testing, documentation, and use case support. Based on this flexible and open platform environment, the full products are composed, integrated, and tested. While in this approach software component technology will play a much bigger role, we also propose in this chapter the use of "architecture slices," which are fragments of the full architecture. These are integrated and tested as part of the compositional software platform. Such architecture slices typically cover one or more subsystem of the architecture. In this way, we can ensure integration and testing that goes beyond component-level testing. This is also important regarding nonfunctional requirements, beyond the scope of individual components. This process is illustrated in Fig. 2.1. A critical point is that the architecture slices are not a full integration and some external component dependencies have to be made explicit.

Adopting a compositional product family approach causes an intentional shift of integration and testing responsibilities to the product creation, where products are

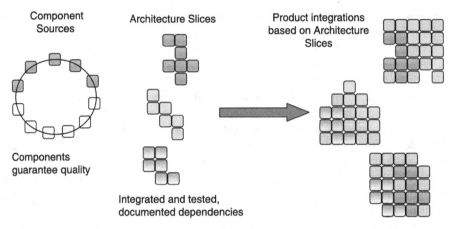

Figure 2.1. Compositional approach.

composed from the aforementioned elements. In our experience, this approach is more adequate for product families with wide scope, fast evolution, and open innovation and competition at the component level.

The motivation and basic characteristics of the compositional product family approach were introduced in reference 5. The approach is detailed and enhanced in this chapter, in particular by the architecture slice concept. The contribution of this chapter is the following. First, we present a detailed and precise assessment of the problems of the integration-oriented platform approach. Second, we impart the consequences of adopting a compositional product family approach on all aspects of SW development, including requirements, process, organization, architecture, and tools.

The remainder of this chapter is organized as follows. In the next section, we introduce the integration-oriented approach, discuss its disadvantages and introduce the compositional approach as an alternative. Subsequently, in Section 2.3, the concept of architecture slices is presented as a key element of the compositional approach. Section 2.4 presents a set of research challenges for the evolving and maturing the compositional approach.

2.2. FROM INTEGRATION-ORIENTED TO THE COMPOSITIONAL APPROACH

This chapter discusses and presents an alternative to the traditional, integration-centric approach to product families. However, before we can discuss this, the concerns of the integration-oriented platform approach need to be defined more clearly. Traditionally, product families are organized using a strict separation between the domain engineering organization and the product organizations. The domain engineering organization employs a periodic release cycle where the domain artifacts are released in a fully integrated and tested fashion, often referred to as a platform. The product organizations use the platform as a basis for creating and evolving their product by extending the platform with product-specific features.

The platform organization is divided in a number of teams, in the best case mirroring the architecture of the platform. Each team develops and evolves the component (or set of related components) that it is responsible for and delivers the result for integration in the platform. Although many organizations have moved to applying a continuous integration process where components are constantly integrated during development, in practice significant verification and validation work is performed in the period before the release of the platform and many critical errors are only found in that stage.

The platform organization delivers the platform as a large, integrated and tested software system with an API that can be used by the product teams from which to derive their products. As platforms bring together a large collection of features and qualities, the release frequency of the platform is often relatively low compared to the frequency of product programs. Consequently, the platform organization often is under significant pressure to deliver as many new features and qualities during the release. Hence, there is a tendency to short-cut processes, especially quality assurance processes. Especially during the period leading up to a major platform release, all validation and verification is often transferred to the integration team. As the components lose quality and the integration team is confronted with both integration problems and component-level problems, in the worst case an interesting cycle appears where errors are identified by testing staff that has no understanding of the system architecture and can consequently only identify symptoms, component teams receive error reports that turn out to originate from other parts in the system and the integration team has to manage highly conflicting messages from the testing and development staff, leading to new error reports, new versions of components that do not solve problems, and so on.

Although several software engineering challenges associated with software platforms have been outlined, the approach often proves highly successful in terms of maximizing R&D efficiency and cost-effectively offering a rich product portfolio. Thus, in its initial scope, the integration-centric approach has often proven itself as a success. However, the success can easily turn into a failure when the organization decides to build on the success of the initial software platform and significantly broadens the scope of the product family. The broadening of the scope can be the result of the company deciding to bring more existing product categories under the platform umbrella or because it decides to diversify its product portfolio as the cost of creating new products has decreased considerably. At this stage, we have identified in a number of companies that broadening the scope of the software product family without adjusting the mode of operation quite fundamentally leads to a number of key concerns and problems that are logical and unavoidable. However, because of the earlier success that the organization has experienced, the problems are insufficiently identified as fundamental, but rather as execution challenges, and fundamental changes to the mode of operation are not made until the company experiences significant financial consequences.

In the following, we detail these problems, first regarding the scope of the platform and then regarding openness.

2.2.1. Problems from Overextended Scope

So, what are the problems causing a mode of operation that was initially so successful to turn into such a problematic approach? In the list below, we discuss the problems regarding scope that one can observe and perceive directly.

- *Lack of Component Generality*: Although most components were useful for most products in the initial scope of the product family, in the expanded scope the number of components that is only used in a subset of products is increasing.
- *Incorporation of Immature Functionality*: As discussed in the previous bullet, in the initial scope most functionality useful for one product is likely to become relevant for other products over time. Hence, there often is a tendency to incorporate product-specific functionality into the platform very early on, sometimes already before it has been used in the first product. When the scope of the family increases, the disadvantages of incorporating immature functionality become apparent.
- *Slow Evolution of Functionality*: As the scope of the product family increases and the organization maintains an integration-oriented approach to developing the shared software artifacts, the response time of the platform in response to requests to add functionality of existing features increases.
- *Implicit Dependencies*: In an integration-oriented approach, a relative high degree of connectivity between components is accepted because there are few disadvantages at that stage and it increases short-term developer productivity. When the scope of the product family increases, the components need to be composed in more creative configurations and suddenly the often implicit dependencies between components become a significant problem for the creation new products.
- *Unresponsiveness of Platform Development*: Especially for product categories early in the maturation cycle, the slow release cycle of software platforms is particularly frustrating. Often, a new feature is required rapidly in a new product. However, the feature requires changes in some platform components. Because the platform has a slow release cycle, the platform is typically unable to respond to the request of the product team. The product team is willing to implement this functionality itself, but the platform team is often not allowing this because of the potential consequences for the quality of the product team.

When analyzing these problems with the intention to understand their underlying causes, among others, the following causes can be identified:

- *Decreasing Complete Commonality*: Before broadening the scope of the product family, the platform formed the common core of product functionality. However, with the increasing scope, the products are increasingly diverse in their requirements and amount of functionality that is required for all products is decreasing, in either absolute or relative terms. Consequently, the (relative) number of components that is shared by all products is decreasing, reducing the relevance of the common platform.

- *Increasing Partial Commonality*: Functionality that is shared by some or many products, though not by all, is increasingly significantly with the increasing scope. Consequently, the (relative) number of components that is shared by some or most products is increasing. The typical approach to this model is the adoption of hierarchical product families. In this case, business groups or teams responsible for certain product categories build a platform on top of the company-wide platform. Although this alleviates part of the problem, it does not provide an effective mechanism to share components between business groups or teams developing products in different product categories.

- *Overengineered Architecture*: With the increasing scope of the product family, the set of business and technical qualities that needs to be supported by the common platform is broadening as well. Although no product needs support for all qualities, the architecture of the platform is required to do so and, consequently, needs to be overengineered to satisfy the needs of all products and product categories. This, however, impedes extensibility and increases maintenance effort.

- *Cross-Cutting Features*: Especially in embedded systems, new features frequently fail to respect the boundaries of the platform. Whereas the typical approach is that differentiating features are implemented in the product-specific code, often these features require changes in the common components as well. Depending on the domain in which the organization develops products, the notion of a platform capturing the common functionality between all products may easily turn into an illusion as the scope of the product family increases.

- *Maturity of Product Categories*: Different product categories developed by one organization frequently are in different phases of the lifecycle. The challenge is that, depending on the maturity of a product category, the requirements on the common platform are quite different. For instance, for mature product categories, cost and reliability are typically the most important whereas for product categories early in the maturity phase, feature richness and time-to-market are the most important drivers. A common platform has to satisfy the requirements of all product categories, which easily leads to tensions between the platform organization and the product categories.

2.2.2. Problems of the Closed Approach

A second major challenge to the traditional integration-oriented approach is growing importance of open source software and components off the shelf (COTS). The core issue is that the integration-oriented approach assumes a strong governance of the requirements, features, and roadmaps of both the platform and the products. In particular, this leads to several problems:

- *Inflexible Base Platform*: If the base platform integrates external software, such as open source software, it does not have control over the roadmap, development process, and release cycles. This leads to a number of constraints and in our experience makes it more challenging to find an architecture which suits all derived products.

- *Evolution*:   In case an individual derived product extends the platform by open source software, it is again difficult to later include this software into the main product line platform.
- *Tools and Organization Mismatch*:   Open source software employs different organizational approaches, tools, and quality assurance and testing practices. These are difficult to integrate into software product lines as discussed in (8).

The consequence is that we need a more open approach that does not assume full control of features, roadmaps, and tools. The compositional approach as discussed below assumes a more open environment and caters much easier to this setting of decentralized management and heterogeneous processes and tools.

2.2.3. The Compositional Product Family Approach

The main idea of the compositional approach to software product lines is that the product line is not an integrated, complete software solution: Instead, it is provided as an open, but integrated, toolbox and software environment. The role of a fully integrated reference platform is now taken over by a set of *architecture slices*, which are integrated and tested component compositions for one or more subsystems. This includes specific components with high cohesion, which is typically a vertical integration of highly dependent components and can extend to small component frameworks. The set of architecture slices shall cover the full scope of the software product line and both exemplify and enable the later product integration. While the concept of architecture slices appears similar to related work on architecture modeling (9, 11, 15), our notion of architecture slice is driven by integration and testing aspect and we consider more the overall software product line approach.

For instance, on a mobile phone a set of multimedia applications that use a built-in camera can be an architecture slice. This may include several interchangeable camera drivers, picture-taking and picture-viewing applications, and several operating system components for fast storage and retrieval of media data. These components can vary, depending on the camera resolution or on the number of cameras. Furthermore, the operating system support for the cameras may depend on the resolution and the performance needed for data storage. In addition, the dependencies to other components and architecture slices must be specified. In this example, the viewer application can interface with messaging application to send pictures directly. Also, a video conferencing application may depend the camera support for recording video calls. While these dependencies must be documented and can be tested with sample code, the actual product creation has the responsibility for the integration. More details on architecture slices are found in the following section.

In summary, a compositional software product family includes the following:

- A set of coherently managed components that facilitate easy integration.
- Overall architecture blueprints and principles that guide the later product development.
- Architecture slices that cover the full scope of the software product line and exemplify the product integration.
- Test cases and test environments for both components and architecture slices.
- Detailed documentation on dependability between components, architecture slices, and their dependencies and recommended compositions.

Based on this flexible and open environment, the full products are composed, integrated, and tested.

The compositional product family approach can, in addition, include a fully integrated platform for certain base products without integrating all components. This can also serve as reference product in order to test integration and nonfunctional requirements. The main difference is that the majority of product derivation is a composition of the above pieces.

In the integration-oriented approach, the fully integrated software package must resolve all dependencies and interactions between components by actual code. In this approach, this is done by integrating typical sets of components by architecture slices and by documenting the external dependencies. This documentation of dependencies is highly important and must be treated as an essential part of the compositional approach. Compared to the traditional approach, we make these dependencies explicit and leave the actual integration to the product creation.

The main advantages and technical characteristics of this approach are as follows:

- *More Flexible Product Architecture*:   The software architecture of products is much more freely defined and not constrained by a platform architecture. This is because there is no enforced platform architecture, although a reference architecture may exist to inspire product architectures.
- *Local Responsibility*:   The reusable components that may be used in product creation accept a much higher level of local responsibility. This responsibility means that each component (a) only uses predefined provided, required, and configuration interfaces, (b) verifies at composition or deployment time that all its interfaces are bound correctly and that the component can provide the use cases or features (or parts thereof) that it promises, and (c) contains intelligence to dynamically adjust itself to client or server components that either offer less than expected functionality or require more than expected functionality.
- *Reduced Integration Cost*:   Integration of reusable and product-specific software components takes place by each product, and no platform integration is performed. Due to the increased intelligence of components, the integration effort is brought down to a fraction of the current effort requirements.

Clearly, this approach leads to several challenges that concern all aspects of software development. We will discuss these in Section 2.4. However, we first discuss the impact of the approach on different aspects of software development.

2.2.4. Key Differences of the Compositional Approach

To more precisely describe the compositional approach in relation to the integration-oriented approach, we discuss the two approaches from five perspectives that we believe are of predominant importance in the context of broadening the scope of software product families—that is, business strategy, architecture, components, product creation, and evolution:

- *Business Strategy*: The original reason for adopting product families is often the reduction of R&D expenditure through the sharing of software artifacts between multiple products. Although this is certainly not ignored in the compositional approach, the main focus is typically to maximize the scope of the product family. Although R&D cost and time-to-market are obviously relevant factors for any technology-driven organization, the most important rationale for the composition-oriented approach is that by giving product developers more flexibility and freedom, the creation of a much broader set of products is facilitated.

- *Architecture*: Initially, the architecture for the product family is specified as a complete structural architecture in terms of components and connectors. The architecture is the same for all products, and variation is primarily captured through variation points in the components. When moving toward a compositional approach, the structural view of the architecture is diminished and increasing focus is directed toward the underlying architectural principles guaranteeing compositionality. As discussed earlier, the key difference between this approach and other approaches is that the architecture is not described in terms of components and connectors, but rather in terms of the architectural slices, design rules and design constraints.

- *Components*: During the first phase of a software product family, the components are implemented for a specific architecture that is specified in all or most of its aspects. The components contain variation points to satisfy the differences between different products in the family, but these do not spread significantly beyond the interfaces of the components. Finally, the components are implemented such that they depend on the implementation of other components rather than on explicit and specified interfaces. When evolving toward a compositional approach, the focus on components remains. However, these components are not developed ad hoc, but are constrained in their implementation by the architecture—that is, the architectural fragments, rules, and constraints discussed earlier. As each component is integrated in one or more architecture slices, compositionality of these slices is ensured.

- *Product Creation*: The integration-oriented model typically assumes a preintegrated platform that contains the generic functionality required by all or most products in the family. A product is created by using the preintegrated platform as a basis and adding the product-specific code on top of the platform. Although not necessarily so, often the company is also organized along this boundary. The approach works very well for narrowly scoped product families, but less well when the scope of the product family is broadening. In the compositional approach, the explicit goal is to facilitate the derivation of a broad range of products that may need to compose components in an equally wide range of configurations. Product creation is, consequently, the selection of the most suitable components, the configuration of these components according to the product requirements, the development of glue code in places where the interaction between components needs to be adjusted for the product specific requirements, and the development of product-specific code on top of the reusable components.

- *Evolution*: Often, in an integration-oriented approach, there is a strong preference toward incorporating new features and requirements into the preintegrated platform. The reasoning behind this is that new features, in due time, need to be provided in all products anyway and, consequently, the most cost-effective approach is to perform this directly. The alternative, intended approach where product-specific functionality evolves and commoditizes over time and is incorporated into the platform is often diminishing. In the compositional approach, product teams as well as component teams can be responsible for the evolution of the code base. Product teams typically extend existing components with functionality that they need for their product but is judged to be useful for future products as well. Product teams may also create new components for the same purpose. Component teams, if used, are more concerned with adding features that are required by multiple products. A typical example is the implementation of a new version of a communication protocol.

2.3. COMPONENTS AND ARCHITECTURAL SLICES

In the above, we have discussed the composition-oriented approach. In this section we elaborate compositional software development based on the key ingredients, components, and architecture slices. The decentral nature of compositional development makes it possible to combine various styles of development because, essentially, the composed artifacts are developed independently.

2.3.1. Component Technology

The key difference between integration-oriented and composition-oriented development is that the compositional approach is decentralized. The components that are being composed are developed independent from each other and from the products they are to be used in. A definition of a component that suits this chapter well is the one provided by Clemens Szyperski in his book on components: "A software component is a unit of composition with contractually specified interfaces and explicit context dependencies only. A software component can be deployed independently and is subject to composition by third parties" (19).

In other words, components are developed indepently and then integrated by a third party. We interpret the "unit of composition" broadly here. In our experience, depending on the level of abstraction, very large software systems are broken down into hundreds of components that may still be very large.

As noted in the introduction, the key activity in the integration-oriented approach is the integration phase during which critical errors in the software and its components are identified and then fixed. A compositional approach to software development allows product and component developers to operate independently. Consequently, it is a more scalable approach that allows more developers to (a) work together (by decentralizing their work) and (b) build larger software products (by combining their output). However, integration testing is inherently difficult to accomplish when developing in a compositional way because of the independent modes of operation of both product and component teams and the absence of a central planning and decision making.

Of course, the product developer will need to test the particular configuration of components that is used in the product as well as any product specifics. However, the product developers shall not change the components in the configuration (aside from manipulating them through the configuration API). Also it is much harder for product developers to demand from the developers of the components that they fix bugs, implement or change features, and so on. This may be hard for various reasons:

- The component is provided by external developers (e.g., subcontractors, a commercial off-the-shelf component (COTS) vendor, or an open source project). These parties may have some commitment toward supporting and maintaining their components (e.g., governed through a support contract) but are unlikely to care much about product-specific issues manifesting themselves during product integration.
- The component is developed according to its own roadmap with planned major and minor releases. Any issues that do not fit in this roadmap are unlikely to be addressed on short notice.
- The required changes conflict with those required by other users of the component. Components may be used by multiple products. In the case of external components, these may even be competing products. When confronted with such conflicts, the solution will have to be provided in the product rather than in the component.

Consequently, the components that are used in the product need to be stable and well-tested well before the product integration phase. In other words, adopting a compositional approach implies putting more emphasis on component testing and makes this the responsibility of the component development teams.

In case essential functionality for a specific product is not provided by the component environment and it cannot be added by extensions or glue code, it may be needed to add a derivative component. This will happen more frequently in the compositional approach as roadmaps and features are less coordinated. We see this option, however, as an advantage as it increases the internal competition. Using the compositional approach for development, it may be expected that these components may eventually become of use to other products developed by the same organization.

2.3.2. Architecture Slices and Components

The approach we outline in this section addresses component integration testing using the notion of architecture slices and partial integration. An architecture slice does not describe a full product architecture. Rather it describes relevant aspects of the environment a component is expected to be used in.

The IEEE 1471 standard defines software architecture as "the fundamental organization of a system embodied in its components, their relationships to each other and to the environment and the principles guiding its design and evolution" (10). In the case of compositional development, it is not possible for component developers to consider all products their component is to be used in. Furthermore, all these products may have little more commonality other than the fact that they use the component. In other words, rather than focusing on the full architecture, component developers need to focus on the part of the architecture that relates directly to their component. We refer to this as an architectural slice.

An architecture slice is a set of densely coupled components that are recommended to be used in this combination in products. In most cases, this represents a subsystem of the architecture. For example, in a mobile phone this can be a set of multimedia applications for a built-in camera and include drivers or a set of components for media playing. An architecture slice also defines its external dependencies on other components or subsystems. An architecture slice is not complete without these external dependencies and must describe its relation to these external subsystem. In other words, architecture slices include assumptions about how other subsystems relate to it.

2.3.3. Architecture Slices and Integration Testing

As argued earlier, an essential part of the compositional approach is the integration testing of architecture slices. For this, a major issue is that the dependencies to external components need to be addressed. In order to test a component or a architecture slice, a developer will need to provide an environment that fulfills these dependencies. Using the resulting architecture slice configurations, simple applications may be implemented that test various aspects of the component functionality. In the case where the intended use is extension by another component, creating such extensions is the preferred way to test.

The dependencies to external components can be categorized in two groups:

- *Uses Dependencies*: The component likely depends on other components. This may either be specific versions of specific components or, as is increasingly common in the Java world, implementations of a specific standard API.

- *Usage Dependencies*:   These dependencies indicate other components that depend on this component or that must at least work correctly with the component.

The dependency relations may also be coupled so that, for example, using component A implies also using component B. Such relations should of course be documented.

The process of integration testing is normally done as part of product development. However, as indicated earlier, this is generally too late to address any component issues. Consequently, integration testing needs to be done earlier at the component and architecture slice level. While it is impossible to realize complete products as a part of the component testing process, it is feasible to provide the environment used for testing representative of known or anticipated uses of the component in actual products:

- For the uses dependencies a selection of components may be used that is likely to be used by product developers. If compatibility is important, various configurations of the architecture slice with different components may be created to, for example, test various versions of the same component or different implementations of the same API. In the situation that a component extends another one, the relation to the extended component can be characterized as a uses relation as well. In that case, selection is easy because it is always the same component that is being extended.
- The usage dependencies may be more difficult. In some cases it may be possible to test using a complete product configuration. However, when developing a new version of the component (and particularly when API changes are involved), it is not likely that existing components are compatible. In that case, usage dependencies may need to be simulated using mock implementations. Additionally, in the case of commercial products, the full product software may not be available to the component developer.

2.3.4. Component Dependencies

While in general it is not possible to test all combinations of all dependencies, it is possible to determine combinations of components that are known to work as expected. This information can be provided in documentation.

This practice is quite common in the software industry. For example, the release notes of Apache's Jakarta Commons Logging component (version 1.1.0) state that: "All core classes were compiled with a 1.2.x JDK. JCL may work on some augmented 1.1 series JREs but it is recommended that those wish to run on 1.1 JREs download the source and create a custom implementation." This is a nice example of a dependency that might work but is not recommended because the component developers did not include it in their testing procedure. The recommendation clearly indicates that users are discouraged from using a 1.1 JRE but that it may be possible to do so if needed. This is also an example where product development may choose to create their own versions of components at their own responsibility.

This practice of documenting working and recommended combinations of components is quite common. Many component vendors will certify that their software works in combination with certain other components and will be able to provide more extensive support to users if they use the recommended components in combination with component releases they produce. This certification and support model is the basis for most open source product companies like MySQL and JBoss.

In practice, this causes product developers to (strongly) prefer release quality components over development releases (if available) and to satisfy any dependencies those components have using the recommended components. Doing so allows them to rely on the test work that has been done already by the component developers and focus more on testing the product specifics.

A second consequence is that this makes fulfilling the dependencies a decision process that is preferably completed early in the product development process. Generally, in a new product, most dependencies will be fulfilled during the product architecture design phase. Upgrades to new versions may of course occur, but it is not likely that product managers will want to risk having to be part of the component integration testing process. These two practices are markedly different from the practice of co-evolving components and products in a software product line. During the integration phase, components are continuously integrated with development versions of the other components. Likewise, product developers will end up using modified versions of the components, thus negating some of the earlier integration testing effort. The above-mentioned practices strongly discourage this from happening and allow product developers to build on a well-tested foundation.

2.3.5. Examples

In this section we have characterized how component developers can do integration level without building a full product based on their component. This is important for creating compositions of components because it allows product developers to rely on the integration testing already done, rather than having to do this themselves.

A convincing example of this is the Debian linux distribution. The Debian linux distribution is a collection of thousands of open source software packages running on linux. The stated goal of the Debian foundation is to provide a stable, fully tested and integrated distribution. Essentially, most of their work consists of integrating the thousands of packages into their distribution. While there is some Debian-specific development, most of it consists of Debian-specific infrastructure and gluecode. Additionally, the integration testing feedback is propagated to the dependent open source packages, often along with patches for the problem.

In reference 1 some impressive statistics are presented regarding the size of this distribution: Release 3.1 (a.k.a. Sarge) was measured to consist of 230 million lines of code (MLOC). The 3.0 release only three years earlier was measured at 105 MLOC, and the 2.1 release (according to reference 20) was 55 MLOC. In other words, the distribution has quadrupled in size in roughly five years. According to Wheeler, who has applied the COCOMO model to these metrics, this corresponds to multiple billions of dollars worth of investment, requiring thousands of software engineers to work together in a timeframe that exceeds the actual time spent delivering these versions of Debian, which is governed by a small foundation funded by donations from industry and individuals. In other words, the fully integrated approach that COCOMO models would not be good enough to produce a software system comparable in size to Debian.

An interesting development in recent years is the emergence of open source projects where software is co-developed by developers working for or financed by competing organizations. This trend is motivated by the above metrics: It is the only cost-effective way to develop large software packages with many software engineers in a short timeframe. If the software is not differentiating the core products, continuing under an open source license may actually make them more differentiating.

The natural tendency of companies to protect investments and intellectual property is in direct conflict with this and poses an organizational and strategic challenge. A good example of a company that has overcome this reluctance is IBM. Five years ago they released the popular Java development environment eclipse under an open source license. Later they even transferred development and ownership of this product to an independent foundation. Doing so had benefits for them that outweighed the lost sales of their visual age product. First of all, many of their competitors have since contributed to the projects, and the resulting development environment is now the industry standard development platform. Because IBM is heavily associated with the eclipse product, this means that other companies have lost differentiating power while IBM gained some. Additionally, while IBM continues to invest much resources in eclipse, much of the investment is now shared with their competitors. So either they cut some cost here or they managed to improve and innovate at a lower cost (compared to doing everything in house). Also some things that IBM was not interested in were financed by others and are now also of use to IBM customers. Finally, their strong involvement in this product makes IBM an interesting partner for related products and services such as the middleware, hardware, and consultancy services IBM provides. Arguments along the same line may be found in the Cathedral and the Bazaar (17).

2.4. RESEARCH CHALLENGES OF THE COMPOSITIONAL APPROACH

The compositional approach represents a potential improvement for organizations currently using a software product line approach for developing their software. However, there are many challenges that will need to be addressed. In this section, we aim to provide an overview of these challenges.

2.4.1. Decentralized Requirements Management

A consequence of using a compositional approach is that requirements of the integrated products are managed separately from those of the individual components that are used in the system.

In the integration-oriented software product line development, requirements are managed centrally. When developing a new product based on the product line software, the product architect identifies which requirements are product-specific and which are fulfilled by the product line. The product line evolution in turn is centrally governed and driven by common requirements across products and other requirements that are believed to be useful for future products. Development of individual components in the product line is driven by these centrally managed requirements.

Characteristic of the compositional approach is that there is no central management of requirements and features. Product developers select components and architecture slices based on how well they support the product requirements but may also consider other factors such as, for example:

- *Ability to Influence Component Requirements*: Even if the requirements do not match 100%, the ability to influence the roadmap of the component may be decisive.
- *Component Roadmap*: The advertised component roadmap may include items that are currently not relevant for the product but might become relevant in the future
- *Reputation*: The component may have an established reputation with respect to important quality attributes.
- *Openness*: While often advertised as black boxes, many components require a level of understanding of the internal component design that effectively makes them white boxes. Arguably, this is an important reason for the apparent lack of success of COTSs. Additionally, it is an important factor in the success of open source components in the current software industry.

A successful component will be used by many products that may have little in common aside from the fact that they somehow depend on the component. Component requirements may be driven by a number of factors:

- Feedback on potential improvements from existing component consumers. In case of a commercial relation between producer and consumer, there may also be some contractual terms (e.g., in the context of a support contract).
- Market analysis of product requirements of products that currently do not use the component. Evolving the component to support those requirements presents an opportunity to grow market share.
- External factors such as standards. Component requirements may be (partially) based on standardized or de facto specifications. When such specifications evolve, supporting the evolved specification can become a requirement.
- Internal factors, such as improving quality factors that are important to the component developers such as, for example, maintainability. Other factors may include the personal interest of the developers that are involved to explore design alternatives or realize small improvements.

This approach results in a more bottom-up approach where instead of being tailored to a specific set of products (i.e., top-down approach), there tends to be an organic bottom-up process where more or less independently components are selected and put together to fulfill products requirements. In this way, potential conflicts between independently developed components are eventually resolved by the component selection and integration process.

2.4.2. Quality Management and Architecture

A characteristic of the compositional approach is that there is no central architecture. Instead, product and architecture slices each have their own architectures. This poses a number of interesting research challenges with respect to, for example, applying quality assessments methodologies, which mostly assume having a centrally managed architecture and full control over the assets governed by this architecture.

The intention of applying quality assessment methods is to verify conformance to centrally managed quality requirements (which do not exist in a compositional approach) and to improve product quality by addressing any identified quality issues. However, performing conventional architecture assessment at the product level makes relatively little sense due to the lack of control over the composed components.

- Consequently, quality assessment and improvements need to happen at the component or possibly architecture slice level. However, given the lack of central quality requirement managed and the lack of control over depending and dependent components, this means that guaranteeing system level quality with respect to quality requirements such as real-time constraints, throughput, security, and so on, is difficult. Component developers need to anticipate quality requirements of their potential customers and convert this anticipated demand into component improvements.
- A second issue is that architecture assessment methods mostly require an already integrated system. In a compositional approach, one would like to consider impact on quality before the components are integrated. Any identified problems might lead to component improvements but might also lead to the selection of alternative components.

A second goal of having explicit software architecture is to enforce architectural style and design rules. The reason for this is that this ensures that the architectural components fit together. A problem with commercial off-the-shelf components (COTS) has been finding components with matching interfaces. The absence of a centrally governed architecture does not mean that there are no guiding architectural principles. Necessarily, components that are going to be used together must share common architecture. At least a significant level of compatibility is required. Small differences can be bridged using glue code. However, it is not very desirable to create significant amounts of glue code when creating products. Consequently, the compositionality poses a number of interesting new challenges:

- How to document architectural properties of components and architecture slices.
- How to optimize product architecture such that is optimal for the components it will be composed off.
- How to design components such that they do not impose too many constraints.

2.4.3. Software Component Technology

Component-oriented programming and later web services have been advocated as a major step forward in building large software systems (18). This has been largely due to providing standardized component infrastructures with well-defined APIs and services as well as interoperability support. While this has been significant progress, it does not address the issues of variability and architecture as in software product lines.

In software product lines as well as in many tools for configuration management, dependencies between components are managed. Managed dependencies are clearly a basic ingredient for our compositional approach. Yet, this covers only the management of syntactic code dependencies—for example, regarding versions and API compatibility. The information in such systems can also include tested configurations and can hence be used to describe architecture slices.

Interesting in this context is also the work presented in (14). Van Ommering is a proponent of so-called populations of product lines and introduces component technology that supports this. His approach is very similar to ours but focuses more on the technical aspects of composing components than on the other aspects that we discuss in this chapter.

For our target of compositional software products lines, we need components that can also work in unforeseen use cases and environments. This, for instance, means more robustness and awareness of dependencies and interactions with other components. More specifically, the two main challenges we discuss here are semantic dependencies that must be managed more explicitly and, secondly, that components are designed in a more robust way.

Semantic interaction between components means that the component behavior has to be adapted when composing with others. This goes well beyond the syntactic compatibility of APIs and has been examined extensively in the context of feature interaction research (6). These interactions can be positive or negative:

- Positive interaction requires additional functionality to be added. For example, if we have an email client on a mobile phone and a picture viewer, it should be possible to email pictures from the viewer.
- Negative interaction requires us to disallow some cases or removal of ambiguities. Typically, two components or features contradict in their behavior or compete for resources which are limited. For instance, the silence mode of a phone should not disable the alarm clock.

In fact, some dependencies occur only when several components are combined and cannot be observed for two features at a time (16). Negative feature interaction-related problems can be very hard to find and are also not likely to be identified in the decentralized integration testing approach outlined earlier.

2.4.4. Process and Organizational Issues

As discussed in reference (4) there are several ways to organize software product line organizations. Adopting a compositional approach makes it both possible and necessary to organize differently. As argued in earlier sections, a key characteristic of a compositional approach is that there is less central management of requirements, architecture, and implementation. Essentially, development and evolution of components happens in a decentralized fashion. Decoupling of product and component development is an explicit goal of a compositional approach because it allows decision making that affects products to be separate from decision making that affects components.

Doing this in one organization introduces a contradiction in the sense that an organization typically has goals, targets, and a mission. All activity conducted by the organization (including component and product development) follows (or should follow from) this overall mission. This implies that product and component development are not independent at all. Consequently, introducing a compositional approach in a product line organization introduces a number of challenges:

- How to organize such that product development teams have the freedom to select external components or initiate development of new components rather than using the internally developed component. The business decision of a product team to not use the in-house developed component has negative consequences for the component team. The best technical solution may not be the best for the organization as a whole. Balancing such difficult and conflicting interests is a key challenge that needs to be addressed.

- Allowing component teams to take responsibility for their own roadmap and architecture may lead to a situation where resources are spent on feature development that is not going to be used by any of the product teams. Balancing innovation of component teams and product development is required to keep development cost under control.

- An issue in any organization is the distribution of resources (money, people, time, etc.) over the organizational units. Essentially, product teams and component teams are all competing for the same resources. However, product teams are typically the only organizational units directly contributing to revenue, which leads to a bias in their favor. Adopting a compositional approach therefore needs to create an internal value chain or market mechanism to distribute the internal development resources.

- While, initially, components may be used only by product teams, components may themselves become products that are potentially interesting for other software developing organizations. Where this does not conflict with product differentiation, it would be desirable to market such components as separate components or share the burden of developing such components with other companies, even if these companies are competitors. Productizing or open sourcing components internally is a natural side effect of a fully implemented compositional approach but may also introduce new requirements that are well outside the scope of product development.

For all these organizational challenges a careful balance needs to be made between the conflicting interests of component and product teams and the overall corporate mission. However, it should be noted that this is also true for a decompositional approach. The reason for converting from a software product line-based development approach to a compositional one is that central management of all these decisions becomes harder as development grows in scale and as the software product line scope widens.

2.5. SUMMARY

Software product families have found broad adoption in the embedded systems industry, as well as in other domains. Due to their success, product families at several companies experience a significant broadening of the scope of the family. We have discussed several key issues that can arise from this and also from other trends like external or open source software which is outside the control of one organization.

For product families that aim primarily to be open and cover a wide range of products, we have proposed the concept of compositional product families. This approach relies on a decentralized organization that gives the product creation more flexibility and responsibility. Also it gives similar freedom to internal component developers.

Instead of a fully integrated platform, we rely on the new concept of architecture slices to ensure integration and testing beyond component level testing. Furthermore, we have shown that this compositional approach must include all aspects of software development in order to be successful. Additionally, we have identified several key research challenges of this new approach with respect to requirements, quality management, and software component technologies, as well as processes and split of responsibility within an organization.

A topic that interests us at Nokia, where development has been based mostly on integration oriented approaches, is that of cross-cutting behavior and nonfunctional requirements such as performance and power consumption. This has proven to be extremely hard in the integration-oriented approach we depend on currently.

REFERENCES

1. J.-J. Amor-Iglesias, J. M. González-Barahona, G. Robles-Martínez, and I. Herráiz-Tabernero. Measuring Libre software using Debian 3.1 (Sarge) as a case study: Preliminary results. *UPGRADE: European Journal for the Informatics Professionals* **6**(3):13–16, 2005.
2. L. Bass, P. Clements, S. Cohen, L. Northrop, and J. Withey. Product Line Practice Workshop Report, Technical Report CMU/SEI-97-TR-003, Software Engineering Institute, June 1997.

3. J. Bosch. *Design and Use of Software Architectures: Adopting and Evolving a Product Line Approach.* Pearson Education (Addison-Wesley & ACM Press), Reading, MA, 2000.

4. J. Bosch. Maturity and evolution in software product lines: Approaches, artefacts and organization. In *Proceedings of the Second Conference Software Product Line Conference (SPLC2)*, pages 257–271, 2002.

5. J. Bosch. Expanding the scope of software product families: Problems and alternative approaches. In *Proceedings of the 2nd International Conference on Quality of Software Architectures (QoSA 2006)*, LNCS 4214, page 1, Springer, 2006.

6. M. Calder, M. Kolberg, E. H. Magill, and S. Reiff-Marganiec. Feature interaction: A critical review and considered forecast. *Computer Networks.* **41**(1):115–141, 2003.

7. D. Dikel, D. Kane, S. Ornburn, W. Loftus, and J. Wilson. Applying software product-line architecture. *IEEE Computer* **30**(8):49–55, 1997.

8. J. van Gurp. OSS Product Family Engineering. First International Workshop on Open Source Software and Product Lines at SPLC 2006. Available from www.sei.cmu.edu/splc2006/

9. J. van Gurp, R. Smedinga, and J. Bosch. Architectural design support for composition and superimposition. In *Proceedings of the 35th Hawaii International Conference on System Sciences (HICSS-35 2002)*, page 287, 2002.

10. IEEE Std P1471-2000. *Recommended Practice for Architectural Description of Software-Intensive Systems.* IEEE, New York, 2000.

11. T. Kim, Y. T. Song, L. Chung, and D. T. Huynh. Dynamic software architecture slicing. In *Proceedings of the 23rd International Computer Software and Applications Conference (COMPSAC '99)*, pages 61–66, 1999.

12. R. R. Macala, L. D. Stuckey Jr., and D. C. Gross. Managing domain-specific product-line development. *IEEE Software* **13**(3):57–67, 1996.

13. R. van Ommering. Building product populations with software components. In *Proceedings of the 24th International Conference on Software Engineering*, pages 255–265, 2002.

14. R. van Ommering and J. Bosch. Widening the scope of software product lines—From variation to composition. In *Proceedings of the 2nd Software Product Line Conference (SPLC2)*, pages 328–347, 2002.

15. W. Pree and K. Koskimies. Framelets—small and loosely coupled frameworks, *ACM Computing Surveys* **32**(1):6, 2000.

16. C. Prehofer. Feature-oriented programming: A new way of object composition. *Concurrency and Computation* **13**(6):465–501, 2001.

17. E. S. Raymond. *The Cathedral and the Bazaar: Musings on Linux and Open Source by an Accidental Revolutionary.* O'Reilly & Associates, Sebastopol, CA, 1999.

18. M. Stal. Web services: Beyond component-based computing. *Communications of the ACM* **45**(10):71–76, 2002.

19. C. Szyperski. *Component Software—Beyond Object Oriented Programming.* Addison-Wesley, Reading, MA, 1997.

20. D. Wheeler. More than a Gigabuck: Estimating GNU/Linux's Size, www.dwheeler.com/sloc/redhat71-v1/redhat71sloc.html, 2002.

3

TEACHING DESIGN PATTERNS

Bernd Brügge and Timo Wolf

3.1. INTRODUCTION

In object-oriented development, design patterns are template solutions that developers have refined over time to solve a range of recurring problems (2). A design pattern consists of a name, a problem description, a solution, and consequences. Design patterns belong to the basic knowledge of software engineers, architects, and object-oriented developers and provide a common language between participants of a software development project. Using design patterns include

- the knowledge of a broad range of design patterns,
- problem analysis and the identification of possible design patterns,
- the implementation of design patterns in source code, and
- the identification of design patterns in source code.

While we were teaching software engineering including design patterns, we recognized that students have problems in understanding and applying design patterns. Some students just look at the design pattern class models, provided from design pattern catalogs, but do not internalize the sense and concepts of the patterns and their dynamic behavior. They have problems to apply the knowledge to a given problem, to separate between

Emerging Methods, Technologies, and Process Management in Software Engineering. Edited by De Lucia, Ferrucci, Tortora, and Tucci
Copyright © 2008 John Wiley & Sons, Inc.

design pattern concepts and their implementation, and to identify implemented design pattern concepts from source code. For instance, we observed students having problems in explaining the observer pattern, but not in explaining the mechanisms of the Java mouse event listener. They were not able to see the same concept.

We recognized that practical experiences are needed to understand and internalize the application of design pattern. Therefore, we developed a set of design pattern exercises that are described in this chapter. The exercises are based on our implementation of the old Asteroids game, which builds the target for applying design pattern. We cover the design pattern concepts by modeling exercises and implement the models in Java. We designed the exercises to be small and simple enough so that beginner students are able to understand them and to realize the exercises within a short time. The system is also large enough so that the advantages of applying design patterns get clear and don't create more overhead than changing the system without a design pattern.

The exercises start with a running system and its initial design. Each following exercise provides a requirement that must be solved by applying a design pattern, including modeling and its implementation. As opposed to the exercises in reference 4, all exercises in the present chapter are incremental and extend the system under development. Each sample solution provides a pattern-based object model and its implementation, building the basis for the following exercise.

Section 3.2 describes the design of our sample system. A short tutorial about compiling and executing the system is covered in Section 3.3. The design pattern exercises are described from Section 3.4 to Section 3.9 and cover the observer, adapter, and strategy pattern. We conclude by describing our experiences of executing the tutorial in Section 3.10.

3.2. THE DESIGN OF ASTEROIDS

In this section we describe the Asteroids game and provide an initial design of the system. All of the following exercises are based on this design.

3.2.1. Game Description

The Asteroids player controls a space shuttle on a game board, representing the outer space. Two different types of asteroids are also present on the game board: (a) small and fast asteroids, which change their direction only when they hit the edge of the game board, and (b) big and slow asteroids, which may change their direction any time. All asteroids can change their speed, ranging from a minimum to a maximum speed. The player can fire rockets and change the direction and speed of the space shuttle by using the keyboard. Striking a big asteroid with a rocket replaces the big asteroid with three small asteroids. Striking a small asteroid removes the asteroid from the game board. The player wins if he destroys all asteroids. He loses if his space shuttle collides with any asteroid. Figure 3.1 shows a screenshot of the initial version of Asteroids.

Figure 3.1. Screenshot of the initial Asteroids game.

Based on the game description, we provide the initial object design in Fig. 3.2. We focus on the main classes and concepts and omit unnecessary details.

In the following we describe the classes of Fig. 3.2:

3.2.2. Class: Game

The Game class represents the main window of the asteroids application. It consists of a GameBoard and a ToolBar class. It is the root component for all graphical user interface classes.

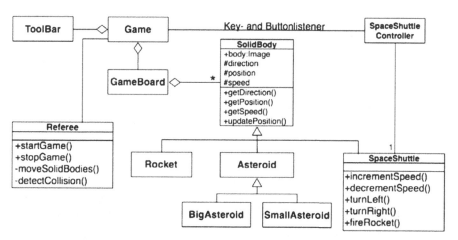

Figure 3.2. Initial object design of Asteroids (UML class diagram).

3.2.3. Class: `ToolBar`

The class `ToolBar` is a graphical component that presents a start and stop button to the Asteroids player.

3.2.4. Class: `SolidBody`

The class `SolidBody` represents an abstraction of all objects that move over the `GameBoard`. The `SolidBody` has a body attribute that represents an image used for painting. The flight direction is stored in the direction attribute. Values from 0 and 360 are valid and represent the direction in degree. Zero degree is the direction pointing to the top. The position attribute has a horizontal and a vertical coordinate and holds the current position of a `SolidBody`. Each `SolidBody` has a speed attribute. All attributes are protected to prevent modifications from foreign objects. Getter operations are provided to access the attributes of the `SolidBody`. The operation `updatePosition ()` computes and sets a new position, based on the speed and direction attribute values. If the new position reaches the boundary of the `GameBoard`, the direction of the solid body gets changed with the rule: the angle of incidence is the angle of reflection.

3.2.5. Class: `Asteroid`

Represents an asteroid that moves over the `GameBoard`. The `Asteroid` class overwrites the `updatePosition ()` operation and randomly increments or decrements the speed.

3.2.6. Class: `BigAsteroid`

The class `BigAsteroid` specializes the `Asteroids` class by adding extra functionality that randomly changes the direction.

3.2.7. Class: `SmallAsteroid`

This represents a small asteroid that moves with higher speed than do objects of the `BigAsteroid` class.

3.2.8. Class: `SpaceShuttle`

The space shuttle is the solid body, controlled by the player. The player loses the game if the space shuttle is destroyed. He wins if the space shuttle is the only solid body that is left on the GameBoard. The class provides public operations to change the speed, the direction, and to fire rockets.

3.2.9. Class: `Rocket`

`Rocket` objects get created by the fireRocket() operation of the `SpaceShuttle` class. Their direction is the space shuttle's direction and do not change. Rockets destroy any other solid bodies. They get removed from the `GameBoard` when reaching the `GameBoard` boundaries or when hitting other solid bodies.

3.2.10. Class: `GameBoard`

The `GameBoard` represents the outer space of the game asteroids. It consists of many `SolidBody` objects. During a game, the solid bodies are moving on the `GameBoard`. The `GameBoard` paints the images of the `SolidBodies` at their position. The positions of the solid bodies are always within the surface of the `GameBoard`.

3.2.11. Class: `Referee`

The `Referee` class is the main controller of the game Asteroids. It is responsible for starting, controlling, and stopping the game. Starting the game creates a separate control thread that invokes the operation moveSolidBodies() in frequent intervals. The operation moveSolidBodies() calls the updatePosition() operation of all solid-body objects and forces the `GameBoard` to repaint, thus enabling the `SolidBody` movement. After moving all solid bodies, the operation -detectCollision (...) : SolidBody is used to identify collisions. It computes if the two solid bodies body1 and body2 intersect and decides which solid body gets destroyed. The destroyed solid body is returned. If two asteroids intersect, none of them get destroyed. If an asteroid or the space shuttle intersects with a rocket, the asteroid or space shuttle gets destroyed. If an asteroid intersects with a space shuttle, the space shuttle gets destroyed. After detecting collisions, the Referee tests if the player has won or lost the game. He wins if no asteroids are left on the `GameBoard`. He loses if the space shuttle gets destroyed. In these cases, or if the stopGame () operation is invoked, the control thread and the game get stopped.

3.2.12. Class: `SpaceShuttleController`

The `SpaceShuttleController` listens to keyboard and mouse events. Depending on the events, space shuttle operations are invoked, to change the direction and speed or to fire a new rocket.

3.3. DOWNLOADING AND EXECUTING ASTEROIDS

This section describes how Asteroids can be downloaded, compiled, and executed. Asteroids is developed and hosted by the Chair for Applied Software Engineering at the Technical University of Munich (TUM). All resources are available from a password-protected Asteroids project portal. The address URL and the password can be received by asking via email. In this chapter, we use the variable $Asteroids as a placeholder for the address. The portal provides subportals for each exercise and solution. We describe the compilation and execution of Asteroids for the initial version of Asteroids, described in Section 3.2.

Download the source code of the initial game of Asteroids from http://$Asteroids/1_InitialGame/downloads and unpack the archived file. You should find the following folders and files.

- **src**: This contains all Java source code files, images and sound files of asteroids.
- **etc**: This contains script files for starting the Asteroids game on different platforms (e.g. Windows, Linux and Mac OS X).
- **build.xml**: This is the Ant build file for compiling and packaging the asteroids game.

For compiling and running the game, Java 1.5 and Apache-Ant is required. Skip the following steps if Ant and Java SDK is already installed.

- Download the Java SDK 1.5 or higher.
  - o Java J2SE 5.0 can be downloaded from
    http://java.sun.com/j2se/1.5.0/download.jsp
- Install Java and follow the installation instructions.
- *Note*: Some applications may require the system environment variable JAVA_HOME. Make sure that the JAVA_HOME environment variable is set correctly.
- Download the latest version of Apache-Ant from
  http://ant.apache.org/bindownload.cgi
- Install Ant by following the Apache Ant Manual
  (http://ant.apache.org/manual/index.html)

After successfully installing Java and Ant, we are able to compile and run Asteroids. Open a command line shell and change to the unpacked folder of Asteroids. On Windows, the execution of the cmd command starts the command line shell, and on Unix-based systems any shell like bash can be used. The steps below describe the Ant tasks, provided by the downloaded build.xml file:

- Type ant compile to compile the Asteroids source code. The Java class files are compiled into a new classes folder. All image and sound files are copied from the src folder into the classes folder.
- Typing ant invokes the default ant target called build, which creates the Asteroids executables for all supported platforms. A new folder build will be created containing two subfolders Asteroids and OSX. The Asteroids folder consists of the Java archive asteroids.jar, containing all compiled

Java classes, as well as startup scripts for Windows and Unix systems. The OSX folder contains an executable application for Mac OS X.

- Type `ant clean` to delete the `classes` and the `build` folders.

After compiling and building, we can execute Asteroids. The compiled java classes, resources and required startup information are packed in the Java archive `build/Asteroids/asteroids.jar`. Double-clicking on the `asteroids.jar` file will start Asteroids on most platforms. In addition, we provide startup scripts for the following:

- **Windows**: Open the Windows Explorer and change to the folder `build/Asteroids`. Double click on the batch file `asteroids.bat`.
- **Unix-Based System**: Open a shell and change to the folder `build/Asteroids`. Type `./asteroids.sh` to start the Asteroids application.
- **Mac OS X**: Open the Finder and change to the folder `build/OSX`. Double click on the Asteroids application to start Asteroids.

3.4. EXERCISE 1: OBSERVER PATTERN MODELING

In the first exercise, the initial object design (see Fig. 3.2) should be changed to meet the requirement:

> The player of Asteroids should see relevant information of the space shuttle during a game. The information must include the current speed, direction, and position of the space shuttle.

To realize the requirement, an instrument panel should be added to the initial object design model of asteroids. The instrument panel consists of instruments that display the required states (e.g., speed, direction, and position) of the SpaceShuttle. The design must be extendible for new instruments and thus require minimal coupling to reduce future change effort. The instruments for this exercise are

- a speedometer, displaying the speed,
- a compass, displaying the direction, and
- a GPS, displaying position of the space shuttle.

The instruments should always display the changing states of the space shuttle. Use the Observer Pattern (see reference 1, page 702) to publish state changes to the instruments.

Exercise Task
- Draw a UML class diagram that realizes the given requirement.
- Draw a UML sequence diagram that shows the interactions between the space shuttle and the instruments.

The required exercise model should focus on the concepts of the Observer Pattern and should only contain attributes and operation that are needed to understand the design. Details about instruments like the GPS or the compass, as well as existing classes that are irrelevant for the solution, can be ignored.

3.4.1. Sample Solution for Exercise 1

The UML class diagram shown in Fig. 3.3 provides a sample solution for Exercise 1. Only relevant classes, focusing on the Observer Pattern and the instruments, are shown.

First, we added the application domain classes described in the exercise. We created a new class `InstrumentPanel`, which consists of many `Instruments`. The class `Instrument` is abstract and generalizes all concrete instrument classes like the `Compass`, `Speedometer` or the `GPS`. The `Instrument` class reduces the amount of associations between the `InstrumentPanel` and the concrete instruments. Otherwise, the `InstrumentPanel` would have an association to each concrete instrument, and new associations are required when adding new instruments.

We applied the Observer Pattern to notify the instruments of space shuttle changes. The `SpaceShuttle` becomes the `Publisher` as it provides the information to present. The `Instrument` class becomes the `Subscriber`. `Subscriber` instances can be subscribed and unsubscribed on the `Publisher` and, thus, on the `SpaceShuttle`. The `notify()` operation of the `Publisher` invokes the `update()` operation of all subscribed instruments to announce changes of the `SpaceShuttle`. All concrete instruments implement the abstract operation `update()`. They retrieve the required information from the `SpaceShuttle` and

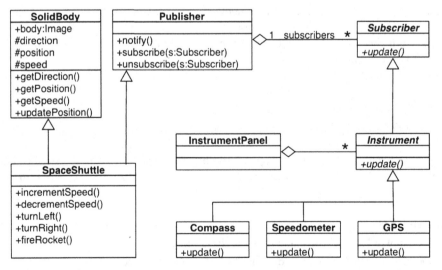

Figure 3.3. Object design including the instruments and the Observer Pattern.

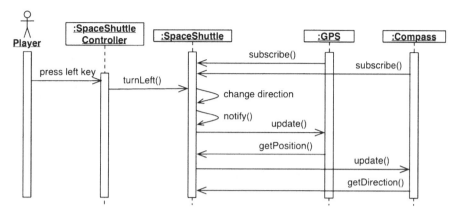

Figure 3.4. Interaction between the space shuttle and its instruments.

update their visualization whenever the `update ()` operation is invoked. Figure 3.4 illustrates the interaction as a UML sequence diagram. The provided design is extensible, because no changes on the `SpaceShuttle`, `InstrumentPanel`, or `Instrument` class are needed when adding new concrete instruments.

Note that the design uses multiple inheritance for the `SpaceShuttle`, which is not supported in all programming languages. We provided an implementation-independent design that explains the concept. The concept can be realized in any programming language. The implementation must not exactly reflect the class structure of the design.

3.5. EXERCISE 2: OBSERVER PATTERN PROGRAMMING

Exercise 2 focuses on the implementation of the object design including the Observer Pattern from Exercise 1. The exercise works on a source code stub that implements parts of the design. Download the source code stub from:

`http://$Asteroids/2_ObserverPatternExercise/downloads.`

Compile and execute Asteroids as described in Section 3.3. The Observer Pattern, the Speedometer and the GPS are already implemented according to the object design of Exercise 1.

Exercise Task

Implement the class `Compass`, showing the direction of the space shuttle. The `Compass` must extend the `Instrument` class and must be added to the `InstrumentPanel`. Subscribe the `Compass` to the space shuttle to receive notifications of the direction changes from the space shuttle.

Before starting the implementation, we want to explain the main classes of this exercise. The design from Exercise 1 uses multiple inheritance for the `SpaceShuttle` class. Java does not support multiple inheritance. Therefore, we merge the `Publisher` class into the `SpaceShuttle` class by adding the required methods.

```java
public class SpaceShuttle extends SolidBody {

  private ArrayList<SpaceShuttleSubscriber> subscribers;
  :
  :
  public void incrementSpeed () {...}
  public void decrementSpeed () {...}
  public void turnRight () {...}
  public void turnLeft () {...}
  public void fireRocket () {...}
  :
  :
  protected void setSpeed(int speed) {
    super.setSpeed(speed);
    notifySpaceShuttleSubscribers ();
  }
  protected void setDirection(int direction) {
    super.setDirection(direction);
    notifySpaceShuttleSubscribers ();
  }
  public void subscribe(SpaceShuttleSubscriber subscriber)
{...}
  public void unsubscribe(SpaceShuttleSubscriber subscriber)
{...}
  public synchronized void notifySpaceShuttleSubscribers ()
{...}
}
```

Note the differences between design and its implementation. In the design we added the class `Subscriber` to show that we use the Observer Pattern. We realize the `Subscriber` class with a Java interface called `SpaceShuttleSubscriber`. The name points out that the subscribers can subscribe on a space shuttle and increases the readability of the source code. The `SpaceShuttle` class just knows the interface `SpaceShuttleSubscriber`, which can be any implementing class. The `SpaceShuttle` class needs no modifications if new concrete `SpaceShuttle Subscriber` classes are added.

```java
public interface SpaceShuttleSubscriber {
  void update();
}
```

The abstract Java class `Instrument` implements the `SpaceShuttle Subscriber` and extends the class `JPanel`, a graphical container of Swing. It provides a protected instance variable that concrete subclasses can use to retrieve the space shuttle information to display. The concrete subclasses like the GPS or the Speedometer can add any graphical Swing components to visualize information of the SpaceShuttle. The update () operation gets invoked whenever the attributes of the SpaceShuttle gets changed.

```
public abstract class Instrument extends JPanel implements
    SpaceShuttleSubscriber {

  protected SpaceShuttle spaceshuttle;

  public Instrument(SpaceShuttle spaceshuttle) {
    this.spaceshuttle = spaceshuttle;
  }

  public abstract void update ();
}
```

The class InstrumentPanel is also a graphical Swing container, which contains all instruments. The InstrumentPanel creates the instrument instances and subscribes them to the SpaceShuttle. The following code extract shows the initialization of the instruments GPS and Speedometer.

```
public class InstrumentPanel extends JToolBar {
  :
  :
  public InstrumentPanel(SpaceShuttle theSpaceShuttle) {
    super(JToolBar.VERTICAL);
    setFloatable(false);
    this.spaceshuttle = theSpaceShuttle;

    :
    :
    speedometer = new Speedometer(theSpaceShuttle);
    theSpaceShuttle.subscribe(speedometer);
    add(speedometer);

    gps = new GPS(theSpaceShuttle);
    theSpaceShuttle.subscribe(gps);
    add(gps);
    :
    :
  }
  :
  :
}
```

3.5.1. Sample Solution for Exercise 2

We only show the main parts of the sample solutions of Exercise 2. The complete source code can be downloaded from

```
http://$Asteroids/2_ObserverPatternSolution/downloads
```

First, we create the requested class Compass that extends the abstract class Instrument. We add a JLabel to the Instrument container, which displays the direction of the SpaceShuttle as text. We update the text, whenever the update() method gets invoked and the direction has changed.

```java
public class Compass extends Instrument {

  private JLabel theLabel = new JLabel("", JLabel.CENTER);
  public Compass(SpaceShuttle spaceshuttle) {
    super(spaceshuttle);
    setLayout(new BorderLayout ());
    add(theLabel, BorderLayout.CENTER);
    theLabel.setText(getText(spaceshuttle.getDirection ()));
  }
  public void update() {
    String newText = getText(spaceshuttle.getDirection ());
    if (!newText.equals(theLabel.getText ())) {
      theLabel.setText(newText);
    }
  }

  private String getText(int direction) {
    return "Direction: " + direction;
  }
}
```

Second, we create a new Compass instance, subscribe it to the SpaceShuttle, and add it to the InstrumentPanel:

```java
public class InstrumentPanel extends JToolBar {
  :
public InstrumentPanel(SpaceShuttle theSpaceShuttle) {
    super(JToolBar.VERTICAL);
    :
    compass = new Compass(theSpaceShuttle);
    theSpaceShuttle.subscribe(compass);
    add(compass);
    :
  }
  :
}
```

3.6. EXERCISE 3: ADAPTER PATTERN MODELING

Exercise 3 focuses on the problem of integrating software components that are not modifiable and that do not fit into the design of the system under development. The components are either third-party components or legacy systems that provide required functionality.

In Exercise 3, we added the class `AnalogSpeedometer` to the Asteroids project, which displays speed with a needle but does not extend the `Instrument` class, does not follow the Observer Pattern from Exercise 1, and does not event know the class `SpaceShuttle` (see Fig. 3.5). The `AnalogSpeedometer` class provides the public operation `setAngle(angle:int)` that sets the angle of the speedometer needle. It takes values between 0 and 180 degrees.

Exercise Tasks

- Draw a UML class diagram, integrating the `AnalogSpeedometer` into the Observer Pattern mechanism (see Fig. 3.5), so that it always displays the current speed of the space shuttle. The `AnalogSpeedometer` is treated as a legacy class that cannot be modified. The Adapter Pattern (see reference 1, page 697) should be used for the integration.
- Draw a UML sequence diagram, illustrating the dynamic behavior of the Adapter Pattern, when updating the `AnalogSpeedometer`.

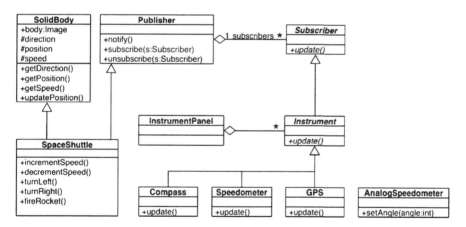

Figure 3.5. Diagram illustrating the legacy class `AnalogSpeedometer`, which should be integrated into the design of Asteroids but cannot be modified.

3.6.1. Sample Solution for Exercise 3

The UML class diagram in Fig. 3.6 shows the integration of the analog speedometer in Asteroids by using the Adapter Pattern. We removed all previous introduced instruments to increase the readability. To integrate the `AnalogSpeedometer` class, we created the new adapter class `AnalogSpeedometerAdapter`. The adapter class is

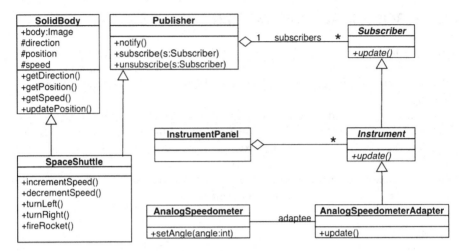

Figure 3.6. Sample solution for integrating the `AnalogSpeedometer` class by applying the Adapter Pattern.

associated with the `AnalogSpeedometer` and extends the `Instrument` class to fit into the Observer Pattern design.

Figure 3.7 shows a UML sequence diagram that illustrates the dynamic behavior of the integration. The `AnalogSpeedometerAdapter` is a subscriber of the space shuttle and the `update()` operation is invoked when any space shuttle attribute value changes. The `update()` operation retrieves the current speed from the space shuttle and computes and sets the related angle to the `AnalogSpeedometer`. The `AnalogSpeedometer` must not be changed.

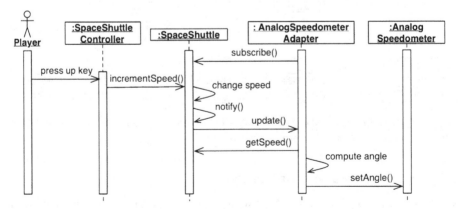

Figure 3.7. UML sequence diagram that illustrates the dynamic behavior of the integrated `AnalogSpeedometer` by using the Adapter Pattern.

3.7. EXERCISE 4: ADAPTER PATTERN PROGRAMMING

Within Exercise 4, we implement the Adapter Pattern integration described in Section 3.6. The exercise source code sub can be downloaded from

```
http://$Asteroids/3_AdapterPatternExercise/downloads
```

We added the Java class `AnalogSpeedometer.java` to the package `legacysystem`, which realizes the analog speedometer. The `Analog Speedometer` extends also the Java class `JPanel` and is already added to the graphical container `InstrumentPanel`:

```
public class InstrumentPanel extends JToolBar {
  :
  public InstrumentPanel(SpaceShuttle theSpaceShuttle){
    :
    analogspeedometer = new AnalogSpeedometer ();
    add(analogspeedometer);
    :
  }
  :
}
```

After compiling and executing Asteroids, you will recognize that the analog speedometer does not show the current speed of the space shuttle.

Exercise Task
- Integrate the analog speedometer into the system by using the adapter pattern. Create a new Java class called `AnalogSpeedometerAdapter.java`, which implements the Adapter Pattern as shown in Section 3.6. It should delegate the speed from the space shuttle to the analog speedometer. The file `AnalogSpeedometer.java` should not be changed.

3.7.1. Sample Solution for Exercise 4

The complete source code of the sample solution for exercise 4 can be downloaded from

```
http://$Asteroids/3_AdapterPatternSolution/downloads
```

We create the class `AnalogSpeedometerAdapter` in the instruments package of Asteroids. The instance of the adapted `AnalogSpeedometer` class is provided in the constructor and set as the private instance variable. The `AnalogSpeedometer`

Adapter class extends the Instrument class. The update() method implementation retrieves the current speed of the space shuttle and computes the angle for the analog speedometer. To reduce needless computations, we store the latest speed value of the space shuttle in a private instance variable and compute the angle only if the current speed is different.

```
public class AnalogSpeedometerAdapter extends Instrument {
  private AnalogSpeedometer adaptee;
  private int speed;

  public AnalogSpeedometerAdapter(SpaceShuttle spaceshuttle,
      AnalogSpeedometer analog_speedometer) {
    super(spaceshuttle);
    this.adaptee = analog_speedometer;
    update();
  }
  public void update() {
    if (this.speed != spaceshuttle.getSpeed()) {
     this.speed = spaceshuttle.getSpeed();

     double percent = 1.0d / (double) spaceshuttle.getMaximumSpeed()
         * (double) this.speed;
     int angle = (int) ((double) adaptee.getMaxAngle() * percent);
     this.adaptee.setAngle(angle);
    }
  }
}
```

To enable the adapter mechanism, we modify the InstrumentPanel class by creating a new AnalogSpeedometerAdapter instance and subscribe it in to the space shuttle.

```
public class InstrumentPanel extends JToolBar {
   :
  private AnalogSpeedometer analogspeedometer;
  private AnalogSpeedometerAdapter analogspeedometeradapter;
   :
  public InstrumentPanel(SpaceShuttle theSpaceShuttle) {
    :
    analogspeedometer = new AnalogSpeedometer();
    analogspeedometeradapter = new AnalogSpeedometerAdapter(spaceshuttle,
        analogspeedometer);
    theSpaceShuttle.subscribe(analogspeedometeradapter);
    add(analogspeedometer);
    :
  }
   :
}
```

3.8. EXERCISE 5: STRATEGY PATTERN MODELING

In the Asteroids system the class `Referee` is responsible for detecting collisions between different solid bodies. After a unit of time, the referee moves each of the bodies and identifies which of the solid bodies intersect with each other. The class `Referee` uses the method `detectCollision()`—shown in the source code below—to identify the intersection of two bodies. The method takes two objects of type `SolidBody` as parameters. If an intersection occurs, the crashed `SolidBody` is returned; otherwise, if no intersection occurs, `null` is returned. The subclass type of the parameter—Asteroids, SpaceShuttle, Rocket—is used to determine if the object is crashed. The implemented collision strategy is very simple: The space shuttle crashes whenever it intersects with any other object, asteroids intersecting with other asteroids never crash, and the rocket crashes any other object, but never crashes itself.

```
public SolidBody detectCollision(SolidBody solidbody1, SolidBody
solidbody2) {
    Point p1 = GameBoard.getInstance().convertPosition(
        solidbody1.getPosition());
    Dimension d1 = solidbody1.getSize();
    Rectangle r1 = new Rectangle(p1, d1);

    Point p2 = GameBoard.getInstance().convertPosition(
        solidbody2.getPosition());
    Dimension d2 = solidbody2.getSize();
    Rectangle r2 = new Rectangle(p2, d2);
    if (r1.intersects(r2)) {
      if (solidbody1 instanceof SpaceShuttle) {
        return solidbody1;

      } else if (solidbody2 instanceof SpaceShuttle) {
        return solidbody2;

    } else if (solidbody1 instanceof Rocket) {
      return solidbody2;

      } else if (solidbody2 instanceof Rocket) {
        return solidbody1;

      } else {
        return null;

      }
    }
    return null;
  }
```

This implementation has several disadvantages: The source code for the method detectCollision() is hard to read, because it contains conditional statements with several nesting levels. Furthermore, the collision strategy is realized outside the class SolidBody and its subclasses. As a result, it is hard to add new requirements, for example:

> The player of Asteroids should be able to change the collision strategy of the space shuttle at run time.

To be able to deal with these types of requirements, we apply refactoring of the source code and model transformations on the class diagram:

1. *Refactoring of the Source Code.* We extract the functionality of checking whether a solid body gets crashed and move it into a new method called +collide(body:SolidBody):boolean of the class SolidBody. Therefore, the Referee has only to detect if two SolidBodies intersect and asks the bodies if they get crashed by calling the collide() method. The following code fragment shows the changes in the Referee class.

```java
private void moveSolidBodies() {
    GameBoard gameBoard = GameBoard.getInstance();
    SolidBody[] solidbodies = gameBoard.getSolidBodies();

    int max_x = gameBoard.getSize().width;
    int max_y = gameBoard.getSize().height;
    for (int i = 0; i < solidbodies.length; i++) {
      solidbodies[i].updatePosition(max_x, max_y);
    }
    gameBoard.repaint();                           /

    HashSet<SolidBody> crashedBodyCache = new HashSet<SolidBody>();
    for (int z = 0; z < solidbodies.length; z++) {
      SolidBody solidbody1 = solidbodies[z];
      if (crashedBodyCache.contains(solidbody1)) {
        continue;
      }

      for (int i = 0; i < solidbodies.length; i++) {
        SolidBody solidbody2 = solidbodies[i];
        if (solidbody1 == solidbody2) {
          continue;
        }
        if (crashedBodyCache.contains(solidbody2)) {
          continue;
        }
        boolean collision = detectCollision(solidbody1, solidbody2);
        if (collision) {
          boolean isCrashed = solidbody1.collide(solidbody2);
```

```
            if (isCrashed) {
              crashedBodyCache.add(solidbody1);
              GameBoard.getInstance ().removeSolidBody(solidbody1);
            }

            isCrashed = solidbody2.collide(solidbody1);
            if (isCrashed) {
              crashedBodyCache.add(solidbody1);
              GameBoard.getInstance ().removeSolidBody(solidbody2);
            }
          }
        }
      }
    }

    if (!gameBoard.hasSolidBody(gameBoard.getSpaceShuttle ())) {
      stopGame ();
      JOptionPane.showMessageDialog(null, "You lost the game in "
          + gameduration_in_seconds + " seconds!", "Information",
          JOptionPane.INFORMATION_MESSAGE);
      int index = (int) (Math.random () * (double) gameoverClips.size ());
      AudioClip clip = (AudioClip) gameoverClips.get(index);
      clip.play ();

      initGame ();

    } else if (GameBoard.getInstance().getSolidBodies().length == 1) {
      stopGame ();
      JOptionPane.showMessageDialog(null,
          "Congratulation, you won the game in "
              + gameduration_in_seconds + " seconds!",
          "Information", JOptionPane.INFORMATION_MESSAGE);
      initGame ();
    }
  }

  public boolean detectCollision(SolidBody solidbody1, SolidBody
  solidbody2) {
    Point p1 = GameBoard.getInstance ().convertPosition(
        solidbody1.getPosition ());
    Dimension d1 = solidbody1.getSize ();
    Rectangle r1 = new Rectangle(p1, d1);

    Point p2 = GameBoard.getInstance ().convertPosition(
        solidbody2.getPosition ());
    Dimension d2 = solidbody2.getSize ();
    Rectangle r2 = new Rectangle(p2, d2);
    if (r1.intersects(r2)) {
      return true;
    } else {
      return false;
    }
  }
```

2. *Model Transformation.* Figure 3.8 shows a UML class diagram according to the changes above. The `Referee` class invokes the operation `collide(...)` of `SolidBody` instances, when the `detectCollision()` operation returned true. Note, that we show only relevant classes.

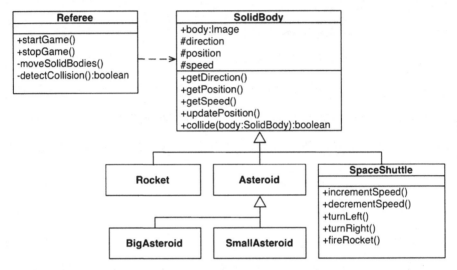

Figure 3.8. UML class diagram showing the refactoring changes. Only relevant classes are shown.

Exercise Task

To meet the requirement "change the collision strategy of the space shuttle at run time," the exercise task is to apply the Strategy Pattern to the UML class diagram.

- The collision strategy must be realized in a separate class called `CollisionStrategy`. The `CollisionStrategy` class is abstract and must provide abstract operations that realize the functionality of the collide(...) operation, so that the `SolidBody` class can delegate all `collide(...)` invocations to its `CollisionStrategy`.
- Provide concrete collision strategies for the space shuttle and the asteroids classes.
- Provide operations to change the collision strategies at run time.

3.8.1. Sample Solution for Exercise 5

The UML class diagram in Fig. 3.9 shows the usage of the strategy pattern to realize the changing of collision strategies at run time. The `Referee` class invokes the `collide(...)` operation of the `SolidBody` class. The solid body delegates the call to the

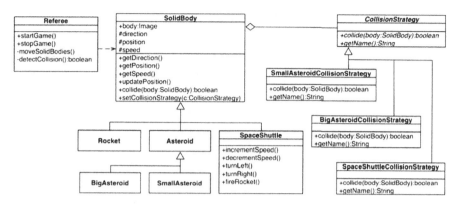

Figure 3.9. The UML class diagram shows the decoupling of the solid bodies and its collision strategies by using the strategy pattern.

associated `CollisionStrategy`. The current concrete implementing collision strategy subclass answers the call, and the solid body returns the result to the referee. The concrete subclass is not known to the solid body and can be changed at run time by the `setCollisionStrategy(...)` operation. We added the operation `getName():String` that returns the name of a collision strategy. The name will be used to display the current collision strategy of the space shuttle. Now, Asteroids is extendable by new collision strategies, without modifying the `Referee` or any `SolidBody` class.

3.9. EXERCISE 6: STRATEGY PATTERN PROGRAMMING

Exercise 6 is based on the Asteroids source code stub, which can be downloaded from

```
http://$Asteroids/4_StrategyPatternExercise/downloads
```

We already implemented the design provided in Section 3.8. The Strategy Pattern classes are located in the package `collisionstrategies`. The following code shows the abstract class `CollisionStrategy`. The implementing subclasses require a reference of the solid bodies on which the method `collide(...)` gets invoked. Therefore, the `CollisionStrategy` class provides a private instance variable with appropriate getter and setter methods.

```
public abstract class CollisionStrategy {
  private SolidBody solidBody;

  public void setSolidBody(SolidBody solidBody) {
    this.solidBody = solidBody;
  }
```

```
   public SolidBody getSolidBody () {
     return solidBody;
   }

   public abstract boolean collide(SolidBody opponent);

   public abstract String getName ();

   public String toString () {
     return getName ();
   }
}
```

The following code fragment shows the changes of the class SolidBody. It delegates the collide invocation to its current collision strategy and provides methods to retrieve and change the strategy. The setSolidBody (...) method of the Collision Strategy class gets invoked from the setCollisionStrategy (...) of the SolidBody class.

```
public abstract class SolidBody {
   :
   private CollisionStrategy collisionStrategy;

   public SolidBody(Point position, int direction) {
      :
     setCollisionStrategy(new DefaultCollision ());
   }
   :
   public boolean collide(SolidBody solidbody) {
     return collisionStrategy.collide(solidbody);
   }
   public void setCollisionStrategy(CollisionStrategy
   collisionStrategy) {
     if (collisionStrategy == null) {
       throw new IllegalArgumentException(
           "The given collision strategy is null.");
     }
     if (this.collisionStrategy != null) {
       this.collisionStrategy.setSolidBody(null);
     }

     this.collisionStrategy = collisionStrategy;
     this.collisionStrategy.setSolidBody(this);
   }
```

```
  public CollisionStrategy getCollisionStrategy () {
    return collisionStrategy;
  }
  :
}
```

After compiling and executing Asteroids, a new drop down list appears within the instrument panel (see the screenshot in Fig. 3.10). The list displays the current collision strategy of the space shuttle and contains all exiting strategies, which are located in the `collisionstrategies` package and get dynamically loaded by using Java Reflection. The collision strategy can be changed at run time.

Exercise Task
- Implement a new collision strategy that enables the space shuttle to collide with three asteroids before getting crashed. The new collision strategy must be located in the `collisionstrategies` package. Otherwise, the dynamic class loading mechanism will not find it.

3.9.1. Sample Solution for Exercise 6

The complete source code of the sample solution for Exercise 6 can be downloaded from

```
http://$Asteroids/4_StrategyPatternSolution/downloads
```

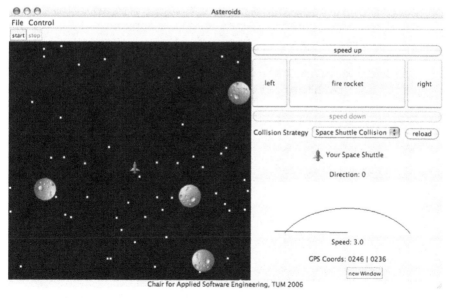

Figure 3.10. Screenshot of Asteroids including the collision strategy selection.

We implemented the following class SpaceShuttle3Credits that extends the
SpaceShuttleCollisionStrategy and reuses its collide (...) method
implementation. To realize the requested requirement, we added a counter called
credits that is initialized with 3. The counter gets decreased whenever the
collide (...) method of the superclass returns true. The collide (...)
method of the class SpaceShuttle3Credits returns false, until the counter
credits reached 0. The intersecting of two solid bodies takes some time, before
they are completely separated again. To avoid decreasing the counter to 0 within one
longer intersection, we only decrease the counter in three-second intervals.

```java
public class SpaceShuttle3Credits extends
SpaceShuttleCollisionStrategy {

  private int credits;

  private long lastCrashInMillis;

  public SpaceShuttle3Credits () {
    super ();
    credits = 3;
    lastCrashInMillis = System.currentTimeMillis ();
  }

  public boolean collide(SolidBody opponent) {

    boolean isCrashed = super.collide(opponent);
    if (isCrashed && credits > 0) {
      if ((System.currentTimeMillis ()
      -lastCrashInMillis)/1000 > 3) {
        lastCrashInMillis=System.currentTimeMillis ();
        credits--;
      }
      return false;
    } else {
      return isCrashed;
    }
  }
  public String getName () {
    return "3 credits";
  }
}
```

3.10. EXPERIENCES AND CONCLUSION

We applied the provided tutorial on design patterns several times in different teaching environments. We used the exercises accompanying to the Software Engineering lectures at the Technical University of Munich in the winter semesters 2004/2005 and 2005/2006. About 100 students from the third semester attended weekly practical sessions in which we performed the modeling exercises interactively with the students. We discussed the problem and asked the students to create a paper-based solution while providing individual help. A selected student introduced his sample solution before we provided and discussed our sample solution. The students had to accomplish the programming exercises individually during the week.

We executed the Asteroids exercises within the Pattern-Driven Development tutorial during the Second International Summer School on Software Engineering (5). Ph.D. students attended the four-hour tutorial, which already had deeper knowledge in design patterns, object-oriented development, and programming.

Patricia Lago used the exercises to teach design patterns within the Software Engineering course at the University Vrije Universiteit Amsterdam in Spring 2006 (3). The Software Engineering course focuses on theoretical principles of software engineering and covers design patterns in only one week. About 120 second-year computer science bachelor students participated in the lecture and were segmented into groups of 30. Each group performed a tutorial within a computer lab. The tutorial started with a 15-minute presentation on design patterns in general. Then, each exercise including the associated pattern was introduced in 15 minutes and individually solved by the students in 30 minutes. We received a positive feedback for the tutorial execution. They were able to teach design patterns including practical experiences within a very limited time and reported a good success in teaching design patterns to students.

We observed that teaching design pattern based on a real system instead of small toy examples improves the students understanding of design pattern-based development. Using a larger system increases difficulties at the beginning, but increases also the student motivation and creativity, when recognizing the ability to understand and extend the system by knowing the concepts behind. We received many exercise solutions that went beyond the requested tasks and got students asking for the realization of additional feature in Asteroids.

REFERENCES

1. B. Bruegge and A. H. Dutoit. *Object-Oriented Software Engineering Using UML, Patterns, and Java*, second edition. Prentice-Hall, Englewood Cliffs, NJ, 2003.

2. E. Gamma, R. Helm, and R. Johnson. *Design Patterns. Elements of Reusable Object-Oriented Software*. Addison-Wesley Professional Computing Series, Addison-Wesley, Reading, MA, 1995.

3. P. Lago, R. Farenhorst, and R. de Boer. *Software Engineering, Vrije Universiteit Amsterdam*, Spring 2006. http://bb.vu.nl/webapps/portal/frameset.jsp?tab=courses&url=%2Fbin%2Fcommon%2Fcourse.pl%3Fcourse_id%3D_17030_

4. A. Schmolitzky. A laboratory for teaching object-oriented language and design concepts with teachlets. In *Proceedings of the Conference on Object Oriented Programming Systems Languages and Applications (OOPSLA '05) Companion to the 20th Annual ACM SIGPLAN Conference on Object-Oriented Programming, Systems, Languages, and Applications.* pages 332–337, 2005.

5. *Second International Summer School on Software Engineering.* September 2005, Salerno. http://www.sesa.dmi.unisa.it/seschool/previousEditions/2005/.

PART II

EMERGING METHODS

4

ON THE IMPACT OF AOSE IN SERVICE-ORIENTED COMPUTING

Laura Bocchi, Paolo Ciancarini, Rocco Moretti, and
Valentina Presutti

4.1. INTRODUCTION

In this chapter we discuss the impact of Agent-Oriented Software Engineering (AOSE) in service-oriented computing. We consider some key ideas of the Service-Oriented Architecture (SOA) (7) in the context of the agents technologies for the coordination and composition of Web and Grid services.

In the last decade the Web as the dominating Internet service has evolved into the most popular and widespread platform for world-wide global information systems. At its core, the Web is a hypertext in which documents are offered by servers, retrieved by clients with the HTTP protocol and displayed by graphical interfaces that are very easy to use. Because of its diffusion, the usage of the Web as a platform for dynamic, distributed applications rapidly attracted the interests of both industry and academia (11).

At the same time, one of the main trends that we observe today within different areas of Computer Science is the creation of complex systems as a composition of simpler, heterogeneous and possibly distributed parts. On the *e-business* scenario, we observe a common trend toward *outsourcing* (24). Outsourcing means contracting workers from outside a company to perform specific tasks instead of using company employees. Applying this term to the Information Technology (IT) infrastructure of a company means exploiting external hardware and software resources and integrating them with

Emerging Methods, Technologies, and Process Management in Software Engineering. Edited by
De Lucia, Ferrucci, Tortora, and Tucci

the internal system of the company. The IT infrastructure of a company might thus comprise external resources, networks, and services as well as internal or legacy parts.

As to *e-science*, the need concerns huge computational power and wide storages to manage a large amount of data to support scientific tasks and experiments. Since the middle of the 1990s, the first Grid prototypes meant to address this issue. The consequent need for a middleware that integrates dynamic services running on distributed, heterogeneous platforms led to different, but in some parts interleaving, solutions.

It is hard to identify a general framework that allows the management of services in a standard and platform independent way. The middleware support for distributed applications can be a valid starting point to implement such a framework. However, the full interoperability among different middleware platforms is still not completely realized (26). In order to support services within a uniform reference architecture, there is the need for a lightweight framework that at least realizes interoperability between current middleware technologies.

Both the Model-Driven Architecture (MDA) (26) and the SOA (7) approaches attempt to address these needs. The MDA starts from the viewpoint of models and model specifications, whereas the SOA starts from an approach to distributed computing that regards software resources as services available on a network (7).

We underline the reasons that make software agents a suitable solution for the design and development of a service-oriented system over a Web and Grid infrastructure. In this context, we focus on the role of AOSE in the Web Services Architecture (WSA) (5) and the Grid.

Different application domains are adopting the Web protocols as a basis for service-oriented middleware infrastructures. For instance, e-business and e-science are currently focusing on middleware platforms merging the notion of SOA with the usage of Web infrastructures and protocols—that is, WSA for e-business and the Open Grid Service Architecture (OGSA) (21) for e-science.

This chapter is organized as follows. Section 4.2 introduces agent systems and the AOSE. Section 4.3 presents an overview of service-oriented computing. Section 4.4 presents issues concerning MDA-based services for Grid Agents. Section 4.5 focuses the discussion on coordination in the WSA. Section 4.6 discusses the central problem of defining an ontology to provide agents in the WSA a machine readable model of the domain of interest. Finally, Section 4.7 presents our conclusions pointing out possible future research directions.

4.2. AGENT SYSTEMS AND AOSE

An *agent* is an "encapsulated computer system, situated in some environment, and capable of flexible autonomous action in that environment in order to meet its design objectives" (37). Starting from this definition, an *agent system* is a way of thinking (a programming metaphor) about systems composed of active entities (i.e., the agents) and their collective behavior. Agent systems can be very heterogeneous: They can include hardware, software, active documents, orchestrated services, whole networks, and even people.

The agent metaphor is especially effective for building software for complex networked systems, where no global control is possible. The choice of having one or several agents depends on modularity, a desirable property when designing complex systems. In this context, a *software agent* is a programming artifact based on a specific computing model related to other computing models like subroutines/coroutines, functions/procedures, processes, and classes/objects. Broadly speaking, in software the term "agent" is used in many different ways: as a persistent process/daemon, a mobile code, autonomous robots, and an "intelligent" agent (in this last meaning, there is not an agreement on what makes it intelligent).

In this chapter, we mean software agents as the logical building blocks of the next generation of middleware. Such a middleware will build on top of the existing middleware (e.g., CORBA, EJB, Jini) and provide run-time integration via dynamic discovery and resource negotiation. In this context, we consider as AOSE a discipline dealing with the design and development of distributed, multi-agent applications (12).

AOSE focuses on intercomponent relationships, their software architecture, and the engineered approach to multi-agent development. Suitable abstractions and frameworks are defined in order to build coherent and well-structured systems from single components and to understand, manage, and maintain complex multi-agent applications.

AOSE provides a conceptual basis rooted in problem domains because agents are natural (simulative) abstractions in several contexts. Other motivations for AOSE are the increasing localization and encapsulation of software components of Internet applications and the strong support for reuse of designs and programs. The AOSE also enables whole subsystem components (design patterns, commercial off-the-shelf (COTS))—that is, multi-agent architectures and flexible interactions (application frameworks) as well as coordination architectures and auction protocols.

Starting from an AOSE-based approach, an agent-oriented software life cycle can be defined:

1. Requirements *specifications* for agent systems
2. Requirements *analysis*
3. *Design*
4. How to *implement* such systems
5. How to *verify* that implemented systems satisfy their specifications

Requirements *specifications* are provided by the user often in terms of desired scenarios or undesired scenarios. Such requirements are often ambiguous and contradictory and generally insufficient for system design. The *analysis* of the requirements is performed in order to determine the overall desired behavior of the system. Such a phase focuses on the main goals of the system, the roles that must be played for solving the problem, the resources available for solving the problem, the human interface, and the requirements. In particular, it is determined what can be varied in order to achieve the expected behavior and what cannot be varied. The *design* phase is for transforming high-level goals and roles into concrete agent types—that is, what agents will perform which roles. In this phase, the number and types of the agents are defined; high-level interactions are transformed into specific interaction protocols; and, finally, low-level functions of each agent type are defined in order to carry out high-level behaviors. In the *implementation* phase, protocols and low-level behavior are transformed into code. Besides, if not part of requirements, one decides on the communication mechanism, communication languages, content languages, and the implementation language. As regards the *verification* phase, one carries out a process for showing the evidence that requirements specifications are satisfied.

The agent-oriented methods for software development, that are a widely discussed topic in the research community (10, 36, 40), seem to be a meaningful starting point toward the definition of service-oriented software development methods. In order to present this possible evolution, we briefly consider two agent-oriented software development methods: Gaia and Tropos.

Gaia is a multi-agent systems engineering method describing the *analysis* and *design* phases on a high abstraction level (36). The *analysis* phase suggests to define a *role* and an *interactions model*. The *design* phase is where such concepts are translated into an agent model, a services model, and an acquaintance model. Gaia seems to be limited to small-scale systems for static organizations, even though an evolution of Gaia (40) enables one to model organizational rules.

Tropos (10) includes many different methods for requirements analysis and design. It enables one to model *actors*, *hard and soft goals*, *plans*, *resources*, and relations/dependencies among them. Tropos seems to be tailored for closed systems because of the model for agents internal architecture that it enables one to define.

In Section 4.7, we will discuss how it will be possible to move from AOSE to Service-Oriented Software Engineering (SOSE) by leveraging agent-oriented methods for designing SOAs.

4.3. THE IMPACT OF AGENTS IN SERVICE-ORIENTED ARCHITECTURES

The SOA is "a set of components which can be invoked, and whose interface descriptions can be published and discovered" (4). Services are network addressable entities with a well-defined and standardized interface. These services have stateless connections and are available to clients by waiting in an idle state until a request comes. They communicate by means of standard protocols, and they can be accessed and readily used with no need for integration. A service may be used in different scenarios because it is not bound to a precise customer context.

The notion of *service* presents analogies with the notion of software *component*. Services like components are loosely coupled and they are often designed independently from the context in which they are used and composed. The two concepts distinguish themselves by the level of abstraction. SOAs typically involve multiple organizations interacting with a networked systems where there is no single designer having full knowledge, control, and ownership. Services are the nonmaterial equivalent of a good; they are owned by a particular organization and they have a semantics that is meaningful for some other customer organization. In this sense, services are more coarse-grained than components.

As to the most known instances of SOA, because of its relationship with e-business scenarios, the WSA can be described as a self-interested system where a server provides some benefits to the client for its own interest (e.g., the service is "bought" by the client).

The OGSA (21) presents similar features, but, because of its connection with the Grid and e-science application scenarios, it has a stronger emphasis on the overall efficiency and optimization of resource usage versus a self-interested behavior.

Coordination and *composition* have a key role in architectures based on the notion of service. The activity of services is typically cooperative: They can be invoked by other services or interact in order to carry on a task. Furthermore, SOAs are multi-organization networked systems where there is no single designer having full knowledge, control, and ownership. Services can be published, modified, and revoked at any time. This implies a *high impact of change*. Finally, a SOA is characterized by *openness and uncertainties* since it is not possible to anticipate all the eventualities or prescribe in advance all the possible responses of the system. In order to address the issues outlined above, it is important to rely on

1. A software entity capable of addressing coordination and composition in a open system characterized by a high impact of change and
2. A machine-readable specification of the domain of interest—in particular, of the data exchanged among services and of the services semantics.

As to item 1, the automation of service coordination and composition can achieve considerable benefits from technologies deriving from the agents scenario. Agents are defined in reference 22 as "programs that operate at a high enough semantic level that they can form new connections to other programs in order to get a job done."

Agents are a goal/role-oriented computing model. The agent metaphor is especially effective for building software for complex networked systems where no global control is possible. In a highly dynamic system, sometimes it is desirable for composition relying not only on *a priori* information. In some cases, the aspects characterizing a service can be known just at run time (e.g., the load of a system) or they are critical for the client service.

The scenario of dynamic automated services composition is similar to Distributed Problem Solving (DPS) in multi-agent systems where some knowledge sources (KSs) have to find a cooperative solution to a problem in a decentralized way. In the context of DPS, each knowledge source is not able to autonomously achieve the solution; thus the problem is decomposed in sub-tasks that are delegated to some other KSs.

Davis and Smith (18) proposed the *Contract Net Protocol* (CNP) (31), enacting a negotiation based on a bidding activity to solve DPS. Negotiation is "... a discussion in which the interested parties exchange information and come to an agreement" (18). In the most general significance, the *discussion* is a process involving parties that can be either human or software agents. The interaction among agents involved in a CNP has been described by the Foundation for Intelligent Physical Agents (FIPA) (20) by means of the following steps:

1. The Initiator sends a call for proposal.
2. Each Participant reviews the received call for proposal (possibly from different initiators) and bids accordingly.
3. The Initiator chooses the best bid, awards the Contract to the respective Participants and rejects the other bids.

Reference 3 discusses the analogy of CNP (and the problem it addresses) with problems and solutions in the WSA.

As to item 2, it is important to have some model describing in a machine readable way the data exchanged and the capabilities provided by a service. In this context, a key issue is to suitably define which aspects of a service are captured by the description (e.g., its functional, nonfunctional and behavioral properties) and which kind of language is used to express them. In reference 23, three approaches to service description are discussed: text-based (i.e., searching is typically done by pattern matching), frame-based (i.e., properties of a service are expressed as attribute-value couples), and ontology-based. The advantage of using the third approach based on ontologies consists of considering recall (i.e., absence of false negative) and precision (i.e., absence of false positive) in the search process.

4.4. A MODEL-DRIVEN ARCHITECTURE OF SERVICES FOR GRID AGENTS

The real improvement provided by the SOA in middleware development is due to the Web service orientation of SOA-based systems. Web services allow a middleware to support standard-based SOAs with loosely coupled services that solve many interoperability problems. In an analogous way, Grid systems can be considered as an emerging service-oriented middleware using loosely coupled components and shifting the emphasis on resource sharing rather than on simple remote object coordination. The Grid was born as a static operating environment where resources are used by batch computations including scarce or none interaction (2, 21). It is evolving to become a more dynamic environment where resources can be discovered and exploited by means of agents embedded into service intensive applications (21).

This scenario implies that a framework for middleware integration consists of the convergence among Grid and Web service technologies and the current middleware in a service oriented model driven architecture. In this process, MDA can be used in order to put together all the technologies and offer a method for the design of platform independent software. These considerations lead to platform-independent modeling of Grid services (1). In a recent draft of the Globus Toolkit 4 (GT4) documentation (30), it is stated that "a service-oriented application is constructed via the composition of components defined by service interfaces (in the current context, Web services)." This sentence synthesizes the vision of convergence among middleware components, Web and Grid services in the SOA.

In order to bridge the gap between the current Grid-related technologies, the OGSA and the Web Service Resource Framework (WSRF) (8) define a model for Grid systems where everything is represented as a service: "a network enabled entity that provides some capabilities through the exchange of messages" (21). Such a model is actually an SOA supporting both local and remote transparency providing for interoperability.

In the OGSA, a Grid service is defined as a special Web service that provides a set of basic interfaces and following specific conventions. The WSRF attempts to concretely integrate the OGSA approach with Web services and the semantic Web technologies. It extends the Web Services Description Language (WSDL) mechanism enabling stateful Web/Grid Services. The existence of a state is a central topic because it enables the distinction of one instance of a service from another one. In this way, OGSA can be viewed as a distributed object system where each service instance has a unique identity and each instance has a state.

The Grid and Web convergence realized by the WSRF has meaningful implications at a higher level too, namely in the Semantic Grid (16) and the semantic Web service (35) envision of the Grid Services Architecture (GSA) described in terms of the OGSA (21). The Semantic Grid attempts to create an Internet-centered environment where resources are shared and managed relying on their interconnection semantics (39). The Semantic Web Services add semantics to Web Services exploiting service ontologies described in the DARPA Markup Language (DAML), Web Ontology Language (OWL) (34) or Unified Modeling Language (UML) (27). Both semantic Grid and semantic Web services researchers aim to apply the Semantic Web technologies to Web and Grid services in order to add semantics to service-oriented software, which is a fundamental requirement to enable agents and autonomous behaviors in SOAs. This vision is orthogonal to the lower-level convergence between Web and Grid achieved by OGSA and WSRF. In order to integrate all technologies exposed above in a service-oriented semantic Grid, the MDA (26) can be used as a harmonizing glue. Model transformations are one of the key features of MDA. A set of rules and techniques is used to transform a model described in UML into another one. In the MDA, the models represent parts of functions, structures or behaviors of a system at different levels of detail. The separation of refined model views from simplified ones allows the zooming-in of multiple alternative models of the same system functionality. The MDA provides the needed high-level approach to services development and allows the management of semantics and life cycle of business applications. It further allows to integrate other technologies and maintains complex applications within a lightweight architecture. Besides, the MDA in SOAs will enable a service-driven approach to the development of enterprise applications (30). Hence, MDA is an effective platform independent tool, just like UML has been and effectively neutral tool for object-oriented software.

In conclusion, the convergence between the Grid and Web services is the next step in the development of the GSA. On the one hand, the Web services simplify programming the Grid and on the other hand, they add some very useful mechanisms like platform independence, thereby allowing us to put together Web services, Grid services, and agents.

4.5. AGENT COORDINATION AND ORCHESTRATION IN THE WEB SERVICE ARCHITECTURE

Services, in their essence, are stateless entities. Besides, many business-to-business scenarios need a stateful, collaborative behavior thus implying complex coordination. It is thus crucial to specify a precise order and causality of the service operations (for example: a purchase should happen after a payment). In the Web service scenario, nothing prevents from coordinating services at the level of application code. Anyway, most coordination languages have their focus on a clear separation between coordination and computation, seen as orthogonal language design issues. A very famous metaphor (9) in the form of a simple equation establishes this orthogonality as follows:

$$\text{application} = \text{computation} + \text{coordination} \tag{4.1}$$

Thus, according to such a metaphor, a programming language should be composed of two orthogonal components: a coordination component and a computational component. This separation is effective from a software engineering viewpoint: keeping the specification of coordination issues separate from computational issues brings interaction to a higher level of abstraction thus simplifying the programming task. This separation is crucial in an SOA: in a loosely coupled system, characterized by a high impact of change, modularity is an important feature. Since the 1990s, the business logic can be expressed and managed separately from the application by means of a centralized Workflow Management System (WfMS). In the context of WfMSs, equation (4.1) has been rewritten as (25)

$$\text{workflow} = \text{activities} + \text{processes} \tag{4.2}$$

where the basic entities involved in a workflow are activities performing working units while processes are employed for coordinating such activities. This approach is followed by current XML-based languages (e.g., orchestration and choreography languages) that attempt to standardize the possibility of service coordination in the WSA. Different languages exist to define the different aspects of a service. For example, WSDL describes the interface, while orchestration-choreography languages describe the process. All these standards, anyway, do not capture the semantic of a service.

4.6. ONTOLOGICAL APPROACH FOR WSA

This section describes the advantages of combining an agent-oriented approach and WSA in the context of the so-called *semantic Web*. Web services provide a standard way for the interoperability of software applications that run on different platforms and frameworks. The Web service activity (38) of W3C has developed a set of technologies leading WSA to its full potential by the way the success of such technologies is growing in both industry and academia and cannot be fully exploited yet. The reason for this situation is in the lack of semantic-based technologies and infrastructures. The semantic Web has the goal of enabling knowledge sharing among heterogeneous, distributed and dynamic sources. Agents represent a natural way of implementing these kind of tasks. In fact, as underlined by reference 33, they are particularly suitable for processing semantic Web content. Furthermore, they expose social ability and autonomy. The agent is the concrete piece of software that acts in order to carry out a task, while the service is the resource characterized by the abstract set of provided functionalities. In reference 6 the vision of the semantic Web is explained with a scenario where

> software agents roaming from page to page can readily carry out sophisticated tasks for users.

Ontologies are the key aspect for the realization of the semantic Web vision. From this point of view, an ontology is a formal description of a conceptualization. It expresses a range of concepts (a domain of knowledge), the relationships among them, and the logical constraints governing the specific domain. It is possible to define an ontology on the Web by means of a set of languages, such as the Resource Description Framework (RDF) (29) and OWL (28). In this context, ontologies provide a basis for addressing the problem of capturing the semantics of a service. The capability of understanding what a service does is crucial for a software agent in order to discover, select, and compose services. In an analogous way, the capability of describing and capturing its own and other agents needs at run time is important in order to cope with problems that are not specifiable *a priori*. In order to address the lack of semantics, several research efforts have been done. There are many aspects that an ontology for services-based computing has to consider. It should provide mechanisms to allow discovery, composition, orchestration, and coordination. For example, OWL-S (13) is an OWL-based ontology for Web services. The main goal of OWL-S is that of facilitating the automation of web service discovery, execution, composition, and inter-operation. OWL-S is built upon three core concepts:

- *Profile*, which captures the information needed for discovering the service, its advertisement;
- *Grounding*, which provides information about transport protocols, how to interact with the service;
- *Model*, which provides a description of how the service is used.

Another contribution is the Web service Modeling Ontology (WSMO) (17) extending the Web service Modeling Framework (WSFM) (19). According to WSMF, WSMO identifies four top-level elements that have to be considered in order to describe Web services. Such elements are: *ontologies*, *Web services*, *goals*, and *mediators*. By the specification of these elements, WSMO provides constructs for defining an ontology, describing Web services capabilities (e.g., assumptions, pre-conditions and post-conditions) and interface (e.g., coordination and orchestration); for describing the goals a user wants to achieve through a Web service; and for specifying mediators that allow to handle aligning, merging, and transforming issues (e.g., resolving possible representation mismatches between ontologies). In the context of the semantic Web, reference 15 presents a choreography mechanism that allows us to handle heterogeneity in Web services interaction. This work realized such a choreography mechanism for IRS-III (14), a platform for developing semantic Web services using the WSMO ontology (17).

Although OWL-S and WSMO cover many issues related to the semantics of Web services, such ontologies do not consider the problems concerning dynamic aspects. For example, they do not consider how to handle situations that are not specifiable *a priori* (i.e., dynamic coordination). The key idea of dynamic coordination relates to open systems where the processes and resources populating the systems are not known at design time. In such a situation, it would be desirable to have a mechanism allowing processes (or a selection of them) to communicate their intentions and needing of resources at run time. A possible ontological approach to this problem is proposed in reference 32, where it is defined an ontology for coordination. The main concepts defined are: *Agent, Process, Resource, Interdependency, Operational Relationship*. In particular, as subclass of *Process* the concept of *Coordinable Activity* is defined. This concept is in turn a composition of activities, some of them atomic (i.e., composed of no further activities). The notion of *Atomic Activity* is comparable with the notion of process in OWL-S. The ontology allows us to express a number of features for a *Coordinable Activity*, such as the earliest date at which the activity may begin, the expected duration, and the agent that will carry it on. Through the concept of *Resource*, it is possible to describe the nature of the resources that may be needed for performing an activity. For example, a resource can be consumable (i.e., its usage reduces its availability) and sharable (i.e., it can be used by more than one agent at a given time). In the model of *Interdependency*, the concept of *Coordination Relation* is specified. It can be in turn either a positive coordination or negative. For example, a negative coordination is a relationship which, if it occurs, will lead to some failure, while a positive coordination, if it occurs, will make possible the execution of another activity. *Operational Relationship* is used for resolving coordination relationships between activities. For example, if two agents have a *Contractual Authority* relationship, then the first agent has priority over the second one because of some rules defined in the context to which they belong.

4.7. CONCLUSIONS

In this work we have underlined the rising interest in putting together agent-oriented abstractions and methods with the support for fully open and distributed systems development provided by the SOA.

Starting from agent-oriented methods for software development, we may hypothesize the work of the research community toward the definition of service-oriented software development methods. In order to leverage the most successful agent-oriented methods to service-oriented software design, such methods should provide a phase of services elicitation where a role, defined according to a specific role model, is associated to each service. Such methods should enable us to define the relationships among the roles involved in the definition of complex services. In this way, these complex services will be built on top of the services directly mapped into the roles defined in the role model. Another phase of role-service deployment may consist of selecting the software components to associate to each role. This method may be iterative and enable the refinement of the services and the role model.

Another meaningful research direction concerns the full bridging of the MDA, the Grid, and the semantic Web services for allowing the development of applications in a service-oriented model driven semantic Web. For this purpose, the concept of service needs a deep investigation in order to exploit it for distributed software development.

Finally, related to the refinement of the concept of service is the research work for a better integration of the agents, the services, and the semantics. In particular, the existence and the semantics of a service "state" is a central issue and it needs to be investigated in order to give a suitable definition in the service-oriented paradigm.

REFERENCES

1. S. Andreozzi, P. Ciancarini, D. Montesi, and R. Moretti. Towards a metamodeling based method for representing and selecting grid services. In M. Jeckle, R. Kowalczyk, and P. Braun, editors. In *Proceedings of the First International Conference on Grid Services Engineering and Management*, LCNS 3270, pages 78–93, Springer, Berlin/Heidelberg, Germany, September 2004.

2. R. Baxter. A Complete History of the Grid. Software Development Group EPCC and NeSC, October 2002.

3. L. Bocchi, P. Ciancarini, and R. Lucchi. Atomic Commit and Negotiation in Service Oriented Computing. Technical Report UBLCS-2005-16, University of Bologna, Italy, 2005. ftp://ftp.cs.unibo.it/pub/techreports/2005/2005-16.pdf.

4. D. Booth, H. Haas, and A. Brown. Web services Glossary. Technical Report, World Wide Web Consortium (W3C), 2004. http://www.w3.org/TR/wsgloss/.

5. D. Booth, H. Haas, F. McCabe, E. Newcomer, M. Champion, C. Ferris, and D. Orchard. Web service Architecture. Technical Report, World Wide Web Consortium (W3C), 2004. http://www.w3.org/TR/wsarch/.

6. T. Berners-Lee, J. Hendler, and O. Lassila. The semantic web. *Scientific American*, **284**(5):28–37, 2001.

7. J. Bloomberg. Principles of SOA. *Application Development Trends Magazine*, **10**(3):22–26, March 2003.

8. K. Czsjkowski, D. Ferguson, I. Foster, J. Frey, S. Graham, D. Snelling, and S. Tueke. *The WS-Resource Framework*, March 2005.

9. N. Carriero and D. Gelernter. Coordination languages and their significance. *Communications of the ACM* **35**(2):97–107, 1992.

10. J. Castro, M. Kolp, and J. Mylopoulos. Towards requirements-driven information systems engineering: The TROPOS project. *Information Systems* **27**(6):365–389, 2002.

11. P. Ciancarini, R. Tolksdorf, and F. Vitali. The World Wide Web as a place for agents. In M. Wooldridge and M. Veloso, editors. *Artificial Intelligence Today. Recent Trends and Developments,* LNAI 1600, pages 175–194. Springer, Berlin, 1999.

12. P. Ciancarini and M. Wooldridge, editors. *First Int. Workshop on Agent Oriented Software Engineering*, LNCS 1957. Limerick, Ireland. Springer, Berlin, 2000.

13. DAML. OWL-S 1.1 Release. http://www.daml.org/services/owls/1.1/.

14. J. Domingue, L. Cabral, F. Hakimpour, D. Sell, and E. Motta. IRS III: A platform and infrastructure for creating WSMO-based semantic web. In *Proceedings, Workshop on WSMO Implementations (WIW)*, Frankfurt, Germany, 2004.

15. J. Domingue, S. Galizia, and L. Cabral. Choreography in IRS-III—coping with heterogeneous interaction patterns in web services. In Y. Gil, E. Motta, V. R. Benjamins, and M. A. Musen, editors. The semantic Web—ISWC 2000: *Proceedings of the Fourth International Semantic Web Conference (ISWC 2005)*, Galway, Ireland. LNCS 3729. pages 171–185, Springer, Berlin, 2005.

16. D. DeRoure, N. Jennings, and N. Shadbolt. Research Agenda for the Semantic Grid: A Future e-Science Infrastructure. Technical Report UKeS-2002-02, National e-Science Centre, December 2001.

17. J. Domingue, D. Roman, and M. Stollberg. Web service Modeling Ontology (WSMO)—An Ontology for Semantic Web services. http://www.w3.org/2005/04/FSWS-/Submissions/1/wsmo_position_paper.html, 2005.

18. R. Davis and R. G. Smith. Negotiation as a metaphor for distributed problem solving. In *Readings in Distributed Artificial Intelligence*, pages 333–356. Morgan Kaufmann Publishers, San Francisco, 1988.

19. D. Fensel and C. Bussler. The Web service Modeling Framework WSMF. *Electronic Commerce Research and Applications* **1**(2):113–137, 2002.

20. FIPA. *FIPA Contract Net Interaction Protocol Specification*. FIPA, 2001. http://www.fipa.org/specs/fipa00029/.

21. I. Foster, C. Kesselman, and S. Tuecke. The anatomy of the grid: Enabling scalable virtual organizations. *International Journal of Supercomputer Applications* **15**(3):200–222, 2001.

22. Y. Gill, E. Motta, V. R. Benjamins, and M. A. Musen. editors. The semantic Web—ISWC 2000: *Proceedings of the Fourth International Semantic Web Conference (ISWC 2005)*, Galway, Ireland. LNCS 3729. Springer, Berlin, 2005.

23. J. Hendler. Agents and the semantic web. *IEEE Intelligent Systems* **16**(2):30–37, 2001.

24. M. Klein and A. Bernstein. Searching for services on the semantic web using process ontologies. In I. Cruz, S. Decker, J. Euzenat, and D. McGuinness, editors. *Proceedings of the First Semantic Web Working Symposium (SWWS'01)*, pages 431–446, July 2001.

25. R. Klepper and W. O. Jones. *Outsourcing Information Technology, Systems and Services*. Prentice-Hall, Englewood Cliffs, NJ, 1998.

26. F. Leymann and D. Roller. *Production Workflow: Concepts and Techniques*. Prentice-Hall PTR, Englewood Cliffs, NJ, 2000.

27. Object Management Group (OMG). Model Driven Architecture (MDA) architecture board, July 2001.

28. Object Management Group (OMG). Omg unified modeling language specification v. 1.5, March 2003.

29. OWL Web Ontology Language Family of Specifications. http://www.w3.org/2004/OWL, 2004.

30. Resource Description Framework (RDF). http://www.w3.org/RDF.

31. R. Radhakrishnan and M. Wookey. Model Driven Architecture Enabling Service Oriented Architectures, March 2004.

32. R. G. Smith. The contract net protocol: high-level communication and control in a distributed problem solver. In *Readings in Distributed Artificial Intelligence*, pages 357–366. Morgan Kaufmann Publishers, San Francisco, 1988.

33. V. A. M. Tamma, C. Aart, T. Moyaux, S. Paurobally, B. Lithgow Smith, and M. Wooldridge. An ontological framework for dynamic coordination. In Y. Gil, E. Motta, V. R. Benjamins, and M. A. Musen, editors. The semantic Web—ISWC 2000: *Proceedings of the Fourth International Semantic Web Conference (ISWC 2005)*, Galway, Ireland. LCNS 3729. Springer, Berlin, 2005, pages 638–652.

34. V. A. M. Tamma, I. Blacoe, B. Lithgow Smith, and M. Wooldridge. Introducing autonomic behaviour in semantic web agents. In Y. Gil, E. Motta, V. R. Benjamins, and M. A. Musen, editors. The semantic Web—ISWC 2000: *Proceedings of the Fourth International Semantic Web Conference (ISWC 2005)*, Galway, Ireland. LCNS 3729. Springer, Berlin, 2005, pages 653–667.

35. World Wide Web Consortium (W3C). OWL. Web Ontology Language, W3C recommendation, February 2004.

36. World Wide Web Consortium (W3C). Web services Semantics (WSDL-S)—W3C member submission, November 2005.

37. M. Wooldridge, N. Jennings, and D. Kinny. The Gaia methodology for agent-oriented analysis and design. *Autonomous Agents and Multi-Agent Systems* **3**(3):285–312, 2000.

38. M. Wooldridge. Agent-based software engineering. *IEE Proc Software Engineering* **144**(1):26–37, 1997.

39. W3C Web services Activity. http://www.w3.org/2002/ws/.

40. H. Zhuge. Semantic Grid: scientific issues, infrastructure, and methodology. *Commun. ACM* **48**(4):117–119, 2005.

41. F. Zambonelli, N. R. Jennings, and M. Wooldridge. Developing multiagent systems: The Gaia methodology. *ACM Transactions on Software Engineering and Methodology* **12**(3):317–370, 2003.

5

TESTING OBJECT-ORIENTED SOFTWARE

Leonardo Mariani and Mauro Pezzè

5.1. INTRODUCTION

Software development is a complex and error-prone process that can fail in meeting its quality goals if the required properties are not properly verified. Quality cannot be added as an afterthought, but must be improved during development and verified on the final product. Test and analysis activities are the elements of the software development processes that aim to identify faults during development and to measure the readiness of the final product.

The software development process translates user needs and constraints into requirements specifications, and it also transforms requirements into architecture and design specifications to produce code that addresses user needs. At each step, developers shape the solution by adding details and choosing from several design alternatives, while quality experts verify the consistency of the models and their correspondence with the previous abstractions as well as with user needs.

Software development methodologies define the interplay of specification, design, and verification activities, determine the models produced during development, and constrain the choices of test and analysis activities.

Many test and analysis techniques have been developed in the context of classic methodologies and coding approaches, which assume procedural models of software—that is, consider software programs as functional transformations from

Emerging Methods, Technologies, and Process Management in Software Engineering. Edited by De Lucia, Ferrucci, Tortora, and Tucci
Copyright © 2008 John Wiley & Sons, Inc.

inputs to outputs. For example, popular functional testing approaches like category partition (31) or catalog-based testing (27) work on input–output relations, while control and data flow testing (13) assume a procedural coding style.

Object-oriented design is characterized by state-dependent behavior, encapsulation, inheritance, polymorphism, and dynamic binding and makes extensive use of genericity and exceptions (28). These features modify classic procedural models and mitigate some well-known design and implementation problems, but introduce new weaknesses that call for new test and analysis techniques. For example, classes and objects force encapsulation and information hiding, thus reducing well-known problems that derive from the excessive use of nonlocal information in classic procedural programs, while inheritance and polymorphism postpone bindings of objects to run time and can lead to failures that depend on the dynamic binding of the objects. Classic approaches are still useful at high abstraction levels, when dealing with requirements expressed independently from design decisions. However, they need to be complemented with new techniques to cope with the new problems that arise when using object-oriented design features.

5.2. IMPACT OF OBJECT-ORIENTED DESIGN ON TESTING

Object-oriented features impact on test and analysis in different ways. Classes and objects are characterized by state, and the results of method invocations do not depend only on parameter values, as in procedural software, but also depend on the state of the objects. For instance, the effect of invoking method commit of the class Cart shown in Fig. 5.1 depends not only on the value of parameter warehouse, but also on the current content of the cart—that is, the state of the cart. Most classic testing approaches are based on input–output relations and do not consider the program state. For instance, they would derive test cases for different values of parameter warehouse of method commit, but would not consider different contents of the cart, thus missing possible problems that depend on the object state. When dealing with object-oriented software, we need to consider not only methods and their integration, as if they were procedures, but also classes and objects, and we need to extend the set of techniques that can deal effectively with state information.

Classes and objects export only part of their state and behavior. Implementation details are hidden to external entities. For example, the class Cart shown in Fig. 5.1 hides the details of fields items and numTotItems which cannot be accessed from outside the object. Classic techniques for generating scaffolding and oracles assume full visibility of the code. Trivially breaking encapsulation by exporting hidden information can alleviate, but not solve, the problem of scaffolding and oracle generation. When dealing with object-oriented software, we need new approaches that safely deal with hidden information.

Classes can be defined by specializing other classes. Child classes inherit characteristics of ancestors, and they add or modify features. We can, for example, create a class SecureCart by specializing the class Cart in Fig. 5.1. Class SecureCart would inherit the characteristics of class Cart, and it would override and add methods to deal with user authentication. The extensive reuse of inherited methods raises new questions

```
1:    public class Cart {
2:        private Hashtable<String, Integer> items;
2:        private int numTotItems;
3:
4:        public Cart() {
5:            items = new Hashtable<String, Integer>();
6:            numTotItems = 0;
7:        }
8:
9:        public void addItem(String itemId, Integer quantity) {
10:           items.put(itemId, quantity);
11:           numTotItems+=quantity;
12:       }
13:
14:       public void removeItem(String itemId) {
15:           Integer qt = getQuantity(itemId);
16:           if (qt != null) {
17:             numTotItems -= qt;
18:             items.remove(itemId);
19:           }
20:       }
21:
22:       public void updateItem(String itemId, Integer quantity) {
23:           if (getQuantity(itemId) != null) {
24:             removeItem(itemId);
25:             addItem(itemId, quantity);
26:           }
27:       }
28:
29:       public Integer getQuantity(String itemId) { return items.get(itemId); }
30:
31:       public int getNumTotItems() { return numTotItems; }
32:
33:       public boolean commit(Warehouse warehouse) {
34:           Enumeration<String> itemIds = items.keys();
35:           if (!itemIds.hasMoreElements()) return true;
36:
37:           warehouse.beginTransaction();
38:
39:           while(itemIds.hasMoreElements()) {
40:               String id = itemIds.nextElement();
41:               if (!warehouse.isAvailable(id, items.get(id))) {
42:                   warehouse.abortTransaction();
43:                   return false;
44:               }
45:           }
46:
47:           itemIds = items.keys();
48:
49:           while(itemIds.hasMoreElements()) {
50:               String id = itemIds.nextElement();
51:               warehouse.remove(id, items.get(id));
52:           }
53:
54:           items = new Hashtable<String, Integer>();
55:           numTotItems = 0;
56:
57:           warehouse.commitTransaction();
58:           return true;
59:       }
60:   }
```

Figure 5.1. An excerpt of a simple Java `Cart`.

about reuse of test cases and optimization of test case execution. Methods shared between ancestors and children without direct or indirect modifications may be tested only once, but testing techniques must be able to identify indirect interactions and avoid problems that may derive from unexpected interactions not properly tested.

In object-oriented programs, variables can change their type dynamically. The scope of changes is restricted by a statically declared base type that binds actual types to be one of its subtypes. For example, a variable myCart declared of type Cart can be dynamically bound to objects of type Cart as well as objects of any other types that specialize Cart (e.g., SecureCart). Dynamic binding follows the inheritance hierarchy, but does not climb it: Variables of type SecureCart cannot be bound to objects of type Cart. Since variables can dynamically change their type, method calls can be bound only at run time. Consider that all possible bindings for each polymorphic call become quickly impractical, since the number of combinations may grow exponentially. Therefore, we need testing techniques that select suitable subsets of possible bindings.

Besides their characteristic features, object-oriented programs make extensive use of additional features, which are not well-exploited in procedural implementations: genericity and exceptions.

Most popular object-oriented languages offer generic classes (i.e., classes implemented with symbolic types) that are bound to concrete types when objects of generic classes are instantiated. For example, the hashtable in Fig. 5.1 is an instance of a generic class Hashtable, which works with two parameters representing key and value that must be instantiated with concrete types when used, (e.g., String and Integer in Fig. 5.1). Testing generic classes must consider all possible instantiations, which may be infinitely many.

Modern object-oriented languages provide explicit constructs to handle exceptional and erroneous cases—for example, the Java try{...}catch(...){...} finally{...} block sizes instructions that can generate exceptions—and define the local exception handler. Exception handlers add implicit control flows, which can be activated explicitly or even implicitly at run time—for example, triggered by a division by zero. In principle, testing techniques can take into account all these erroneous and implicit execution flows when generating test cases. However, the number of possible executions grows exponentially, even for simple programs.

5.3. SPECIFICATION-BASED TESTING TECHNIQUES

The main specification-based testing techniques proposed so far for object-oriented software focus on either diagrammatic specifications [in particular, the Unified Modeling Language (UML) (29)], or formal specifications [in particular, algebraic specifications (16)].

UML provides many specification and modeling languages that capture different views and abstractions during the various phases of requirements analysis and design. So far, research on intraclass testing has focused mainly on Statecharts, which specify the state-based behavior of a class, while research on interclass testing has considered various models, such as sequence, collaboration, and class diagrams.

Algebraic specifications describe method signatures and semantics, and they are used for automatic generation of test cases and oracles. The technique known as *equivalent scenarios* does not break encapsulation and information hiding, and it can be adapted to other kinds of specifications.

5.4. UML INTRACLASS TESTING

UML specifications describe the state-based behavior of classes by means of Statecharts, which are sometimes used as simple finite state machines (FSMs). A finite state machine consists of a set of states and a set of transitions between states. States represent sets of attribute values that produce the same reactions to stimuli issued by any external observer, while transitions represent events that can change the state. Transitions are labeled with event names that correspond to either method calls or internal actions. In the former case, the transition occurs when the method is executed, while in the latter case the transition occurs when the internal action is executed.

A FSM is characterized by an initial state that corresponds to the initial state of the object, and a set of final states that represent the set of states where the execution can terminate. A new object enters its initial state and evolves according to the behavior specified by transition up to a final state.

Figure 5.2 shows an example of a FSM that specifies a secure cart that extends the cart implementation presented in Fig. 5.1. We assume *implicitly defined transitions semantics* (4)—that is, events that do not correspond to any explicit transition exiting a given state are mapped to implicit self loops. For example, a call to method addItem() in state notLogged corresponds to a self loop; that is, the call does not modify the state. Lee and Yannakakis (26) present the formal details of FSMs.

Statecharts extend FSMs by augmenting transition labels to represent side effects and guards and by introducing composition mechanisms to model states and transitions in a compact way. Side effects are actions executed when transitions are triggered—for

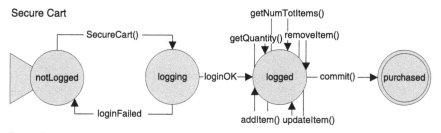

Legend:
The initial state is identified by a triangle, while the final states are identified with double circles. Transitions with labels ending with () correspond to method invocations, while plain labels correspond to internal actions.

Figure 5.2. An FSM specification of SecureCart.

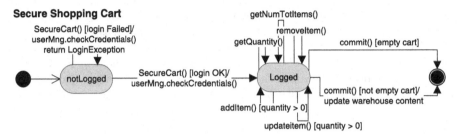

Figure 5.3. A Statechart specification of SecureCart.

example, the invocation of methods of external objects or the updating of local variables. A Statechart transition is labeled with a single event and a possibly empty sequence of actions. Event names and actions are separated by a back slash (/). Guards are conditions associated to transitions. A transition can be triggered only if its guard evaluates to true. Guards are specified after the event name within square brackets.

Figure 5.3 shows the Statechart specification of SecureCart. This specification is more accurate than the FSM specification shown in Figure 5.2, since the Statechart specifies that constructor SecureCart causes an interaction with object userMng, the target state depends on the result of the login attempt, and methods addItem and updateItem can be executed only if variable quantity is assigned to a positive value.

Composition mechanisms specify compound states (i.e., states obtained as the union of multiple states) and concurrency structures (i.e., subparts of a state that can evolve concurrently). Statecharts are described in detail by David Harel in his seminal paper (17).

A simple way of generating test cases from FSM and Statecharts consists of invoking all possible sequences of transitions. This criterion, which corresponds to path coverage in structural testing, quickly leads to infinitely many test cases. Practical testing techniques identify smaller, yet relevant, sets of test cases by referring to states, transitions, and relevant combinations of states and transitions (4, 15, 26). The most popular testing criteria for FSMs are state coverage, transition coverage, and boundary interior loop coverage.

State coverage requires all states to be traversed at least once. Traversing all states without considering the events that can occur in the state selects small test suites, but is seldom sufficient for a thorough test. For instance, the single test case

(*TC*1)   SecureCart(), loginOK, commit()

traverses all states of the FSM in Fig. 5.2, but does not exercise many methods and thus cannot reveal faults that may exist in those methods.

Transition coverage requires all transitions to be traversed at least once, including implicit transitions, if required by the considered semantics. Transition coverage subsumes state coverage; that is, it assures coverage of all states as well. For example, the only test case *TC*1, which is enough to guarantee state coverage, does not guarantee transition coverage of the FSM in Fig. 5.2. We need additional test cases, for example[1]:

(*TC*2) `SecureCart(), loginOK, addItem(), removeItem(),`
`commit()`

(*TC*3) `SecureCart(),         loginFailed,         addItem(),`
`getQuantity(),       updateItem(),         removeItem(),`
`getNumTotItems(),        SecureCart(),         loginOK,`
`addItem(), updateItem(), commit()`

(*TC*4) `SecureCart(), loginOK, addItem(), getQuantity(),`
`getNumTotItems(), commit()`

Transition coverage improves state coverage, but can miss incorrect behaviors that depend on repeated executions of loops.

Boundary interior loop coverage requires loops and simple paths to be exercised. A simple path is a path that starts from the initial state and terminates to a final state, and it traverses all states at most once. A loop is a path that begins and ends at the same state. Loops can be traversed many times in a single execution. Boundary interior loop coverage requires each simple path to be traversed at least once, and it requires each loop to be traversed the minimum and maximum number of times. It also requires each loop to be traversed a number of times between minimum and maximum. Boundary interior path coverage guarantees better coverage than previous criteria, at the price of larger test suites.

If we consider again the FSM in Fig. 5.2, and we limit the number of repetitions of loops to 3, we fulfill boundary interior loop coverage by adding the following cases to test cases *TC*1 – *TC*4:

(*TC*5) `SecureCart(),    loginOK,    addItem(),    addItem(),`
`addItem(), commit()`

(*TC*6) `SecureCart(),         loginFailed,         SecureCart(),`
`loginFailed,         SecureCart(),         loginFailed,`
`SecureCart(), loginOK, addItem(), getQuantity(),`
`getQuantity(), getQuantity(), commit()`

...   ...

Many researchers defined additional criteria for Statecharts and other variants of FSM, such as I/O automata (3, 6). A particularly interesting method is Wp, which generates test cases in presence of information about observable behavior (10). The Wp method augments transition coverage by introducing the concept of distinguishing sequences and requiring the coverage of at least a distinguishing sequence for each state. A distinguishing sequence for a state is a sequence that distinguishes the state

---

[1]Since state `logging` represents only the possible outcomes of `login` attempts, we do not consider implicit transitions for this state.

from any other state in the input/output (I/O) automaton by producing a distinct output. Transition coverage guarantees covering all events for all states. Distinguishing sequence coverage guarantees the observability of the different effects from the external outputs. Intuitively, test cases are obtained by concatenating sequences that guarantee transition coverage with distinguishing sequences. For example, distinguishing sequences can be obtained for the Statechart in Fig. 5.3 by exploiting outputs and signals issued by methods `SecureCart` and `commit()`. Details and variants of Wp are described in references 10 and 15.

If the Statechart contains guards, we can apply branch and condition coverage criteria to guards. For example, we can apply the modified condition decision criterion (MC/DC) by requiring each clause in the guards to evaluate to both true and false, while determining the final result of the whole expression (30). The rational behind this criterion is that each clause should be tested independently from other clauses, to avoid masking effects between different clauses. This criterion includes test cases that violate guard conditions. These cases are useful to check how the target object responds to stimuli that are not acceptable because of particular data values.

For instance, this criterion applied to the Statechart in Fig. 5.3 requires test cases that execute (a) method `SecureCart()` when the login succeeds and fails, (b) method `commit()` when the cart is empty and not empty, and (c) methods `addItem()` and `updateItem()` with positive and nonpositive quantity. If guards are specified with the Object Constraint Language (OCL), test cases can be generated semiautomatically (5).

The semantics of Statecharts' composition mechanisms can be expressed in terms of simple Statecharts, thus test cases can be derived by referring to the flattened Statecharts, as discussed by Binder (3). The flattening process causes the explosion of hierarchy and concurrency structures into large flat Statecharts that represent all possible behaviors.

The cart in Fig. 5.1 contains a fault: if method `addItem` is invoked to add an item already in the cart, the quantity stored in the hashtable is overridden, while state variable `numTotItems` is incremented, thus the items in the cart and the quantity recorder by `numTotItems` become different. For instance, invoking `addItem("Java Book",1)`, `addItem("Java Book",2)` on an empty cart results in a cart that contains two copies of "Java Book", while `numTotItems` records three copies. This fault can be revealed by executing method `addItem` at least twice with the same item followed by method `getNumTotItems()`. State and transition coverage may be satisfied by test suites that do not contain repetitions of method invocations and thus are not able to reveal this fault, while boundary interior loop coverage is more likely to reveal the fault, because it requires test cases with multiple executions of `addItem`.

5.5. UML INTERCLASS TESTING

Statecharts are mainly used to describe intraclass behavior, but the events and method invocations that annotate transitions provide information about interclass collaboration as well. UML offers some other languages to describe the interclass relations: *Class* and *object diagrams* describe the structure of the system statically, while *sequence* and *collaboration diagrams* describe dynamic interactions. Other UML diagrams, like use case, package, and activity diagrams, have not been the object of interesting research on testing yet.

To derive interclass test cases from Statecharts, we need to interpret transition annotations and define their semantics. Events and method invocations that label Statecharts' transitions have been formalized in many ways. *Communicating Statecharts* formalize labels by means of communicating sequential processes (CSP) (23). Labels are given as sequences of communication actions with the following structure:

_channel?inVal   represents a synchronous input operation; *channel* is the name of the channel supporting communication and *inVal* is the symbolic name of the input received by the channel.

^*_channel!outVal*   represents a synchronous output operation; *channel* is the name of the channel supporting communication and *outVal* is the symbolic name of the output sent by the channel.

Synchronous I/O actions that refer to the same channel are paired, to model the communication between two objects. For instance, action SecureCart in Fig. 5.3 can be annotated with the sequence of output and input operations ^*_userAuthChannel!credential_userAuthChannel?result*, which matches the I/O operations *_userAuthChannel?credential* ^*_userAuthChannel?result* executed by the user authentication manager, to model the communication between the two objects required to authenticate a user.

Test cases can be derived from communicating Statecharts by (a) selecting the integrated set of objects that must be tested, (b) automatically composing communicating Statecharts into a single Statechart that represents the behavior of the integrated subsystem, and (c) deriving test cases from the integrated statechart with traditional techniques.

The states of the composed Statechart are the Cartesian product of the states of the original Statecharts; transitions not involved in communication connect all states that generalize the original states connected to the transitions, while communicating transitions are merged in single transitions that substitute the pairs of transitions involved in the communications. Hartmann, Imoberdorf, and Meisinger (22) present an incremental composition algorithm to compose sets of Statecharts. The algorithm is based on a heuristic to incrementally select Statecharts that must be included in the composition. The heuristic aims at minimizing the intermediate size of the Statechart in order to limit the effect of state explosion.

Sequence and collaboration diagrams complement Statecharts specifications by describing typical interaction sequences among objects. Figure 5.4 shows a sequence diagram representing a typical interaction between a secure cart, a user manager, a warehouse, and an external agent. The diagram shows the case of a successful login followed by the order of two items.

Sequence diagrams are usually derived from requirements and early system specifications to model scenarios that can be executed and verified on the target system

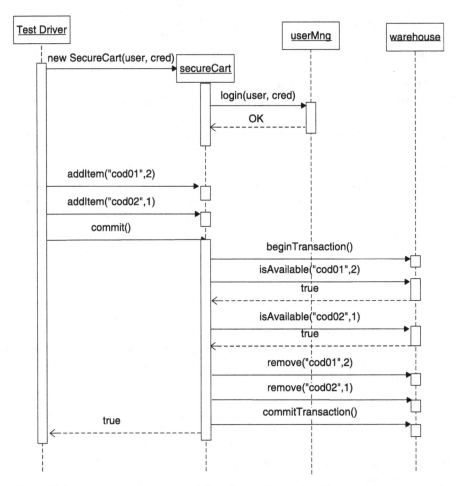

Figure 5.4. A sequence diagram modeling the purchase of two items with a secure cart.

(sequence diagrams usually provide details about the expected sequences of interactions and the data values that should be exchanged), thus they represent potential test cases. For instance, the sequence diagram in Fig. 5.4 specifies that the cart should call twice method `isAvailable` and then twice method `remove` on the `warehouse`. In both cases, the first call should pass parameters `"cod01"` and `2`, while the second call should pass parameters `"cod02"` and `1`.

Sequence diagrams are usually derived in the early development stages, and thus they are seldom directly executable, since they lack implementation details. For instance, the sequence diagram in Fig. 5.4 does not specify that method `isAvailable` of `warehouse` returns `true` only if the requested item and quantity are available in the database. To execute the test case corresponding to this diagram, test designers must properly prepare the database.

In general, missing details cannot be automatically added, but there are tools, like SeDiTeC, that generate stubs to execute sequence diagrams and monitor the run-time behavior of the corresponding application to check if executions satisfy the behavior specified by sequence diagrams (12).

Collaboration diagrams provide an alternative way for describing sequences of interactions among objects. In collaboration diagrams, objects are linked by direct lines that represent communications. Interactions take place by invoking methods. Each line is labeled with the corresponding method or message and with a number that indicates the communication order. Collaboration diagrams can also represent the variables that are exchanged during computation. Figure 5.5 shows an example of a collaboration diagram that represents the interactions between backendController, orderingSystem, supplierManager, warehouse, and moneyAdmin to successfully complete an order. The backendController extracts the default supplier for the ordered product, the product is effectively ordered by issuing a request to orderingSystem, which extracts the expected delivery time and informs the warehouse of the pending order, and finally, backendController notifies moneyAdmin to complete the ordering process.

Similarly to sequence diagrams, collaboration diagrams model typical interaction sequences and can indicate interesting test cases. Abdurazik and Offutt (1) define a simple testing approach that requires covering all collaborations specified by the diagrams.

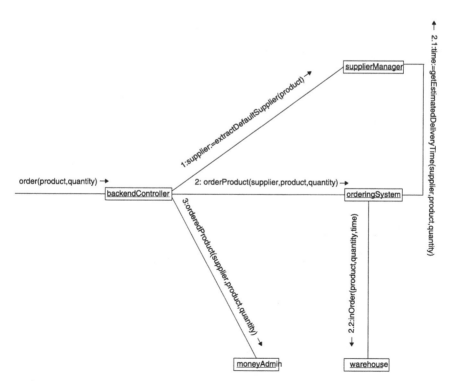

Figure 5.5. A collaboration diagram representing the ordering of a new product.

Andrews, France, Ghosh, and Craig suggest alternative criteria based on conditions that can occur in the diagrams: They require covering all conditions (*condition coverage*), all clauses (*full predicate coverage*), each individual message (each *message on link coverage*), complete paths that are represented in collaboration diagrams (*message paths coverage*), and messages that exchange collections by varying the size of the exchanged collections (*collection coverage*) (2).

Class and object diagrams specify relations among classes and objects. Common relations represented in class and object diagrams are (a) associations, which represent links between classes, (b) specializations, which represent classes inheriting from other classes, and (c) compositions, which represent objects obtained by aggregation. Figure 5.6 shows an example of a class diagram for an online shopping system.

Andrews *et al.* (2) derive test cases from class diagrams by covering structural elements. They define three main criteria: association-end multiplicity coverage, generalization coverage, and class attribute coverage. *Association-end multiplicity coverage*

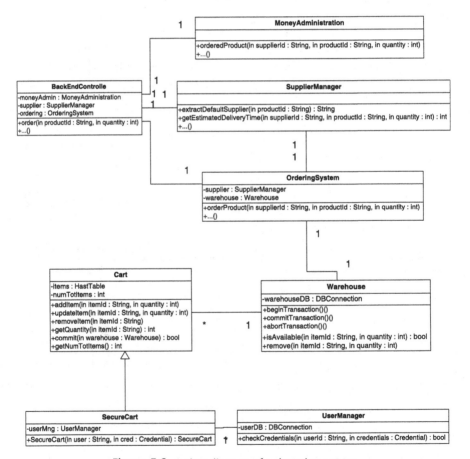

Figure 5.6. A class diagram of a shopping system.

requires test cases that instantiate each association zero, an intermediate, and a maximum amount of times. In case of multiple associations, the criterion requires test cases for the Cartesian product of the single cases.

For example, the association between Cart and Warehouse in Fig. 5.6 can be covered by three test cases. The first test case instantiates a Warehouse without any associated Cart (zero instances), the second test case instantiates a Warehouse and two Carts (intermediate amount of instances), and the third test case instantiates a Warehouse and 100 Carts (maximum instances).

The *generalization criterion* requires test cases that instantiate each subtype of a type at least once. This criterion tests the possibility to replace an object type with any of its subtypes. For example, the generalization between Cart and SecureCart in Fig. 5.6 can be covered by two test cases. The first test case instantiates and uses a Cart, while the second test case instantiates and uses a SecureCart.

The *class attribute criterion* requires test cases that exercise all combinations of state attributes for each single class. States to be tested can be obtained with the category partition method (31). For instance, Cart class in Fig. 5.6 can be covered by generating test cases that create all possible configurations for state attributes items and numTotItems, according to the cart specification.

FSM or Statecharts specifications are often available and there are good powerful tools to generate test cases, which guarantee a complete coverage of object behaviors according to the specifications and the chosen criteria. Several successful experiences are reported by Briand, Cui, and Labiche (5) and by Hartmann, Imoberdorf, and Meisinger (22).

Sequence, collaboration, and class diagrams are commonly available as well. Test cases can be easily generated from these diagrams, but the completeness of the derived test suites depends on the accuracy of the diagrams.

Interclass techniques do not have many chances of finding the fault in method addItem, because they aim to reveal integration faults, while this is a unit fault.

5.6. ALGEBRAIC TESTING TECHNIQUES

Formal specifications support automatic generation of test cases, scaffolding, and oracles. Doong and Frankl (11) proposed an interesting technique for automatic generation of test cases and oracles from algebraic specification in the ASTOOT system. Chen *et al.* (8, 9) extended the original ASTOOT proposal to the TACCLE system, which deals with a larger set of cases.

Test cases are automatically generated by suitably combining algebraic rules, while oracles are created by means of equivalent and nonequivalent scenarios. Given a class C and a sequence s of method invocations, an equivalent sequence is a sequence of invocations that produces the same results of s, while a nonequivalent one is a sequence that produces different results. An equivalent scenario is a pair of equivalent sequences, while a nonequivalent scenario is a pair of nonequivalent sequences. The technique starts with a set of test cases for a class C and automatically generates equivalent and nonequivalent scenarios from algebraic specifications. The results of executing test

```
1:    Cart()
2:    addItem(code, qt)
3:    removeItem(code)
4:    updateItem(code, qt)
5:    getQuantity(code)
6:    getNumTotItems()
7:    commit()
```

Figure 5.7. The interface of class `Cart`.

type Cart
syntax
    create: $\rightarrow$ Cart
    addItem: Cart $\times$ String $\times$ Integer $\rightarrow$ Cart
    removeItem: Cart $\times$ String $\rightarrow$ Cart
    updateItem: Cart $\times$ String $\times$ Integer $\rightarrow$ Cart
    getQuantity: Cart $\times$ String $\rightarrow$ Integer
    getNumTotItems: Cart $\rightarrow$ Integer
    commit: Cart $\rightarrow$ Cart
declare
    C: Cart
    x, y: Integer
    s: String
semantics
    1: getQuantity(create, s) $\rightarrow$ 0
    2: getQuantity(addItem(C, s, x), s) $\rightarrow$ x
    3: getQuantity(addItem(C, t, x), s) $\rightarrow$ getQuantity(C, s)
    4: updateItem(create, s, x) $\rightarrow$ create
    5: updateItem(addItem(C, s, y), s, x) $\rightarrow$ addItem(C, s, x)
    6: updateItem(addItem(C, t, y), s, x) $\rightarrow$ addItem(updateItem(C, s, x), t, y)
    7: removeItem(create, s) $\rightarrow$ create
    8: removeItem(addItem(C, s, y), s) $\rightarrow$ removeItem(C, s)
    9: removeItem(addItem(C, t, y), s) $\rightarrow$ addItem(removeItem(C, s), t, y)
    10: getNumTotItems(create) $\rightarrow$ 0
    11: getNumTotItems(addItem(C, s, x)) $\rightarrow$ $x+$ getNumTotItems(removeItem(C, s))
    12: commit(C) $\rightarrow$ create

Figure 5.8. A specification of class `Cart`.

cases are automatically evaluated by comparing the results of equivalent and non-equivalent scenarios.

For example, consider a class `Cart` that implements the interface shown in Fig. 5.7 and the algebraic specification shown in Fig. 5.8. The algebraic specification defines all possible sequences of method invocations. In general, the set of all sequences that can be generated by applying algebraic rules is infinite. We can reduce the set of sequences by considering only ground terms—that is, terms that can be directly derived from axioms by replacing variables with normal forms (8). Unfortunately, the number of ground terms is often too large to be of any practical use.

ASTOOT reduces the set of test cases by heuristically identifying long sequences of method invocations with many occurrences of different non-inspector methods[2] and by

---

[2]An inspector method of a class C is a method that both returns a value and does not modify the state of the instance where it is applied.

considering all the combinations of parameter values that occur in the conditional specifications (11). For example, a test case for class `Cart` is

$$s_{cart} = \texttt{Cart(), addItem("001",1), addItem("002",3),}$$
$$\texttt{addItem("003",4), removeItem("003")}$$

ASTOOT generates equivalent sequences by automatically applying transformation axioms to the ADT tree representation of the initial sequence (transformation axioms are part of the original specification). For example, for s_{cart}, ASTOOT can generate the equivalent sequence

$$s_{equivalent} = \texttt{Cart(), addItem("001",1), addItem("002",3)}$$

obtained from s_{cart} by applying axioms 7, 8 and 9 in Fig. 5.8.

ASTOOT generates nonequivalent sequences by modifying parameter values of equivalent sequences to violate necessary conditions. For example, for s_{cart} ASTOOT can generate the nonequivalent sequence

$$s_{non\_equivalent} = \texttt{Cart(), addItem("001",1), addItem("002",3),}$$
$$\texttt{addItem("003",4) removeItem("002")}$$

by modifying the parameter of the last invocation in $s_{equivalent}$, thus violating the condition that requires the parameter of method `removeItem` to be equal to the parameter of the last invocation of method `addItem`.

TACCLE refines the technique proposed by ASTOOT by extending the definition of equivalent sequences (8). ASTOOT considers two sequences to be equivalent when one of them can be transformed into the other by applying rewriting rules of the specification. This definition does not consider sequences that lead to equivalent states, even if they cannot be transformed into each other by rewriting rules. TACCLE captures these cases by considering two sequences to be equivalent if both can be transformed into the same equivalent term (9).

ASTOOT compares the results of executing equivalent and nonequivalent scenarios with a (possibly recursive) class method `eqn`. Method `eqn` can be implemented referring to its algebraic specification or by comparing the values of the implemented state attributes. A *specification-driven* `eqn` is simpler, but may omit some implementation details, while an *implementation-driven* `eqn` considers all details, but may fail when comparing logically equivalent states that differ from irrelevant implementation details.

Method `eqn` may be quite complex for large objects. TACCLE introduces relevant observable contexts to narrow the space of the behaviors that must be checked to verify equivalence between objects (8). Intuitively, TACCLE compares object states by matching object attributes and by checking only the result produced by invocation sequences that depend from the different attributes (i.e., the relevant observable context of the attributes). Relevant observable contexts are identified by using a data member relevance graph, which can be built from the class source code (8). With little additional information provided by test designers, such as the set of inspector methods, the technique can automatically verify equivalence between object instances.

Algebraic techniques can reveal the fault in the cart shown in Fig. 5.1, if the initial testing strategy includes tests with at least two invocations to addItem. Equivalent scenarios provide automatic oracles, which can identify the fault if the test suite includes revealing test cases. Techniques based on algebraic specifications introduce important ideas for oracle generation that can be used in different contexts.

Specification-based testing is typically the base-line technique for designing test cases. Black box test cases can be derived early in the software life cycle, without detailed knowledge of the code, and are effective in revealing many faults. However, specification-based testing may miss some classes of faults, in particular the ones that depend on detailed design and implementation choices that are not reflected in the specifications. Moreover, measuring coverage of specification-based test suites may not always be easy. Specification-based testing is typically paired with code-based testing to capture design and implementation faults, and to provide simple coverage measurements.

5.7. CODE-BASED TESTING TECHNIQUES

Code-based testing criteria are defined in terms of code entities that are exercised during test case execution. Classic criteria require covering statements, branches, conditions, decisions, paths, and interprocedural relations (33), but ignore state-dependent behavior, and thus do not apply well to intra- and inter-class testing.

New structural criteria have been proposed to cope with state-based behavior. An interesting family of state-based structural criteria has been defined by applying classic data flow testing criteria (14, 21, 32) to state information, by computing definitions and uses of object attributes (7, 20, 35). Data flow (DF) testing criteria consider *definitions* and *uses* of state attributes, i.e., statements that affect the value associated to the attributes or depend on the value associated to the attributes, respectively. DF criteria pair definitions and uses that refer to the same object attribute (*def-use pairs*) and require covering program paths that traverse def-use pairs—that is, paths that first exercise the definition and then the use of the same attribute without traversing additional definitions of the attribute between the considered definition and use. In this way, they exercise executions that first change the state of the objects (definitions of object attributes) and then use the new state, thus leading to possible failures that depend on erroneous states. There are many data flow testing criteria, which differ for the set of def-use pairs to be covered. In this section we refer to the most popular criterion: the *all-uses* criterion, which requires covering all feasible def-use pairs of a program.

5.8. INTRACLASS STRUCTURAL TESTING

Intraclass techniques test state-based behaviors of single classes. They test definitions and uses of variables whose visibility does not cross the boundary of the class; that is, they do not interact with other classes. We can identify definitions and uses of object attributes referring to the *Class Control Flow Graph* (CCFG) representation of the class. The CCFG can be constructed with the algorithm proposed by Harrold and Rothermel (20). A CCFG is a graph that represents a class where:

- Each method is represented by its control-flow graph, which can be computed by the algorithm defined by Pande, Landi, and Ryder (32).
- Each method call is represented by a call and return node, which are connected to the invoked method entry and exit points, respectively.
- All public methods are represented by a class driver that models the possibility of invoking the public methods in any order. The class driver is composed of an entry, a loop, a call, a return, and an exit node. The call and return nodes are directly connected to all public methods; the loop node is connected with call and return nodes to represent the possibility of repeating invocations an arbitrary amount of times; entry and exit nodes represent the beginning and termination of the execution.

Figure 5.9 shows the CCFG of class Cart, whose code is shown in Fig. 5.1. The state of class Cart is composed of two variables: items and numTotItems. CCFGs can be used to compute def-use pairs, by first annotating the CCFG with definitions and uses, and then traversing the CCFG to compute all pairs. For example, for variable numTotItems of class Cart, we can identify definitions in methods Cart(), commit(), addItem(), and removeItem() and identify uses in methods getNumTotItems(), addItem(), and removeItem(), and we can compute a total of 12 feasible def-use pairs.

Data flow tests can reveal the fault in class Cart, because the def-use pairs to be covered include a definition of variable numTotItems in method addItem() and a use in method addItem(). As it always happens, exercising the faulty statement in the faulty state does not guarantee that the fault will be revealed, since fault occurrence may not result in a visible failure in all executions.

Continuing with the Cart example, variable items is defined in methods Cart() and commit() and is used in methods addItem(), removeItem(), updateItem(), getQuantity(), and commit() (twice at lines 34 and 47). These definitions and uses generate 12 def-use pairs that must be covered to satisfy the criterion.

The above analysis of the variable items is incomplete, since it does not consider its member variables: Variable items is an object with a complex state structure; if we analyze it as a primitive variable, we miss the effect of invocations of its methods. For instance, the invocation of method put at line 10 is not considered as a definition of items in the above analysis, even if it changes the state of items.

Data flow analysis of class Hashtable improves the situation only partially, since def-use pairs computed for class Hashtable generate test requirements that refer to methods of class Hashtable,[3] but do not consider how these methods are used in class Cart. For example, the test requirement for class Hashtable that requires the

---

[3]Test requirements do not refer to methods but to program statements; to simplify this example, we specify test requirements of class Hashtable in terms of the methods that contain definitions and uses, instead of single program statements.

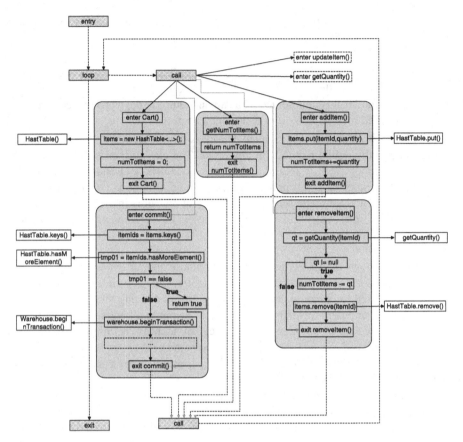

Figure 5.9. The CCFG of class Cart whose code is given in Figure 5.1.

execution of method put followed by method get can be satisfied by one pair of statements of class Cart(). However, class Cart contains several different pairs (⟨10, 29⟩,
⟨10, 41⟩, ⟨10, 51⟩) that deserve to be exercised, but would not, since they refer to the
same pair in class Hashtable. Replacing the invocations of methods of external
classes in the CCFG with their ICFG would generate interprocedural def-use pairs,
but would still miss definitions and uses induced by one class on another.

Interclass def-use analysis can be improved by computing definitions and uses that
include the context in which variables are defined and used. In this way, for instance, we
would be able to identify all def-use pairs induced by Cart on Hashtable. Context-
sensitive techniques are illustrated in the next section.

5.9. INTERCLASS STRUCTURAL TESTING

Context-sensitive techniques address interclass testing by augmenting definitions and
uses with the chains of calls that lead to variable modifications and accesses (35).
A def-use pair for a state variable *o* can be defined as a pair of call sequences (*d, u*),

```
1:    public synchronized V put(K key, V value) {
2:        if (value == null) {
3:            throw new NullPointerException();
4:        }
5:
6:        Entry tab[] = table;
7:        int hash = key.hashCode();
          ...
```

Figure 5.10. An excerpt of the implementation of class HashTable.

where $d = CD_1CD_2...CD_mD$, $U = CU_1CU_2...CU_nU$, CD_i and CU_j are method invocations, D is a program statement that defines o, and U is a program statement that uses o. An example of a call chain of length 3 for the Hashtable implementation in Fig. 5.10 is Cart-25, Cart-10, Hashtable-6, which indicates a definition of variable tab that derives from the execution of line 6 of Hashtable, caused by the execution of line 10 of class Cart induced by the execution of line 25 of class Cart.

A contextual def-use pair (d, u) of a variable o is exercised by an execution that includes the call sequence d, followed by any sequence of method calls that do not modify o and ends with the call sequence u.

This analysis can be executed at different levels of depth. Souter and Pollock (35) define four levels called $cdu - 0$, $cdu - 1$, $cdu - 2$, and $cdu - 3$. Level $cdu - 0$ corresponds to context-free def-use analysis, as presented in Section 5.8. In this case, call sequences d and u includes only the program statements that define and use the variable. Level $cdu - 1$ refers to call sequences of length 2—that is, sequences that include only the caller and the program statement that modifies/uses the variable. Levels $cdu - 2$ and $cdu - 3$ extend the analysis to calls of length 3 and 4, respectively.

Referring to the class Hashtable used by class Cart as shown in Fig. 5.1, level $cdu - 1$ would pair the definitions of Hashtable that derive from an invocation of putItem at statement 10 of class Cart, with the uses of Hashtable that derive from invocations of addItem at statements 29, 34, 41, 47, and 51 (definitions and uses of single state variables are obtained by analysis of the source code of the Hashtable class).

Data flow testing criteria measure the completeness of test suites, but do not provide a method for generating test cases. Buy, Orso, and Pezzè (7) combine data-flow analysis with symbolic execution and automatic deduction to generate test cases that satisfy data flow criteria. The technique first computes def-use pairs as discussed in Section 5.8 and then generates test cases that cover the identified pairs. Test cases are generated in two steps: (a) Symbolic execution identifies (i) paths that cover def-use pairs and (ii) corresponding path conditions (i.e., the constraints on state variables that cause the paths to be executed), and (b) automatic deduction creates complete invocation sequences, by composing path conditions to create feasible test cases.

5.10. TESTING IN THE PRESENCE OF INHERITANCE

Inheritance allows software engineers to implement new classes as subtypes of existing ones. Child classes reuse some functionality of the ancestor classes, modify other functionality, and add new ones. Although, in principle, child classes can be tested as if they were new classes, information about the tests of the ancestor class may reduce the number of test cases needed to thoroughly test the child class.

For example, the class `SecureCart` specified by the class diagram in Fig. 5.6 extends the class `Cart` shown in Fig. 5.10. Class `SecureCart` reuses all methods of class `Cart`, except for the constructor, which is redefined to require user identity and credentials. In this case, methods `addItem`, `removeItem`, `updateItem`, `getQuantity`, `getNumTotItems`, and `commit` are not affected by the added functionality and do not need to be retested. We can thus test class `SecureCart` by testing only the new constructor.

In general, we need to retest all methods that are affected either directly or indirectly by new or modified methods. Harrold, McGregor, and Fitzpatrick (19) group structural and functional test cases according to the methods they test and the kind of test (unit or integration), and they identify the test cases to be added to the test suite and the ones to be re-executed, according to the methods added or modified in the child class:

New methods—that is, methods that are added in the child class—require new unit and integration test cases (if they interact with other entities). Abstract methods require only functional test cases, while concrete methods require both functional and structural test cases.

Unchanged methods—that is, methods inherited from the parent class without changes—do not require additional test cases. Integration test cases must be re-executed if the child class modifies interactions with the reused method.

Redefined methods—that is, methods changed in the child class—require new functional and structural test cases to be added to the exiting ones that must be re-executed. If the method interacts with other entities, we must derive both unit and integration test cases.

5.11. REGRESSION TESTING

During development, software engineers produce many versions of classes that compose software systems. As in the case of inheritance, testing all versions as if they were new classes, without considering the test cases derived for the former versions, results in a waste of time and resources. Regression testing techniques use information about the changes in the new versions to identify which test cases should be re-executed to guarantee that the new versions do not introduce faults. Regression testing techniques focus on functionality that should not be affected by the changes, functionality added or modified in the new versions may require new test cases that can be added to the regression suites and can be generated according to techniques described earlier in this chapter.

Simple regression testing approaches would require re-executing all test cases derived for the previous versions, thus eliminating test design effort but not test execution time. These approaches can lead to the execution of many test cases even for changes limited in size and scope. Several researchers proposed techniques to select subsets of regression test cases for object-oriented software (18, 24, 25, 34). Some of these techniques are safe, whereas others are unsafe. Safe regression testing techniques guarantee that the selected subset of test cases does not miss any fault that can be revealed by the original test suite, while unsafe techniques do not.

Popular approaches for object oriented systems are based on the identification of *firewalls* that represent the set of classes that can be affected by changes in new versions (24, 25, 36). Firewalls are computed by first identifying the changes in the new version and then identifying the classes affected by the changes. Changes can be automatically identified by comparing the source code of two versions, while the set of classes that can be affected by a change can be computed by considering inheritance, aggregation, and association relations (some approaches also consider polymorphism and dynamic binding). Most methods approximate firewalls by considering only some relations of interest. Only perfect identification of firewalls guarantees safeness, but perfect identification is often too expensive. The set of regression test cases to be re-executed is the set of cases that executes classes belonging to the firewalls of all modified classes. Both computing firewalls and determining test cases to be re-executed are simple. However, the technique is not always efficient: Many changes can select almost all the test cases of the original suite, thus reducing the saving of execution time. Therefore, this technique should be used for small and incremental changes.

Other approaches select regression suites for object-oriented software from control flow information. Rothermel, Harrold, and Dedhia (34) proposed techniques based on *CCFG*. Differences between classes are identified by comparing their CCFGs. CCFGs annotated with coverage information—that is, with the set of test cases that cover each edge—provide the information required to automatically select the test cases that need to be re-executed. This technique is safe, and it works for intraclass testing, but does not scale immediately to interclass testing, and features such as polymorphism and dynamic binding can severely complicate the analysis.

The basic idea presented in reference 34 has been further investigated and extended by Harrold *et al.* (18), where they address Java programs that are represented with Java Interclass Graphs (JIGs). JIG represents all features of the Java language, including exception handling and incomplete applications, thus also supporting analysis of many of the features not included in CCFGs.

5.12. CONCLUSIONS

Object-oriented design reduces the occurrence of some critical classes of traditional faults, but introduces new problems that are not adequately addressed by classic test and analysis techniques. The many solutions help us understand the scope of the problems and indicate some useful approaches. So far, however, research has concentrated mostly on some problems—for example, the ones that derive from state-dependent behavior, encapsulation, inheritance, and polymorphism, leaving largely unexplored some others—for example, the ones that derive from the use of generics and exceptions. But more importantly, solutions do not provide a complete and mature framework for testing object-oriented systems.

Researchers are actively investigating new approaches to cope with the whole set of object-oriented features, as well as to scale well from unit to integration and system testing. Practitioners are collecting data about fault occurrence and distribution in object-oriented software; increasingly, they are understanding the new challenges of object-oriented testing, and they are appreciating the solutions proposed by research groups.

Growing awareness of problems and maturity of solutions will soon lead to a new generation of CASE tools, which will effectively deal with test and analysis of object-oriented software.

REFERENCES

1. A. Abdurazik and J. Offutt. Using UML collaboration diagrams for static checking and test generation. In A. Evans, S. Kent, and B. Selic, editors. In *Proceedings of the Third International Conference on the Unified Modeling Language,* LNCS 1939, pages 383–395. Springer, Berlin, 2000.

2. A. Andrews, R. France, S. Ghosh, and G. Craig. Test adequacy criteria for UML design models. *Software Testing, Verification and Reliability,* Vol. 13, Pages 95–127. John Wiley & Sons, Hoboken, NJ, 2003.

3. R. V. Binder. *Object-Oriented Systems—Models, Patterns and Tools.* Addison-Wesley, Reading, MA, 1999.

4. G. V. Bochmann and A. Petrenko. Protocol testing: Review of methods and relevance for software testing. In *Proceedings of the 1994 ACM SIGSOFT International Symposium on Software Testing and Analysis,* pages 109–124. ACM Press, New York, 1994.

5. L. C. Briand, J. Cui, and Y. Labiche. Towards automated support for deriving test data from UML statecharts. In P. Stevens, J. Whittle, and G. Booch editors. In *Proceedings of the International Conference on the Unified Modeling Languages and Applications,* LNCS 2863, pages 249–264. Springer, Berlin, 2003.

6. L. C. Briand, Y. Labiche, and Y. Wang. Using simulation to empirically investigate test coverage criteria based on statechart. In *Proceedings of the 26th International Conference on Software Engineering,* pages 86–95. IEEE Computer Society, New York, 2004.

7. U. Buy, A. Orso, and M. Pezzè. Automated testing of classes. In *Proceedings of the 2000 ACM SIGSOFT International Symposium on Software Testing and Analysis,* pages 39–48. ACM Press, New York, 2000.

8. H. Y. Chen, T. H. Tse, F. T. Chan, and T. Y. Chen. In black and white: An integrated approach to class-level testing of object-oriented programs. *ACM Transactions on Software Engineering and Methodology (TOSEM)* 7(3):250–295, 1998.

9. H. Y. Chen, T. H. Tse, and T. Y. Chen. TACCLE: A methodology for object-oriented software testing at the class and cluster levels. *ACM Transactions on Software Engineering and Methodology (TOSEM)* 10(1):56–109, 2001.

10. T. S. Chow. Testing design modeled by finite-state machines. *IEEE Transactions on Software Engineering* 4(3):178–187, 1978.

11. R.-K. Doong and P. G. Frankl. The ASTOOT approach to testing object-oriented programs. *ACM Transactions on Software Engineering and Methodology (TOSEM)* 3(2):101–130, 1994.

12. F. Fraikin and T. Leonhardt. SeDiTeC—testing based on sequence diagrams. In *Proceedings of the International Conference on Automated Software Engineering (ASE)*, pages 261–266. IEEE Computer Society, New York, 2002.

13. P. G. Frankl and E. J. Weyuker. An applicable family of data flow testing criteria. *IEEE Transactions on Software Engineering* **14**(10):1483–1498, 1988.

14. P. G. Frankl and E. J. Weyuker. An analytical comparison of the fault-detecting ability of data flow testing techniques. In *Proceedings of the 15th International Conference on Software Engineering*, pages 415–424. IEEE Computer Society Press, New York, 1993.

15. S. Fujiwara, G. V. Bochmann, F. Khendek, M. Amalou, and A. Ghedamsi. Test selection based on finite state models. *IEEE Transactions on Software Engineering* **17**(6):591–603, 1991.

16. J. A. Goguen and J. Meseguer. Unifying functional, object-oriented, and relational programming with logical semantics. In *Research Directions in Object-Oriented Programming*, pages 417–477. MIT Press, Cambridge, MA, 1987.

17. D. Harel. Statecharts: A visual formalism for complex systems. *Science of Computer Programming* **8**(3):231–274, 1987.

18. M. J. Harrold, J. A. Jones, T. Li, D. Liang, A. Orso, M. Pennings, S. Sinha, S. A. Spoon, and A. Gujarathi. Regression test selection for java software. In *Proceedings of the ACM Conference on Object-Oriented Programming, Systems, Languages, and Applications*. ACM Press, New York, 2001.

19. M. J. Harrold, J. D. McGregor, and K. J. Fitzpatrick. Incremental testing of object-oriented class structures. In *Proceedings of the 14th International Conference on Software Engineering*, pages 68–80. IEEE Computer Society Press, New York, 1992.

20. M. J. Harrold and G. Rothermel. Performing data flow testing on classes. In *Proceedings of the 2nd ACM SIGSOFT Symposium on Foundations of Software Engineering*, pages 154–163. ACM Press, New York, 1994.

21. M. J. Harrold and M. L. Soffa. Efficient computation of interprocedural definition-use chains. *ACM Transactions on Programming Languages and Systems* **16**(2):175–204, 1994.

22. J. Hartmann, C. Imoberdorf, and M. Meisinger. UML-based integration testing. In *Proceedings of the 2000 International Symposium on Software Testing and Analysis (ISSTA)*, pages 60–70. ACM Press, New York, 2000.

23. C. A. R. Hoare. *Communicating Sequential Processes*. Prentice-Hall, Englewood Cliffs, NJ, 1987.

24. P. Hsia, X. Li, D. C. Kung, C.-T. Hsu, L. Li, Y. Toyoshima, and C. Chen. A technique for the selective revalidation of OO software. *Journal of Software Maintenance: Research and Practice* **9**(4):217–233, 1997.

25. D. C. Kung, J. Gao, P. Hsia, F. Wen, Y. Toyoshima, and C. Chen. Change impact identification in object oriented software maintenance. In *Proceedings of the International Conference on Software Maintenance*, pages 202–211. IEEE Computer Society, Washington, DC, 1994.

26. D. Lee and M. Yannakakis. Principles and methods of testing finite state machines—A survey. In *Proceedings of the IEEE* **84**(8):1090–1123, 1996.

27. B. Marick. *The Craft of Software Testing: Subsystems Testing Including Object-Based and Object-Oriented Testing*. Prentice-Hall, Englewood Cliffs, NJ, 1997.

28. B. Meyer. *Object-Oriented Software Construction*, 2nd edition. Prentice-Hall International Series in Computer Science. Prentice-Hall, Englewood Cliffs, NJ, 2000.

29. Object Management Group (OMG). Unified modeling language: Infrastructure, v2.0. Technical Report formal/05-07-05, OMG, March 2006.

30. A. J. Offutt, Y. Xiong, and S. Liu. Criteria for generating specification-based tests. In *Proceedings of the Internationcal Conference on Engineering of Complex Computer Systems (ICECCS)*, pages 119–129. IEEE Computer Society, Washington, DC, 1999.

31. T. J. Ostrand and M. J. Balcer. The category-partition method for specifying and generating functional tests. *Communications of the ACM* **31**(6):676–686, 1988.

32. H. D. Pande, W. A. Landi, and B. G. Ryder. Interprocedural def-use associations for C systems with single level pointers. *IEEE Transactions on Software Engineering* **20**(5):385–403, 1994.

33. M. Pezzè and M. Young. *Software Test and Analysis: Process, Principles and Techniques*. John Wiley & Sons, Hoboken, NJ, 2006.

34. G. Rothermel, M. J. Harrold, and J. Dedhia. Regression test selection for C++ software. *Journal of Software Testing, Verification and Reliability* **10**(6):77–109, 2000.

35. A. L. Souter and L. L. Pollock. The construction of contextual def-use associations for object-oriented systems. *IEEE Transactions on Software Engineering* **29**(11):1005–1018, 2003.

36. L. White and K. Abdullah. A firewall approach for the regression testing of object-oriented software. In *Proceedings of the Software Quality Week*, 1997.

6

THE UML AND FORMAL METHODS: A CASE STUDY

Carlo Montangero

6.1. INTRODUCTION

Most of the popular approaches to software development, like the agile methods (2) and the unified process (UP) (12), are currently evolutionary; that is, they are based on a cyclic approach, as shown in Fig. 6.1. After a preliminary analysis, which targets the overall feasibility and assesses the major risks, the development enters a loop where, at each iteration, a part of the system (a feature, a use case, etc.) is analyzed and designed and then built and shipped, thereby providing the user with a succession of systems of increasing functionality and quality. The advantage of this approach is a great flexibility in answering to the changes in the requirements that the ever-evolving environment of current business generates.

The two phases in the loop are different in that implementation is focused on code and has a narrow scope, since the code is produced against some specification, while analysis and design is focused on a wide variety of models and have a larger scope, since these models are produced against the requirements. The models that are built in analysis and design are containers for knowledge about the *what* and the *why* of a system. They allow the developer to reach a deep understanding of the properties of the system, long before it is built. They are also the key to the *collaborative design process*, which is at the core of modern software development.

Emerging Methods, Technologies, and Process Management in Software Engineering. Edited by De Lucia, Ferrucci, Tortora, and Tucci
Copyright © 2008 John Wiley & Sons, Inc.

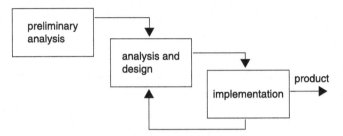

Figure 6.1. Evolutionary life cycle.

However, the two phases are also similar, insofar as they are both based on tighter loops of construction, review, and fix. So, they differ in the artefacts they work on, but are similar in the process (*do and fix*), and the effectiveness of the development process is largely dependent on the degree of automatic support. Nowadays, the two phases are supported in different degrees, in this respect. Implementation is mature, since it has a long story of research and formal grounding in programming languages, and is supported by a wealth of tools, like compilers, static checkers, debuggers, builders, test harnessers, and so on, that are widely used by the practitioners. There are also a number of tools to support analysis and design that have been developed by the formal methods research community, and more are being investigated and developed. Still their adoption by the practitioners is not widely accepted. Part of the problem is related to the great variety of approaches, each with its own formalism targeted at a specific goal. Besides, the level of formality itself can be a problem, since it may entail a steep learning curve requiring a degree of education that is often not available in the average development environment.

The DEGAS project (7) has taken steps to foster the direct use of formal analysis tools by the average designers. The idea, as illustrated in Fig. 6.2, is to let developers use their own development environment while the formal analysis takes place in its own verification environment. In order to perform analysis of the development models in the verification environment, the first step is to use an *extractor*, which extracts the parts of the model that will be relevant for the analysis and put these into the verification environment. After the analysis has been completed, the analysis result is made

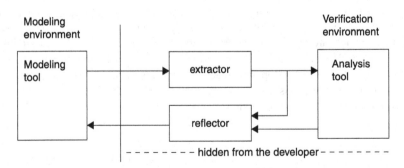

Figure 6.2. The DEGAS approach.

available to the developer using a *reflector*. Often, the results are presented as decoration of the original model. To make this approach practical, from the point of view of the developer, the extractor, the analysis, and the reflector will all be automated and hidden from the developer. Thus, the developer will not need to know the finer details of these elements but may concentrate on the design of the system.

In DEGAS, the development environment exploits the Unified Modeling Language (UML) (16), whose recent popularity in industry has a direct influence on many real-world applications. Among the advantages of using the UML, there are the emphasis on the graphical presentation with the ability to customize it via stereotyping, the view-driven approach, and the support for (temporary) incompleteness and inconsistency. These characteristics foster the dialogue with all the stakeholders, even the less technical-oriented. At the same time, the language is precise enough to let the designer express all the necessary information to extract the formal models for analysis. Another appealing characteristic of the UML is the quite large choice of commercial and free supporting environments, along with the fact that the UML integrates smoothly in a single bundle a choice of well-established modeling approaches that are pretty popular among the practitioners.

The DEGAS verification environment uses process calculi, which are behavioral models of systems, and the analysis of these calculi will therefore concentrate on behavioral aspects of systems. This nicely complements analyses of structural aspects such that object hierarchies are well-typed and diagrams are internally consistent, which are the types of analysis that are typically carried out on UML today.

The main practical result of DEGAS is Choreographer, an integrated design platform for qualitative and quantitative modeling of software systems (4). The qualitative analysis is deployed to investigate the security of the communication protocols used in the application. The analysis guarantees that there are no successful attacks on the authentication of the communicated messages, provided that there are no attacks on the underlying crypto-system used to protect messages. In the case where authentication may be breached, the analysis reports where the breach may occur. The quantitative analysis that is provided is a performance analysis of the system model. This identifies components that are underutilized or overutilized, indicating poor deployment of computational resources. The rest of this chapter is concerned with the security analysis. Taking seriously the DEGAS manifesto, we stick to the developer's point of view and delve no longer into the process-algebra formal basis of the approach. The interested reader may refer to reference 5 for an overview and refer to reference 3 for a thorough discussion. Similarly, the quantitative analysis is overviewed in reference 4 and discussed in reference 10.

The next section highlights some aspects of the UML that are relevant to our discussion; the knowledgeable reader may well skip it. Then, we present *ForLySa*, the framework that, in Choreographer, supports the designer in modeling in the UML the protocols that are to be analyzed for authentication breaches. We discuss how to exploit the framework to build a dynamic model of the protocol, in the context of a static model, thus providing all the information needed for the analysis. Before concluding, we discuss how the results of the analysis are presented to the designer and how he can interpret them, in case flaws are detected in the protocol.

6.2. A BIASED VIEW OF THE UML

We start reviewing some basic general concepts of the UML. A *design* is a set of models that describe the system under construction from different perspectives, and each *model* is an abstract description of (a part of) the system. A design is organized in *views*, and each view collects models that offer coherent perspectives on the system. Typical views are the "Use case" view, which offers scenarios of system usage, the "Operational" view, which is concerned with control flow and performance issues, the "Physical" view, which is concerned with the hardware–software association, and the "Development" view, which is concerned with the organization of the software components. For our purposes, the relevant view is the "Logical" one, which considers the components of the system at a high level of abstraction.

A model can be time-independent (i.e., *static*) and describe some system elements and their relationships: In the logical view it may use concepts in the application domain and express them as *classes* and *associations*. For instance, we will make use of the concepts of principal, key, message, and so on. Or, a model can be *dynamic* and describe part of the behavior of the system in terms of *interactions* of the entities in a related static model (that is, a dynamic model assumes a static one). For instance, we will consider the interactions among the principals involved in a protocol.

Models are usually built in the UML by drawing *diagrams*. It is important to understand the difference between models and diagrams. A diagram is a graphical presentation of a collection of model elements, rendered as a connected graph of arcs (relationships) and vertices (other model elements). A model is also a graph, but of *semantic* elements; a diagram is a graph of *visual* elements that *map* onto the semantic ones. So, in a support tool, a model is a working structure, whereas a diagram is a presentation structure. It may happen that not all the elements in a model are presented in at least a diagram, as shown in Fig. 6.3: this situation may arise if Class2 and its relationship to Class3 were drawn in Diagram2 and then *cut* from the diagram, but not *deleted* from the model. Although diagrams are the principal way to enter a model in a supporting UML tool, there usually are ways to enter elements via dialogue panes and structural editors, acting directly on the model.

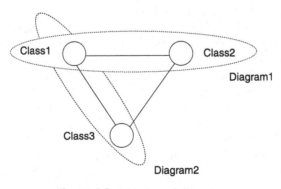

Figure 6.3. Models and diagrams.

In ForLySa we specify a security protocol in a UML logical view, providing two models: a static one, describing the structure of the protocol, and a dynamic one, describing its behavior. The static model is presented as a *class diagram*, whereas the dynamic one is presented as a *sequence diagram*. The UML version in use is 1.5. In the sequel, we introduce briefly the elements that are needed to understand the diagrams in the next section. A quick introduction to the UML can be found in reference 9.

A class diagram describes a part of the real word in terms of *objects*. More precisely, a class diagram characterizes the objects of interest, by classifying them and presenting their structure. A class is a named collection of objects with the same structure, given as a set of *attributes*, and a set of *operations*. A class is drawn as a rectangle with three compartments: one for the name, one for the attributes, and one for the operations. It is always possible not to present the attribute or operation compartment when it is not interesting—for example, because it is empty. This is the case for the classes other than Principal in Fig. 6.4 (*beware*: at the moment, we look at this diagram only

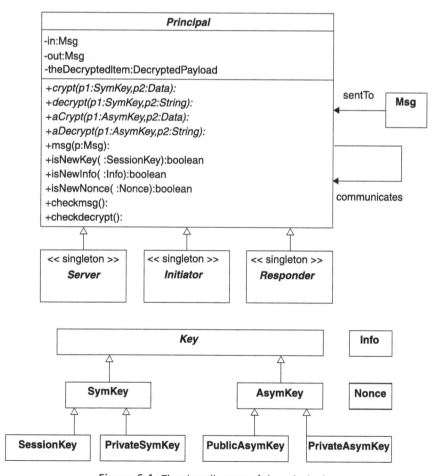

Figure 6.4. The class diagram of the principals.

syntactically; we will consider its meaning in the next section). Attributes, like in and out in Fig. 6.4, have a name and a type, which can be either primitive, like boolean and String, or another class in the model. Operations, like msg, have a name and typed parameters, and possibly a return value. Attributes and operations have a visibility, which in our case is either *private* to the object (denoted by a prefixed minus sign) or *public* (denoted by a plus sign).

Classes may be in the Is-A relationship (denoted by an arrow with an empty triangular head); for instance, Fig. 6.4 tells us that an object of type SymKey is also a Key—that is, SymKey *specializes* Key, or Key *generalizes* SymKey. A class name in italic, like Key, denotes an abstract class (i.e., one for which there are no objects) but is introduced to provide common features to the classes it generalizes. Similarly, an operation in italic is also abstract, meaning that its definition is left to the specializing classes.

Another kind of relationships is shown in Fig. 6.4. A line with a stick head denotes an *association*, which is used to denote generic relationships between the objects: for instance, a Principal can communicate with another, a message (of type Msg) can be sent to a Principal. Still another kind is shown in Fig. 6.7: a line with an empty diamonds denotes the 'part of' relationship, or *aggregation*. The object on the diamond side of the relation has the other one as its part. For instance, in Fig. 6.7, an object of type CryptedPayload has a part "dest," which is of type SetOfCryptoPoints.

The behavioral model is given by a sequence diagram, an example of which is given in Fig. 6.5. Sequence diagrams specify part of the behavior of a system by describing a specific sequence of interactions among a set of objects. In these diagrams, time flows top-down, while the involved partners are listed from right to left. These objects are specified by name and type; for example, i is of type A, and s is of type S. The time periods during which these objects are active is shown by the rectangle superimposed to its *lifeline* (the dashed line). The interactions are shown by the arrows with black heads. Each arrow is labeled by the operation invoked on the target object to perform the interaction. Objects can interact with themselves, calling their own operations, like preMsg1A.

The rectangles with the flipped corner in Fig. 6.5 are not specific to sequence diagrams, but are of general use in UML to attach comments to elements of a model. As we will see later, these *notes* play a crucial role in ForLySa, in the modeling of the authentication requirements.

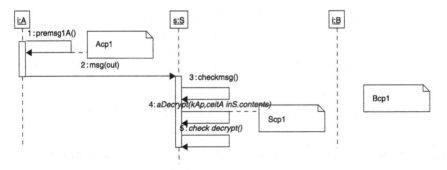

Figure 6.5. A typical protocol step.

6.3. ForLySa

In this section we describe how to build protocols models in UML, so that they can be analyzed for authentication properties in the DEGAS framework. To this purpose, we introduce a couple of reusable UML packages, which should be used in Poseidon, to make protocol models amenable to analysis in DEGAS Choreographer. In other terms, this section specifies how to generate models that the extractor for LySa will accept and that the reflector will be able to use to produce feedback.

Our verification relies on a control flow analysis (3) that is implemented in the LySatool (14). The analysis tells whether the authentication properties are satisfied for all executions of the protocol executed in parallel with an arbitrary attacker process. The analysis reports all possible breaches of the authentication properties in an error component; a pair (c, d) in this component means that something encrypted at c was decrypted at d breaking the specified authentication property. The analysis computes overapproximations; that is, it may report an error that is not actually there. However, reference 3 illustrates that this is not a big problem in practice.

To specify a protocol in UML so that the ForLySa extractor can feed the analyzer, the designer first of all must specify the intended communications and the involved messages. The structure of each message type is specified in a distinct diagram that includes the decorations needed to specify the authentication property. Then, the local information of each principal, like session keys or temporary storage, must be introduced, as well as the operations to build and dissect messages. Then, the designer presents the dynamics of the protocol in a sequence diagram, which formally specifies a canonical run of the protocol. Each message exchange in the protocol is divided into three steps: (a) The sender packages the message, (b) the message is communicated, and (c) the recipient processes the incoming message. Each step is described by one or more UML arrows in the sequence diagram, each associated to an operation of their target. Each operation is specified by pre- and post-conditions—for instance, to specify how to decrypt part of a message, what to check in an incoming message, or what to store for later usage in the principal. The language for these conditions is presented to the designer with a semantics in terms of the UML modeling concepts. This semantics reflects the precise one given by the translation in the underlying process calculus, LySa (3). Finally, the places mentioned in the authentication properties are specified as notes associated with the arrows in steps 1 and 3 above, to provide the necessary hooks for the feedback from the analysis. These notes are placeholders that will support the notification of errors resulting from the analysis. If the analysis reports an error being the pair (c, d), the note introducing c will be modified by the reflector to list d, thereby signaling the breach in authentication reported by the analysis.

As shown in Fig. 6.6, the classes and associations that define the verification scenario assumed by the extractor come in two packages. In the first package, ForLySa, we model general concepts like principals, keys, messages, and so on; the actual protocol model is derived extending the second package, Protocol. Some classes in Protocol inherits from ForLySa, since they specialize the general concepts to the scenario considered by the LySa tool.

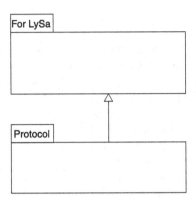

Figure 6.6. General structure of ForLySa.

6.3.1. The Static Model

The contents of package ForLySa are shown in Fig. 6.4 and in Fig. 6.7 with respect to the general aspects and the principals and with respect to the details of the messages, respectively. Three-party protocols are considered, with one kind of principal being the *initiator* of the protocol, while another kind is the *responder*. Additionally, there is a *server*, sometimes referred to as a trusted third party, a key distribution center, a certificate authority, and so on. In a protocol specification there is only one initiator, responder, and server, as indicated by the keyword "singleton" in the diagram. The principals communicate and exchange *messages* as indicated by the *communicates* association. To express communication, the operation msg() can be invoked on the principal that the message is *sentTo*. The specification of this operation is that it copies its argument into attribute *in* of the receiver. For uniformity, and to ease the extraction process, we expect that the value of attribute *out* is passed to msg(). In summary, whenever a principal contributes to a step of the protocol, it needs to keep track of two messages: (a) an incoming message that is left by msg() in its *in* variable and triggers the contribution and (b) the outgoing message that it builds in its *out* variable and then sends.

There are two different kind of admissible cryptography: symmetric, which uses either *private* or *session keys*, and asymmetric, which uses *public/private key* pairs. There are some generic operations that can be used to build and open the messages. They are left abstract, since we leave the choice of the cryptographic algorithms open to further specializations. In fact, the analysis treats encryption as abstract operations so we would not get more precise analysis results by specializing these operations further. Encryption and decryption are performed by *crypt()* and *decrypt()* for the symmetric case, and *aCrypt()* and *aDecrypt()* are performed for the asymmetric case. We assume that decrypt() and aDecrypt() leave their result in attribute *theDecryptedItem*. The type of this variable, and those of the parameters, will be discussed below, when considering the structure of the messages in detail. These operations must be immediately followed by a *checkdecrypt()* operation, as discussed below.

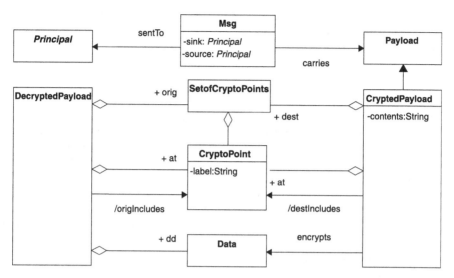

Figure 6.7. The class diagram of the messages.

Class *Info* represents what is being communicated, and is no further specified here, and *Nonce* represents numbers used only once, which is a standard tool when specifying protocols.

As shown in Fig. 6.7, messages (of type *Msg*) carry *Payloads*, some of which can be *CryptedPayloads*; these encrypt *Data* in their *contents*. The CryptedPayloads are returned by the encryption operations that we introduced above. Dually, the decryption operations leave in the local variable theDecryptedItem, values of type *DecryptedData*, which contain the information in clear in the field *dd*.

To support the analysis, the result of each encryption/decryption operation may be decorated with labels, called *Cryptopoints*, that (a) identify uniquely the point in the protocol where the operation is performed (the *at* field of the payloads) and (b) specify the points in which the payload was originated (*orig*, in case of a decryption) or is intended to be used (*dest*, in case of an encryption).

Moreover, always to support the analysis, each message is decorated with a *source* field, which will contain the name of the sender of the message, and a *sink* field, which should contain the name of the recipient.

Operations *checkmsg()* and *checkdecrypt()* are used to open and check the messages and the decrypted payloads, respectively. The specific semantics of each use of these operations will be specified in the protocol model, using invariant and post-condition constraints. The details are given below, when discussing the specification language.

Finally, there are no standard operations to build the outgoing messages. These operations should be introduced explicitly, albeit named in standardized ways that we discuss in the next section, and specified by pre- and post-conditions. They can use the parts of the incoming messages, saved in local variables by previous checkmsg/ checkdecrypt operations, as well as specific information held by the principal in private attributes. Since it often happens, when specifying a protocol, that one needs a "fresh" value of some kind, the Principal specification introduces three "isNew" operations, to express the need of a correct initialization of some variable. These predicates can be used in the pre-condition of the message building operations.

6.3.2. The Dynamic Model

To specify a protocol in our approach, one needs to specify subtypes of the initiator, responder, and server that introduce local variable to held parts of the incoming messages and other specific information, as well as introduce specific operations to build the outgoing messages. Then one needs to build a sequence diagram, which (a) represents the interaction between the involved principals, and (b) holds, as constraints on the arrows, the specification of each operation.

The Protocol package contains the essential starting point for this activity, in a way that reflects the current verification scenario, as shown in Figs 6.8, 6.9, and 6.5. The names for the initiator, server, and responder in Fig. 6.8 come from the tradition in informal protocol narrations.

In the scenario, each principal shares a unique *key* for symmetric key encryption with the server. These *private keys* are known as *kA* and *kB* for the initiator and the responder, respectively. Furthermore, an asymmetric key pair is assigned to each principal. These keys are known as *kAp*, *kAm*, *kBp*, *kBm*, *kSp*, and *kSm* for the initiator, the responder, and the server, respectively. The ending characters of these names are chosen to remind us of the *plus* and *minus* signs that are used in UML to denote public and private attributes/operations, respectively. Indeed, the negative keys in the key pairs are kept secret by the principal they belong to, while the positive key are known to all other principals. This is in agreement with the UML visibility rules.

The remaining attributes are not standard but are simply examples of what a protocol designer may introduce. The choice given here is compatible with a scenario in which the initiator encrypts and sends the information for a certificate to the server, which accepts them in certAinS, and then returns the Certificate (i.e., the received

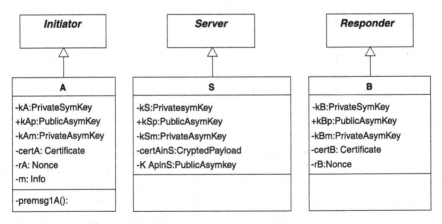

Figure 6.8. The principals in the verification scenario.

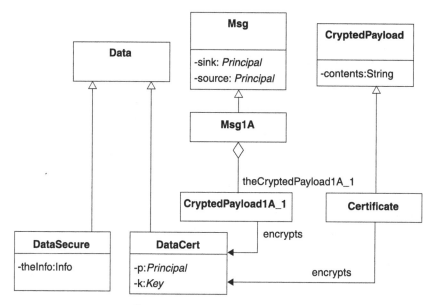

Figure 6.9. Typical data structures.

information to A, encrypted with its private asymmetric key, kSm) to A, which stores it in its variable certA, for future use. It is also expected that the initiator will use a Nonce, rA, and a piece of information m. Similarly, the responder will have its own Certificate and Nonce. The typical (once more) structure of the involved data is given in Fig. 6.9. This figure shows also the structure of a typical message, *Msg1A*, used by the initiator in the scenario above to send the information needed for a certificate, and the naming conventions for its payloads.

Finally, since it has the burden to start the protocol, the initiator shows a typical message building operation, *premsg1A()*. Here we are following a requirement (i.e., that the building operations have names that start by "premsg") and showing a standard way of introducing names (i.e., numbering the operations in the order they occur and tagging them with the principal they pertain). The semantics of this operation, as well as of the other, as already mentioned, is given by pre-/post-conditions and invariant constraints in the sequence diagram, using a specification language defined below.

Finally, Fig. 6.5 shows, as the starting point of the sequence diagram, a typical protocol step. The initiator builds the first message, and the encryption is marked as occurring at cryptopoint Acp1, then sends it to the server, which inputs it with checkmsg and opens it with aDecrypt and checkdecrypt. The diagram shows both the conventional name of the cryptopoints and the way we represent in the diagram the association between the operations and the labels—that is, by placing the latter in a comment linked to the former. Besides, the diagram shows the conventional names of the Principal objects participating in the protocol, namely i, j, and s for the initiator, responder and server, respectively.

To continue the protocol specification, the designer shall introduce new messages and complete each one with pre/post/invariant conditions. The specification of the messages introduced here will be discussed after introducing the specification language in the next section.

6.3.3. The Specification Language

The syntax of the language used to specify the operations in the protocol is given in Table 6.1, where we adopt the following standard meta-conventions: Square brackets denote optional items, curly brackets represent zero or more occurrences, and bold items are terminal. We give the semantics of the Spec language informally, as follows. We will call *destination* of an operation the object that is the destination of the arrow with which the specified operation is associated.

Spec. Each *specification* is evaluated in a namespace that merges the names of the parameters of the operation with the namespace of the sequence diagram, which contains the object names (i, j, and s) and with the namespace of the destination. If the name denotes an object, its fields are also accessible, and so on, recursively, in the usual fashion. Besides, the evaluation namespace includes all the standard public keys kXp. When the destination is the server, the namespace includes also all the private symmetric keys kX, since the server knows them all, in our scenario. The designer is responsible for the absence of clashes; the naming conventions should make this task easy.

Inv. An *invariant* can be associated with checkmsg and checkdecrypt, to specify checks on an incoming message or on the result of a decryption, respectively. The purpose of an invariant is the same as a UML condition on a message: It blocks the protocol if not satisfied. Apparently, the community edition of Poseidon did not provide for explicit conditions on messages in sequence diagrams at the moment of building Choreographer, so we went for this turnaround. The only constraint that can be

TABLE 6.1. The Syntax of the Specification Language

```
Spec ::= Inv | Pre | Post | Comment
Inv ::= Cond { , Cond }
Pre ::= TypeRestriction | EncryptedType |
        Initialization { & Initialization }
TypeRestriction ::= Ide : Type
EncryptedType :: Ide encrypts DataConstructor
Initialization ::= isNewKey( Ide ) | isNewInfo( Ide ) |
isNewNonce( Ide )
Post ::= [ with TypeRestriction ] Cond { & Cond }
Cond ::= Name = Expr
Name ::= Ide { . Ide }
Expr ::= Name | Fun( [ Expr { , Expr } ] )
Fun ::= crypt | aCrypt | cp | Constructor
Ide ::= <any name defined in the namespace of the destination>
Constructor ::= SetofCryptpoints | DataConstructor
DataConstructor ::= <any data constructor>
Comment ::= $$ <string> $$
```

imposed in an invariant is that the values of the two sides of the conditions are equal. Usually, the source and sink of each message are checked against the expected value. Additional checks depend on the specifics of the protocol; for example, a clear payload must be equal to the name of the message source—that is, the sender can only speak for itself. Similarly, another check may be that the incoming responder is indeed the intended one. These checks make the protocol more robust, blocking malicious attacks at run time.

Pre. A *precondition* must be associated with each call of the operation msg(), to specify the actual type of the current message, by a *type restriction*. Similarly, a pre-condition must be associated with each decrypt/aDecrypt operation, to specify the type of the encrypted data, by an *encrypted data* declaration. Finally, preconditions allow the designer to express initializations concisely in premsg (see below).

Initialization. The intended meaning is that before the specified operation, the arguments of these predicates have been assigned fresh values. Initializations can be used to this purpose, as the precondition of a premsg operation. With respect to the analysis, the lack of proper initialization will likely lead to more errors revealed, since it amounts to leave some values unprotected.

The choice of operators in the initialization clause reflects a couple of assumptions, with respect to keys:

- Private keys, either symmetric or asymmetric, can be freely used in the operations of the owner, since they are assumed to be initialised before the protocol starts.
- Asymmetric public keys can be used everywhere, for their own nature; however, some protocols may restrict themselves to use public keys that have been explicitly exchanged.
- Session keys must be initialized explicitly before they are used.

Similarly, nonces and any information that is generated and exchanged during the execution of the protocol must be initialized before their use.

Post. The *post-condition* clause is used to specify the effect of an operation on the state of the destination. The post-condition of operation msg is standard, namely "in = p," meaning that the sent message (the value of the parameter p, which is assigned the value of the 'out' attribute of the sender) is copied into the "in" attribute of the destination.

In the case of premsg, we usually use the optional element, which is a record scope opener à la Pascal, for readability; the fields need not be prefixed by the identifier, in the left-hand sides of the conditions that follow. The restriction is "out: MsgM" if the operation is premsgM.[1] This entails that the names of the Payload of MsgM can be used to denotes fields to be assigned.

The intended effect of the operation is given by the conditions (see below).

---

[1]The same restriction should appear as a precondition in the following msg operation.

Cond. When used in an invariant, a *condition* expresses a check, as seen above.

When used in a post-condition, it defines the value of an attribute or one of its fields, as a result of the execution of the operation it specifies; the name on the left-hand side denotes the element that takes the value defined by the expression on the right-hand side.

Name. A *name* denotes a variable. The standard dot notation is used to access object fields: N.I denotes the variable denoted by I in the namespace of the object denoted by N.

Expr. An *expression* denotes a variable. The standard dot notation is used to access object fields: N.I denotes the value denoted by I in the namespace of the object denoted by N.

Ide. An *identifier* denotes a value or a variable, depending on the context, and evaluates as follows:

- The operation parameters evaluate to the corresponding arguments, as specified in the sequence diagram.
- The identifiers in the sequence diagram evaluate to the corresponding objects.
- The attributes of an object (including the standard ones) denote the corresponding object or value, according to its type.
- The standard key names evaluate to the corresponding key.

The operation arguments are evaluated similarly, in the namespace of the origin of the arrow.

Fun. The admissible operations include the encryption actions, the creation of data to be encrypted, and the creation of cryptopoints and sets of cryptopoints. Following Java, a constructor has the name of the class of the objects it builds. The arguments must correspond in number and order to the fields of the class. The labels in cryptopoints are implicitly quoted, and cp is used as an abbreviation of CryptoPoint.

Before considering an example, we need to list some standard operations and naming conventions.

Messages. The messages shall have types *MsgM*, where M is unique for a given structure of the message. Their payloads shall be named *thePayloadY* and *theCryptedPayloadZ*, where Y and Z usually concatenate the M of the message with a number reflecting the order in the message.

Data. The encrypted data shall have types *DataM*, where M is unique for a given structure of the data.

Principals. Each principal shall have as many *premsgM* operations as messages it sends, where M is the same as in the type of the sent message. The parameters of each operation (if any) shall be named $p1, p2, \ldots$ in the order of appearance. Principal *objects* shall be named i, j, and s.

TABLE 6.2. Exemplar Narration

```
1:premsg1A()                 $$ A -> S: {A,kAp}:kSp $$
<postcondition>: with out:Msg1A source = i & sink = s &
  theCryptedPayload1A_1.contents = acrypt(kSp,DataCert(i,kAp)) &
  theCryptedPayload1A_1.dest = SetofCryptpoint(Scp1) &
  theCryptedPayload1A_1.at = cp(Acp1)
2:msg(out)
<precondition>: out : Msg1A
<postcondition>: in = p
3:checkmsg()                 $$ A -> S: {A,kAp}:kSp $$
<invariant>: in.source=i, in.sink=s
<postcondition>: certAinS.contents =
in.theCryptedPayload1A_1.contents
4:aDecrypt(kAp,certAinS.contents)
<precondition>: certAinS encrypts DataCert
<postcondition>: theDecryptedItem.at = cp(Scp1) &
                 theDecryptedItem.orig = SetofCryptpoint(Acp1)
5:checkdecrypt()
<invariant>: theDecryptedItem.dd.p=i
<postcondition>: kApInS = theDecryptedItem.dd.k
```

Cryptopoints. They should be named in a standard way: TcpN, where T is the type of the owner and N is a progressive number.

6.3.4. An Example of Operation Specification

To discuss the use of the specification language, we exploit the diagram in Fig. 6.1 and the *narration* in Table 6.2, which lists all the conditions associated with the operations in the model and can be generated automatically in Choreographer from the UML model described above.[2]

The protocol fragment discussed here would be expressed in the informal style used to discuss cryptographic issues as

$$A -> S: \{A, kAp\}: kSp$$

to express that the initiator A sends a message to the server S, consisting of the pair <initiator name, initiator public key>, encrypted with the server public key. The fact that asymmetric cryptography is used is left implicit, based on the name of the key. It turns out that reporting this description of the step as a comment in the operations that build and receive the message is a useful way of documenting the protocol.

---

[2]This feature of the Choreographer is very useful when debugging the model. Indeed, these conditons have been associated with the arrows in the diagram through specific I/O panes in the model editor and can only be inspected singularly, so that it is very difficult to have a global view of the specification.

Besides the name and number of each operation, each entry in Table 6.2 displays the following information, when present, per each arrow in the sequence diagram: the comment from the Documentation field, embraced by a couple of double dollar signs, and the constraint fields, tagged with their type.

The first operation in this step of the protocol (*premsg1A*) has to construct the message, which, having type *Msg1A* as declared in the type restriction of the post-condition, requires the definition of five fields:

- The message source, set to the initiator object name, *i*.
- The message sink, set to the server object name, *s*.
- The standard field of the CryptedPayload, *contents*, set to the result of encrypting asymmetrically with the public key of the server a *Data* of type DataCert (according to what declared in Fig. 6.9 by the *encrypts* association). The fields of the encrypted data are, as defined above, the initiator's name and public key.
- The standard field of the CryptedPayload, *dest*, set to the cryptopoint associated with the intended place of decryption, which the designer's foresight sets to *Scp1*, according to Fig. 6.5.
- The standard field of the CryptedPayload, *at*, set to Acp1, the cryptopoint associated with this operation, in Fig. 6.5.

The second entry in Table 6.2 is standard and provides all the information needed to specify the transfer from *out* in the initiator to *in* in the server.

The third entry repeats the comment; this is useful to the cultivated designer who may have a look at the generated LySa code. Since *premsg* and *checkmsg* there are no longer contiguous, the comment, which is reported also in the LySa code, helps in relating the pieces there. Next, the invariant expresses that the standard message fields, *source* and *sink*, are checked, to verify if they are what the designer expects. Moreover, the post-condition asserts that the informative part of the CryptedPayload of the incoming message is stored in the local variable certAinS, for further processing. The other fields, *dest* and *at*, are not relevant here.

The last two entries should be considered together, since they cooperate in opening the encrypted payload, checking its contents, and saving parts for future reference. The pre-condition of operation number 4 is needed to declare the actual type of the *dd* field of the local variable that accepts the result of the decryption, *theDecryptedItem*. The post-condition of the same operation defines the other fields, namely

- the one labeling this decryption point, *at*, which is set to *Scp1*, according to Fig. 6.5;
- the one stating the expected origin—that is, the place of encryption—set to *Acp1*.

The last entry defines the checks on the result of the decryption (we require that the principal in the certificate is the initiator) and that the key must be saved locally, to be used later by the server to build the certificate for the initiator.

6.3.5. Reflection

We now discuss briefly how the results of the analysis are presented to the designer in Choreographer. Figure 6.10 shows the outcome of the reflection for a flowed version of the well-known Wide-Mouthed Frog protocol. The protocol describes key exchange between two principals A and B through a trusted server. The protocol has three steps.

1. Principal A sends a message to the server including the name of B and the new session key K_{AB}, encrypted with its public key K_{AS}.
2. The server decrypts this and sends the name of A and the new key K_{AB} to B, encrypted under B's public key K_{BS}.
3. Principal A sends a message to B encrypted under K_{AB}.

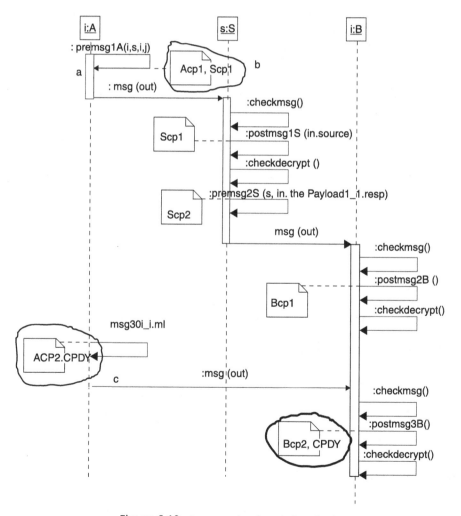

Figure 6.10. An example of analysis output.

Analyzing this protocol, the tool finds the errors circled on Fig. 6.10. For example, the decryption at Bcp2 may decrypt messages coming from the attacker (denoted CPDY) instead of coming only from Acp2 as intended. Based on these errors, the modeler may pinpoint the problem, modify the protocol description in UML, and rerun the analysis until the analyzer guarantees that there are no errors in the protocol.

6.3.6. Experience

Besides a number of small examples used to test the tools, the major experience with the verification approach was made in DEGAS with the case studies of the project. There were two of them, put forward by the industrial partners.

The first case study is a video game in which a large number of players can play simultaneously in a global context, open environment. There is a main server that has just a coordination role, whereas the interactions among players take place directly between mobile devices on a peer-to-peer basis, via data connection or SMS messages. It is essential that the communication between players and between a player and the server is secure to avoid that an attacker could alter the parameters of the players and of the objects they collect during the game. In accordance to the peer-to-peer nature of the project, the security protocol should minimize the involvement of the server.

The second case study comprises a web-based service to enable micro e-business based on a peer-to-peer authentication and communication paradigm. The aim is to provide a simple peer-to-peer e-commerce mechanism for a community of buyers and sellers by offering Web-based business facilities to sellers who do not have the resources to develop a proprietary solution, as well as offering easy access to information about available products and services to the buyers. Transfer of money is handled by standard banking services. Communication should be possible via wired Internet connections as well as via mobile devices, using standard protocols such as WAP. The security requirements for this case study can be reduced to establishing authenticity of messages, which is the main security property addressed in DEGAS.

In both cases it is better to use symmetric encryption for the peer-to-peer exchanges between the mobile devices, since their computational load is smaller than that of asymmetric encryption. However, the keys to be used have to be protected form malicious intruders. So, a protocol in two parts was devised: one in which public keys are distributed, and another in which pairs of players agree on a session key. The analysis showed that other means to establish authentication of messages have to be used: Both players have to provide certificates to the other player in order to prevent the spy from supplying his own key instead of the public key of some player.

The resulting protocol, dubbed *SecureSend*, has a sequence diagram with 38 arrows and has been successfully analyzed in Choreographer. More details can be found in references 15 and 17.

6.4. CONCLUSIONS

The overall aim of our work is somewhat similar to the aim of frameworks such as Casper (13), CAPSL (6), CVS (8), and AVISS (1). These frameworks all aim at providing developers of security protocols with high-level interfaces for formal analysis tools; but unlike our approach, they are based on ad hoc notation. On one hand, this may lead to more compact description of protocols than ours; but on the other hand, we have all the advantages of using a general-purpose modeling language. On the technical side, the information found in protocol descriptions in the above frameworks is quite similar to the information captured in our message sequence diagrams. Also, in the extraction we find similarities—in particular, with Casper, which also has a target analysis formalism using a process calculus. The extraction made in Casper is, however, somewhat simpler than ours because its high-level language is designed so that it directly includes process calculi expression at convenient places.

An important effort that shares the DEGAS focus on the UML is centered on UMLsec. This is a UML profile to express security-relevant information within the diagrams in a system specification, as well as on the related approach to secure system development (11). UMLsec allows the designer to express recurring security requirements, like fair exchange, secrecy/confidentiality, secure information flow, secure communication link. Rules are given to validate a model against included security requirements, based on a formal semantics for the used fragment of UML, with a formal notion of adversary. This semantic base permits us, in principle, to check whether the constraints associated with the UML stereotypes are fulfilled in a given specification. Work is ongoing to provide automatic analysis support, with an approach similar to that of DEGAS. In our opinion, ForLySa provides a more intuitive way to express authentication requirements that are less central in UMLsec: it should be worthwhile to assess the feasibility of the integration of the two approaches.

The experience with the DEGAS cases studies suggests that the representation of a protocol for analysis, which we have seen above, is too detailed to be effectively used when exploiting the protocol in the design of an application. The designer should be able to use a protocol in an application simply, once the protocol has been certified. Essentially, one doesn't want to draw more than one arrow for each step of the protocol, when designing an application, or even one might only want to state that some information is exchanged using the protocol. The best way to link these short-hands and the full-fledge representation for the analysis is left to further research.

Another open issue is related to the implementation of the protocol. It is well known that the implementation process can introduce defects, even if we start from a proven correct specification. Now, in our case the specification used to analyze the protocol contains enough information to support an implementation, and the goal of deriving a correct implementation automatically is worth pursuing.

The solution used to report the error information at the UML level is somewhat minimalist and is made possible by the fact that the diagram is somewhat prepared so to provide hooks for the insertion: the notes attached to the arrows. However, this minimalist attitude seems a good trade-off, until the ongoing standard for UML diagram interchange matures (18). Indeed, it does not seem worthwhile to put too much effort in unraveling the specific graphical representation of the diagram in a single modeling environment. Once the standard is here, it may be worthwhile to design an algorithm for a more flexible update of the diagram with the results of the analysis, which would then have a general validity within the standard.

To conclude, we recall that the work reported here, like the one on quantitative analysis also embedded in Choreographer, is a sort of short-term attack to the problem highlighted in the introduction—that is, that of smoothing, via an UML interface, the negative impact on the development process of the large diversity of formal approaches. In the long run, the problem can only be solved by convergent attacks involving all the players in the game: Industry should invest more in R&D and in the training of personnel, so that formality is no longer daunting the professionals, academia should educate more cultivated engineers to start with, and research should target a basic integration of the diverse theories for formal specifications.

ACKNOWLEDGMENTS

This work profited from many discussions with the DEGAS people, in meetings in Pisa, Trento, and Edinburgh. Special thanks are due to Chiara Bodei, Pierpaolo Degano, and Mikael Buchholtz, for introducing us to (some of) LySa's *arcana*; to Michela Vasari and Monika Maidl, for insights on the case study protocol, and to Lara Perrone, Simone Semprini, and Daniele Picciaia, for programming the extractor. Val Haenel integrated the extractor in Choreographer and built the reflector.

REFERENCES

1. A. Armando, D. Basin, M. Bouallagui, Y. Chevalier, L. Compagna, S. Modersheim, M. Rusinowitch, M. Turuani, L. Vigano, and L. Vigneron. The AVISS security protocol analysis tool. In *Proceedings of the 14th International Conference on Computer Aided Verification (CAV 2002)*, LNCS 2404, pages 349–353. Springer, Berlin, 2002.

2. K. Beck *et al.* Manifesto for Agile Software Development. Available at http://www.agilemanifesto.org/.

3. C. Bodei, M. Buchholtz, P. Degano, F. Nielson, and H. Riis Nielson. Automatic validation of protocol narration. In *Proceedings of the 16th Computer Security Foundations Workshop (CSFW 2003)*, pages 126–140. IEEE Computer Society Press, New York, 2003.

4. M. Buchholtz, S. Gilmore, V. Haenel, and C. Montangero. End-to-end integrated security and performance analysis on the DEGAS Choreographer platform. In *Proceedings of Formal Methods 2005*, LNCS 3582, pages 286–301. Springer, Berlin, 2005.

5. M. Buchholtz, C. Montangero, L. Perrone, S. Semprini. For-LySa: UML for authentication analysis. In *Proceedings of the 2nd International Workshop on Global Computing, (GC'04)*, LNCS 3267, pages 92–105. Springer, Berlin, 2004.

6. G. Denker, J. Millen, and H. Rue. The CAPSL integrated protocol environment. Technical Report SRI-CLS-2000-02, SRI International, 2000.

7. Design Environments for Global ApplicationS—DEGAS, project IST-2001-32072, Information Society Technologies programme of the European Commission, Future and Emerging Technologies. Available at http://www.omnys.it/degas/main.html.

8. A. Durante, R. Focardi, and R. Gorrieri. A compiler for analyzing cryptographic protocols using non-interference. *ACM Transactions on Software Engineering and Methodology* **9**(4):488–528, 2000.

9. M. Fowler. *UML Distilled: A Brief Guide to the Standard Object Modelling Language.* Pearson Education, New York, 2004.

10. J. Hillston. *A Compositional Approach to Performance Modelling.* Cambridge University Press, New York, 1996.

11. J. Jürjens. *Secure Systems Development with UML.* Springer, Berlin, 2005.

12. P. Kruchten. *The Rational Unified Process. An Introduction.* Addison-Wesley, Reading, MA, 1998.

13. G. Lowe. Casper: A compiler for the analysis of security protocols. *Journal of Computer Security* **6**(1):53–84, 1998.

14. Mikael Buchholtz. LySa—A process calculus. Web site hosted by Informatics and Mathematical Modeling at the Technical University of Denmark, April 2004. http://www2.imm.dtu.dk/cs_LySa/lysatool/.

15. C. Montangero. ForLysa User's Guide. DEGAS Document WP3-UNIPI-I02-Int-001, 18/2/05. Available at http://www.di.unipi.it/~monta/ForLySa/ForLySaManual.pdf.

16. J. Rumbaugh, I. Jacobson, and G. Booch. *The Unified Modeling Language*, 2nd edition. Addison-Wesley, Reading, MA, 2005.

17. D. Spunton, I. Mura, M. Vasari, and D. Piazza. Case Studies. DEGAS Deliverable 26, March 8, 2005. Available at http://www.omnys.it/degas/documents.html#D26.

18. Unified Modeling Language: Diagram Interchange version 2.0. 2005. Available at http://www.omg.org/docs/ptc/05-06-04.pdf.

7

MODERN WEB APPLICATION DEVELOPMENT

Mehdi Jazayeri, Cédric Mesnage, and Jeffrey Rose

7.1. INTRODUCTION

The World Wide Web was introduced in 1994 with the goal of making it possible to access information from any source in a consistent and simple way. Developed at CERN, in Geneva, Switzerland, it was aimed at physicists and other scientists who generate huge amounts of data and documents and need to share them with other scientists. Hypertext was adopted as a simple way to both give access to documents and link them together. The HTTP protocol was designed to allow one computer—the client computer—to request data and documents from another computer—the server computer—so that it could make that document available to the users on the client computer. In this way, the World Wide Web was viewed as a vast repository of information that provided access to a large number of users. This view of the Web as a static repository has evolved considerably over time. Now the Web is a sophisticated platform offering a vast array of tools and components to application developers. A new generation of applications offers users the opportunities to communicate, collaborate, and even update the capabilities of the application. Applications support small businesses or communities of users as well as large company businesses.

The Web continues to evolve at a rapid pace. There are many ideas about what trends will predominate in the future. One all-encompassing concept is to consider the emerging trends as forming the basis of Web 2.0. Compared to traditional Web

Emerging Methods, Technologies, and Process Management in Software Engineering. Edited by
De Lucia, Ferrucci, Tortora, and Tucci
Copyright © 2008 John Wiley & Sons, Inc.

applications—those of Web 1.0—Web 2.0 applications are dynamic, they invite user participation, and they are responsive to user requests as are desktop applications. Perhaps the best description of Web 2.0 is given by O'Reilly (http://www.oreillynet.com/pub/a/oreilly/tim/news/2005/09/30/what-is-web-20.html). That article contrasts the applications and technologies from Web 1.0 to Web 2.0. Some telling examples of applications are: Wikipedia versus *Encylcopaedia Brittanica*, in which the former engages the help of users to create data and the latter draws a sharp distinction between producers and consumers of the data. Another example is publishing websites versus blogging, which again differ by their views of allowing user participation. As a third example, we can regard the use of search engines for finding websites as opposed to the earlier approaches of remembering or guessing website addresses. What has made Web 2.0 possible and what will come next?

In this chapter, we look at the state of the art, important concepts that underlie and spur the development of Web 2.0, and, finally, the coming trends in Web applications and the underlying infrastructure support.

7.2. FOUNDATIONS OF THE WEB

Despite the enormous developments over the last decade, the fundamental principles upon which the World Wide Web was based have remained constant. Structurally, the World Wide Web is based on client–server computing, in which servers store documents and clients access documents. The same computer may act as a client and as a server at different times. The World Wide Web introduced three fundamental concepts on top of client–server computing: a method of naming and referring to documents (URL), a language for writing documents that can contain data and links to other documents (HTML), and a method for client and server machines to communicate with each other (HTTP).

URL. A naming system is a fundamental component of computer systems, especially so for distributed systems. A naming system prescribes the way objects are named so that the objects can be identified and located. Depending on the characteristics of the naming system, objects may be searched for on the basis of their exact names only or on the basis of their attributes. For example, one might want to tell the system to "fetch the paper written by Alan Turing about intelligence test." The World Wide Web's naming scheme had the goal of uniquely identifying all objects stored on the computers on the Internet. The naming scheme is based on Uniform Resource Locators (URLs), which are composite names identifying the computer (IP address) and the document in the file system of that computer. URLs are now defined as a standard in IETF RFC 1630.

HTML. The documents on the Web are written in the HyperText Markup Language. HTML documents contain content to be displayed, formatting instructions that tell the browser how to display the contents of the document, and links to other documents. HTML has evolved along with browsers to achieve better visual presentations and standardization.

Initially, HTML was viewed as a language for instructing browsers what to display for humans. But as the number of documents written in HTML has grown, and as many applications started to generate HTML documents, computer processing of HTML documents became important. The eXtended Markup Language (XML) was created to standardize the definition of other specialized markup languages. XHTML is an XML compliant HTML that has become the dominant variant of HTML.

Currently, the Web Hypertext Application Technology Working Group (www.whatwg.org) is working on defining an evolutionary path for HTML and reconciling the discrepancies between XHTML and HTML. Other groups such as W3C are working on XHTML as a standard.

HTTP. The communication protocol for the Web is the HTTP (see RFC 2616) protocol, which defines eight basic operations: OPTIONS, GET, HEAD, POST, PUT, DELETE, TRACE, CONNECT. The most used of these operations or methods are GET and POST. The method GET retrieves from a given URL the data associated with the requested URL. The method POST sends data to the program listening at the requested URL.

These simple concepts have proven to be surprisingly powerful. Application developers have found ingenious ways of using URLs to name a variety of things and not only documents. For example, one of the early ideas was to use the URL to name a program to execute on the server, which would then produce output that would be returned to the client. Likewise, documents are used not only to contain information to be displayed by the browser but to contain code scripts to be executed. A whole array of languages have been created to write code to be executed by the browser (e.g., JavaScript) or on the server (e.g., PHP). Web applications take advantage of a variety of languages and design patterns to combine the capabilities of clients and servers.

7.3. SOFTWARE ENGINEERING AND WEB APPLICATIONS

Software engineering was born in 1968 as a vision of taming the software development difficulties encountered in the 1960s in early large software development projects. It was becoming clear that large monolithic software, which was the only kind of software being built, had many limitations. Such software could not be extended beyond a certain size, could not be maintained, and therefore rarely met customer expectations. Software engineering promised a systematic approach to software construction based on modular designs and standard software components. This vision of software engineering is becoming more real as the years go by.

Web application development followed a history similar to software engineering but at a much more rapid pace. Early Web applications consisted of many scripts scattered over many files and lacked a systematic structure. Perhaps because Web applications are naturally distributed, however, the idea of individual components that can be composed to build applications has become a reality in Web applications much more easily. Web applications commonly use standard components such as payment or registration modules. In this section, we look at several aspects of Web applications that are closely related to software engineering issues.

7.3.1. Static–Dynamic–Live

The early Web was constructed by a set of documents that could freely link to each other. These were simple text files, which had static content and static links connecting to pages. Over time, people realized that in fact these text documents sent from a Web server to the Web browser could just as easily be generated by a program. This led to CGI (common gateway interface) applications, where the URL referred to small scripts or even large compiled programs that would be run on the server to dynamically generate Web pages. The CGI program that ran on the server could, for example, extract data from a database. This became cumbersome for many applications, because putting all of the content and formatting for a website into the code of an application, as software engineers know well, can become tedious and hard to manage. This realization led to a sort of hybrid model, where the language PHP was an early influence. With PHP, the typical structure is to create Web pages that have small bits of code directly in the text of the pages. At the time of a request, the code would be executed and its results inserted into the current document. This led to much more flexibility and easier reuse of page components; but over time, people realized that it was often hard to make changes to code when it was spread out over all of the pages in a website. This led to a further refinement of the model, into what is typical in today's Web applications, where a central component in the application manages access to data, while the code which is dispersed in the HTML pages is limited to just what is displayed to the user.

7.3.2. The Model View Controller Design Pattern

From the software engineering point of view, the concerns of many Web applications are similar: They have a user interface, based in the browser, that interacts with the user, and they manage a possibly large amount of data, stored on the server, on behalf of the user. It took a number of years before Web developers realized that the standard MVC pattern, well known in software engineering, applies just as well to such Web applications.

The Model View Controller (22) was first introduced at Xerox PARC in 1978, first used in Smalltalk, 20 years before the widespread use of the Web and 30 years before many Web application development frameworks started to use it as their core structuring pattern. The purpose of the MVC design pattern, according to its creator, was to "bridge the gap between the human user's mental model and the digital model that exists in the computer." Originally, it was a system composed of four terms: model, view, controller, and editor. We explain the Model View Controller in the context of Web applications. Typically the model is a set of object-oriented classes to interact with the data store (usually a database), the controller contains the logic of the application or processes, and the view is a script that generates an editor (in our case, HTML pages). The controller is also responsible for preparing the data from the model for the view to be created. The controller creates the views and responds to queries made from the views.

7.3.3. Web Applications Frameworks

It took software engineering decades to arrive at usable application development frameworks that support the development of complex applications based on similar components and designs. The underlying idea is to provide these components in a configurable and extensible framework. A plethora of component-based Web engineering methodologies are now available (11, 19) supporting object-oriented composition (10), exploring aspect-oriented and context dependency (3), and searching for patterns using UML (2). Recently, a more robust and agile framework has appeared in different programming languages, many of them based on the Model View Controller design pattern.

Ruby on Rails. Ruby is a dynamic object-oriented programming language (27) that has become popular for writing Web applications. It supports the writing of complete programs and scripts that can be embedded in HTML files. It has a very active and dynamic community that has created many lightweight solutions. One of the best known of these is Ruby on Rails (28). Ruby on Rails is a framework for Web application development based on the model view controller pattern. To this it adds a set of powerful functionalities such as scaffolding, active record, migrations, routing, environments, and many helpers.

The scaffolding is a Ruby on Rails concept in which by means of scripts the developer generates the first version of an application. The scaffolding generates models, views, and controllers as needed based on the predefined database schema. The framework supports an agile development methodology (5) as you start your application with a basic set of files that give you the essential operations on your model, namely: show, edit, create, update, and delete.

ActiveRecord is a library that allows the developer to interact with the backend database only by managing Ruby objects, making the development easier as the developer operates completely in the Ruby environment, without explicitly using the Structured Query Language (SQL).

Migration is a way of managing the database schema by a set of Ruby classes. Changes in the database schema during software maintenance are automatically supported by migration.

The routing facilities of Rails maps a URL query to the desired controller and action to handle the query.

The framework provides three environments by default: development, testing, and production. These different working environments simplify the work on the same code at different stages of implementation in parallel. Furthermore, deployment on different servers, with different databases and operating systems, are specified once and handled automatically by the framework.

Other Frameworks. Popular programming languages are now supported by their own Web application frameworks. J2EE is the Java Web application framework that evolved into a Model View Controller with the introduction of Struts. Its views system is implemented by Java Server Pages (JSP), and controllers and models are typically Java Beans or Java Servlets.

Seaside is a powerful framework that extends the power, flexibility, and simplicity of Smalltalk to Web application development. Django is based on Python.

The common characteristic of these frameworks is that they support (a) the model-view-controller, (b) object-relational mapping to map databases to objects so that the programmer can program in the object-oriented language without explicit database operations and (c) generators for creating routine parts of the application.

7.3.4. Releasing a Web Application

Managing releases is a laborious and expensive part of traditional software engineering. The situation is dramatically different for Web applications.

In a desktop application, adding features and fixing bugs requires either a new version to be installed or a patch to be applied. This upgrade process has proved to be difficult for a number of reasons. First is the simple problem of distribution. Users of an application have to know that an upgrade is available, and then they have to take the time to download and install. Second, the upgrade process is often error-prone. Over time, software installations tend to diverge from the "clean install," and this leads to a large number of potential cases that an upgrade might have to deal with. Differing versions of the application, libraries, and resources require upgrades to be much more complex than what would be needed for moving from one version to the next, for example. In a server situation, this is all dramatically simplified. Features and bug fixes can be added to a running application as soon as they are ready, and instantly all users will benefit from the upgrade. This allows developers to focus on improving the application rather than dealing with complex maintenance and upgrade issues, and it benefits application users because they get instant access to the latest version of the software.

Web application development is therefore more open to agile methods because even small units of functionality may be made available to users instantly rather than having to be bundled with other functionality subject to an arbitrary release schedule. As opposed to desktop applications that may have release cycles of several months or even years, it is not unusual for Web applications to be updated several times a day.

7.4. CURRENT TRENDS

We can identify at least two forces that influence the current trends in the evolution of Web applications. On the one hand, new functionality is driving the development of new types of Web applications. On the other hand, new engineering approaches to building Web applications is driving the way applications are structured, and, consequently, enabling a new range of applications. In this section, we review (a) the phenomenon of user participation as an example of a functionality that affects the evolution of Web applications and (b) the concept of "from desktop to the Web" as a concept that leads to restructuring of Web applications.

7.4.1. Application Trend: Participation

Some still view Web applications as "means to communicate content" for stakeholders (21). While providing content is certainly one use of Web applications, a new generation of Web applications is including the user in the application by offering more interactivity, communication, and collaboration among users and enrolling the user to create value in the application. Recent studies (14) show that Websites considered as "good Websites" over the last years tend to offer more interaction to the user than content. The phenomenon of enlisting the user in the evolution of the Web application is referred to as "user participation." O'Reilly lists participation as one of the major drivers of Web 2.0. In this section we present some types of Web applications that derive their power from the participation of users.

Blog Systems. According to Wikipedia, "A blog is a website where entries are made in journal style and displayed in a reverse chronological order." The ability of readers to interactively leave comments for others to see and comment on is a fundamental feature of blogs. Blogs (Web logs) first appeared on the Blogger.com system. A blog is a website managed by the user in which content is added by "posting." These posts are often organized in categories and can be commented on by other users. The traffic on blogs is intense, and bloggers often cite other blogs within their posts. Blogs therefore have very high link density. As of today, there exist over 60 million blogs on the Web.

Closely related to blogs is the concept of dynamic data feeds. Recently, the very primitive syndication scheme of RSS, which requires polling websites for updated XML content, has taken off among consumers. Many blogs use RSS to notify their readers of changes in the blog. Aggregator applications merge different RSS feeds to produce sites with richer content. Blogs are an obvious example of a phenomenon that has changed the paradigm of news delivery. Blogs offer a different paradigm than the traditional printed newspapers. They enable a new model for society to access up-to-date information about what is going on in the world, albeit without the newspaper's editorial process.

Wiki Systems. Wiki Systems such as wikipedia.org are similar to blogs in principle because they are based on user participation to add content. The fundamental element of wikis are pages as in typical websites, as opposed to blogs in which basic elements are posts (which can be displayed together within the same pages). Wikis allow users not only to read but also to update the content of the pages. The underlying assumption is that over time the wiki will represent the consensus knowledge (or at least the opinions) of all the users. As blogs, wikis exhibit high link density. In addition, wikis have high linking within the same wiki because they provide a simple syntax for the user to link to pages, both to existing pages and to those yet to be created. Most wikis also provide authentication and versioning to restrict editing by users and to be able to recover the history.

Collaborative Tagging Systems. Tagging refers to the ability of a user to associate a term (a *tag*) to a Web page or a Web resource. Tags may then be used to find resources, instead of naming the resource. Tags may also be used to classify resources. Emerging applications to organize information follow a new paradigm named *collaborative tagging*. Its principle is based on the simple assumption that users know how to describe Web resources in their own terms and that collaboratively they cover more aspects of the resources than experts or automatic indexing. Flickr.com is a Yahoo application to store, share, and organize images using terms. Del.icio.us is another Yahoo application that references Web pages by the discovery of users when they browse the Web, assigning terms to Web pages. Bibsonomy.com and citeUlike.com are collaborative tagging applications to organize and share scientific publications. RealTravel.com is a blog system organized using collaborative tagging.

The empirical study of collaborative tagging data (13, 17) reveals the collective behaviors of users. Inductive studies (18) discusses the collaborative tagging system as being the collaborative transcription of users' observations on the basis of terms. The academic and Web engineering world are now considering this paradigm in many new applications, even on the desktop.

Human Computation. Human Computation systems studied in reference 30 are based on the principle that some complex tasks can be simply effected by humans and are difficult for machines. One good example is CAPTCHA, which stands for "Completely Automated Public Turing Test to Tell Computers and Humans Apart." The name speaks for itself and you can encounter them on many websites nowadays. Basically, the idea is to distort text on colorful images and ask the agent in communication to tell what the text is. If the agent is a human, he can simply read it; if the agent is a computer, it cannot do it in a short period of time. This test distinguishes humans from machines. Other uses are image indexation made collectively (Google does that with the ESP Game.) Collaborative tagging, more generally, is an example of human computation for indexing based on simple observations whose substance are terms.

7.4.2. Moving the Desktop to the Web

One of the growing trends in recent Web applications has been moving functionality, which in the past was always implemented as a typical desktop application, into the browser. Word processors, spreadsheets, calendars, email, and other personal information managers are some of the core user applications that have recently shown up in online form. This means that the functionality that was earlier implemented on every user desktop is now supported instead by the Web server and made available to the user through the Web browser. This implies that the application and its data are centralized and are offered as a service to the desktop user.

Ease of collaboration is one of the primary benefits of moving any application from the desktop to the Web. By moving the data to a central location that is accessible by multiple parties, online applications have the advantage of providing easier collaboration platforms. Documents cannot only be viewed and edited by multiple parties without having to manage the back-and-forth transfer of different versions, but real-time collaboration over the Internet is a major step in facilitating telecommuting and long-distance interaction.

Centralization brings many advantages (as well as some disadvantages). Automatic data management and backup is a standard feature that can be offered by a hosted application. By keeping the data on a managed server, a backup scheme can be put in place to serve thousands of users simultaneously, as opposed to each person having to manage their own personal backups when data are stored locally. This model does require that the data server(s) have access controls and adequate security, but in the end it might prove to be easier to maintain security over a small number of servers rather than over a large number of user machines all of which have copies of potentially sensitive data.

So what holds back every application from moving to the Web? This can be broken into two primary issues, interactivity and resource usage. The latency incurred by having all interaction bounce back and forth between a browser and a server means that many Web applications don't feel as responsive as their desktop counterparts. The speed of light and the latency introduced by Internet routers cannot be easily overcome by typical websites, but large Web-based services such as Google are applying standard distributed system solutions to the problem by simply replicating their application servers all over the world. As the typical connection bandwidth increases and latency decreases, by moving to fiber links for example, this will become less of a problem for all but the most data-intensive applications. In some situations, moving to a peer-to-peer model, as described in Section 7.5.2, will help improve latency, but this is a fundamental problem incurred by any sort of distributed processing system. The other major source of poor performance in terms of interactivity is the fact that Web application logic can only be implemented in a high-level scripting language such as Javascript. Although a factor today, as with most resource issues, this problem is not likely to persist, at least in its current form.

As language implementations improve and processor speeds continue to increase, this will not be a problem in the near term future for all but the most processor-intensive applications. Nowadays, even mobile phones contain very powerful processors. Memory and storage are additional resource constraints that limit some applications to the desktop today; but as with processing power, storage capacity has also increased at such a rate that it is now affordable for large companies to offer all customers multiple gigabytes of storage for free.

There are surely advantages and disadvantages to this trend; but as the quality of Internet connectivity and Web technologies improve, the main disadvantages of latency and interactivity will probably succumb to the improvements offered by the online model.

7.4.3. From Web Pages to Web Services

Another trend that is changing the way Web applications are built is the emergence of Web services. A Web service is a piece of functionality accessible over the Internet with a standard interface. The message format is encoded with XML and services are invoked with a remote procedure call (RPC) style. The service is viewed as an object that provides interfaces to access its methods remotely. Many websites now offer not only their own application services to human users but also Web services so that programs (e.g., other Web applications) can access the services automatically. Web services make it possible to build applications by composing services from many different websites. For example, Google search facilities or Amazon book databases may be accessed through Web services and thus be offered as components or basic features of Web applications.

The use of Web services to construct Web applications holds the promise of fulfilling many software engineering goals such as component orientation and reuse. In the context of Web applications, component orientation is indeed a powerful notion since components can provide services ranging from highly specialized to very generic. For example, the search service offered by Google is rather generic, but the Google maps services offer access to data that was expensive to collect and required the use of satellites not available to every Web developer.

Google and many other data-intensive sites, such as the photo sharing site Flickr, are also providing Web developers with API's that allow for remote access to data and images. This allows third parties to create new applications on top of this data, and it gives immense flexibility to users because their data are easily accessed from anywhere in the world with a browser and an Internet connection.

7.4.4. Social Semantic Desktop

Web engineering issues are also brought to the desktop with new software systems using Web technologies on the desktop as means to represent, communicate, and organize information. This is the case of the social semantic desktop (8) of which Gnowsis is an implementation (24, 25). The social semantic desktop is an extension of typical operating systems, which aims at bringing to the desktop a "semantic" view of the file system and a collaborative infrastructure for different desktops to communicate with. Such an infrastructure is intended to support new applications in support of social networking, knowledge work, community management and discovery, file sharing, information discovery, knowledge articulation, and visualization.

7.5. FUTURE DIRECTIONS

The Web is expanding rapidly in many areas. The Web application development area is no exception. It is possible that revolutionary technologies will come along to change the current paradigms. Such things can obviously not be predicted. By looking at current trends and the technology roadmaps for the key application developers, however, it is possible to anticipate at least a few developments of the near future.

We can classify the areas in which developments will affect Web application development into four areas: client support (e.g., the browser), infrastructure support (e.g., the network), application requirements (e.g., social networking), and engineering approaches (e.g., application layers).

7.5.1. Browser Issues

Programming languages used for building Web applications encode the accumulated wisdom of the community about the best ways to build such applications. Over time, application trends and features influence new generations of programming languages that ease the development of more advanced features. Early Web languages, such as PERL, PHP, or JavaScript, were aimed at supporting primarily the browser or the server. More recent languages such as Ruby are general purpose and cover the whole range of browser, application logic, and server functionalities.

Recently, untyped dynamic languages (such as Ruby) have become more popular in the area of Web development, and as processor speeds increase and language implementations become more advanced, this trend is sure to continue. Such languages free the programmer from dealing with machine and operating system specific details so that the logic of the application becomes the focus of development. In this context, it is important to mention the development of ECMAScript, the standard for scripting of interactive Web pages, which continues to evolve into a full-fledged dynamic programming language that can be used to develop software just as sophisticated as a regular desktop application. JavaScript may be viewed as a variant of ECMAScript.

The programming language or languages that enable next-generation Web applications are important, but equally vital is the environment in which they operate, the Web browser. What was once a simple interpreter of simple text files with small bits of markup has now become a sophisticated rendering engine and application platform. Web browsers have almost inadvertently become the primary operating environment of the most widespread applications in computing, and this seems to be the beginning of a major paradigm shift in software deployment. Moving to the next stage will require a considerable effort, however.

Since it is the browser that provides all capabilities to a Web application developer, it is this that will continue to be the focus of much development in the Web community. The long-term functionality included in the browser environment will most likely be driven by the most common applications run in the upcoming generation of dynamic Web applications, but there are a number of developments already visible on the near horizon.

For many reasons, including security, Web browsers have traditionally been given limited access to the local resources on the client computer. The idea was that the main functionality of the application was on the server and the browser only had to provide a simple Graphic User Interface (GUI) to the user for accessing the functionality on the server. The inability to take advantage of local resources is a hindrance to many Web applications, however. Cookies, which have been the only mechanism to store information within the standard browser environment, are a very limited form of key-value storage. Starting with the Flash plugin and then implemented natively in Internet Explorer, in the very latest browsers, cookies have been augmented to allow for the storage model presented in WHATWG (9). In this model, applications can store structured data with a key-value interface, but unlike cookies, the data are not sent to the server on every page request. In the new storage model, this session data or global data always resides locally with the browser, and scripts running within the client can explicitly access the data. This is expected to ease many of the subtle difficulties with session management in Web applications, and it will allow a number of new application models to surface.

Another aspect of browser technology that will continue to improve the capabilities of Web applications is the graphics subsystem now included in many browsers. The *canvas* tag, first introduced by Apple in the Safari browser, is now a WHATWG standard that has been included in Firefox (6) and Opera. This block-level HTML element provides client side scripts with a vector-based two-dimensional drawing context similar to the typical postscript or pdf model. This in-browser graphics environment gives Web applications greater flexibility in creating content that was once limited to server side generation. Spreadsheet charts and graphs, for example, can now be generated in the browser environment for greater interactivity as well as offline display and manipulation. This canvas is the beginning of moving what were once system level libraries into the browser environment, and there is no reason to expect this trend to stop here. Two obvious further improvements are a three-dimensional graphics context and canvas-item-based event handling. Including support for a hardware accelerated three-dimensional rendering context, which is hinted at in both the WHATWG specification and the Firefox roadmap, would for the first time open the Web up to become a true three-dimensional environment. Currently, the canvas widget produces an element that is equivalent to an image in the page, but more fine-grain event handling would allow for the creation of more dynamic content such as custom interface components and interactive games.

7.5.2. Network Infrastructure

If the desktop-to-Web trend is to continue, another major roadblock will be the need for a permanent Internet connection or the ability of the application to deal with intermittent connectivity to the server. In order to address this issue, the WHATWG has also been standardizing on a set of events that can notify running applications of the network status. This would allow a spreadsheet, for example, to store the most recent data locally so that once connectivity is regained, nothing will be lost. Furthermore, by notifying an application that it will be taken offline, both data and application logic could be stored locally so that at least some aspects of a Web application might be continued without access to a network. In this model, the Web becomes an application deployment mechanism and browsers become an execution environment, as opposed to just a data surfing application.

The increasing use of RSS has gone hand in hand with the rapid growth of decentralized media production over the Internet. As we have seen earlier, blogs have created a new paradigm of news delivery. But the current method of first posting data to a website, and then having users poll for updates to the data, is really the only feasible way to distribute content to a large number of people. To address the scalability problems of this method of data distribution, an obvious approach is to exploit a peer-to-peer distribution scheme. BitTorrent is probably the most popular peer-to-peer file distribution protocol, and it can be used for this purpose. BitTorrent allows any number of clients to simultaneously download a piece of content by creating a large, amorphous tree of sharing. Both the Opera and Firefox (7) browsers are working on integrating this peer-to-peer download protocol so that torrents can seemlessly be downloaded from within the browser. This is most likely just the beginning for peer-to-peer (P2P) integration in the browser. In future browsers or browser plugins, many other types of P2P services will most likely be integrated. Data that were once published at a single, centralized Web server will move onto distributed P2P networks that allow for fast data access and virtually limitless scalability.

Besides fast access to Web data, Web applications also need large amounts of storage. One example of a recent service that acts as an example of third-party data source is the Amazon Simple Storage Service, or S3. In S3, Amazon is providing its global storage network as a general-purpose tool for any Web developer with scalable storage needs. With a simple Web services interface, which can be accessed by either a server application or a browser script, data can be stored and retrieved from the S3 service.

7.5.3. Engineering of the Web

As in any software products, Web applications must deliver reliability and performance and other quality requirements. The field of *Web Engineering* deals with systematic development of Web applications. The Web development problems raised by Ginige and Chair in 1999 (4, 12) regarding navigation, accessibility, scalability, maintainability, usability, compatibility, interoperability, security, and reliability are still real. The use of Web frameworks such as presented in the previous sections helps (as a component reuse paradigm) to address most of these issues and leads to incremental improvements in Web application development. In this section we view two approaches that look in fundamentally new ways to the engineering of Web applications.

Specification of Services. The Web currently offers a large array of services that are combined by Web applications to offer yet more useful and complex services to users. The compositional approach of Web services has served the Web application community well. But the large number of services and applications interact in many non-obvious ways. It is difficult from an outside point of view to understand the complex interactions, operations, and data structures of Web systems, often because the developer does not have access to the code, or simply because the code is so large that it takes too long to get a full idea of its function. We see the need of precise specifications of Web applications and Web services as an important task. Specifying Web systems can help both as a bridge between requirements and implementation and as a reference for the understanding of the system. We experimented with the use of temporal logic specifications (16) in the case of collaborative tagging. Having a one-page specification as a communication device of a whole system makes it easier to interact with developers and stakeholders in sharing the same understanding of the system.

Semantic Web. Most of the current data available on the Web are isolated files with occasional links among them. These documents are created primarily to be "processed" by humans. The goal of the semantic Web is to enrich these data so that they can also be processed by computer programs. The idea is to augment the available data with additional information (metadata) that describes the what and why of the data. This additional data are seen as providing the "semantics" of the data. Clearly, if such machine-processible information is available, a completely new generation of Web applications become possible. Applications can exchange data and their semantics, avoiding many interoperability issues.

Semantic Web Fundamentals. In our Web fundamentals section, we defined URLs as being the substance of interactions on the Web as a system, and we defined its language as HTML. The semantic Web substance is URIs (Uniform Resource Identifier), a generalized model of URLs, and its language is RDF (Resource Description Framework). The very language of the semantic Web is a language of interactions which naturally supports the increasingly important applications that offer interactions in content, between applications and between people. The semantic Web's vision is to support such interactions as a basic mechanism.

Attempts to introduce other semantic representations embedded in HTML documents such as microformat (15) or RDFa seem to be good temporary solutions. On the other hand, information grids (1) seems a rather good example of a way to bootstrap the semantic Web by providing access to legacy information systems using semantic Web standards.

Engineering Vision of the Semantic Web. We described the model view controller design pattern in Section 7.3.2. Many Web application frameworks use this pattern successfully today. It took a long time and many experiments for this pattern to become a standard in the case of Web applications. What about in the case of the Web? What if we engineer the whole Web according to this design pattern. This would solve many Web engineering problems such as interoperability, compatibility, accessibility, and so on. The Semantic Web is a Web designed with the Model View Controller design pattern. The model is quite complex but uniform in its representation. As opposed to the current state of the set of all models of the Web in different databases, databases systems, file formats, and so on, the model is the RDF language of URIs, the Controllers are Web applications, and the Views are the generated XHTML pages. From any application, we would be able to access directly a distant model (having an object-oriented representation of it) regardless of networking issues, data transformation, structure, and formats. This is certainly a high-level abstract view and its implementation is years away. But as a vision, it can drive the creation of novel, well-structured applications.

Semantic Web Applications. To build well-structured semantic Web applications routinely, well-engineered semantic Web application frameworks that provide an infrastructure for the semantic web are necessary. One example of such an infrastructure is the Application Server for the Semantic Web (KAON) (20). Currently, semantic Web applications appear only in primitive forms as extensions of existing applications such as semantic blogs, semantic wikis (29), semantic stores, and semantic address books.

An interesting case study of semantic Web applications are those for Cultural Heritage (23, 26) giving the possibility to browse, link, and complete descriptions of the world's artworks.

7.6. SUMMARY AND CONCLUSIONS

In this chapter, we have reviewed the current and future trends in Web application development. We have looked at user participation as a primary driver of applications in the future. We have examined Web application development from a software engineering point of view. And we have evaluated the infrastructure developments that are driving the restructuring of Web applications. Some trends are clear: Some highly data-intensive applications are moving from the desktop to the Web; applications are increasingly composed of widely distributed services; applications are increasingly supporting collaboration and interactions among users. What will come next is hard to predict. Definitely, a better-engineered Web infrastructure is necessary and the semantic Web is one (ambitious) way of achieving that. At the very least, new design patterns for Web application development will be necessary. These design patterns must allow for high levels of interaction among users. Web application development must be agile, and processes and frameworks will need to continue to respect this requirement.

Web application development has been quick to pick up the lessons of software engineering, and it is now in many ways leading in the application of agile methods to build novel, sophisticated distributed, component-oriented software systems.

REFERENCES

1. O. Alonso, S. Banerjee, and M. Drake. Gio: A semantic Web application using the information grid framework. In *Proceedings of the 15th International Conference on World Wide Web (WWW '06),* pages 857–858. ACM Press, New York, 2006.

2. D. Bonura, R. Culmone, and E. Merelli. Patterns for Web applications. In *Proceedings of the 14th International Conference on Software Engineering and Knowledge Engineering (SEKE '02),* pages 739–746. ACM Press, New York, 2002.

3. S. Casteleyn, Z. Fiala, G.-J. Houben, and K. van der Sluijis. From adaptation engineering to aspect-oriented context-dependency. In *Proceedings of the 15th International Conference on World Wide Web (WWW '06),* pages 897–898. ACM Press, New York, 2006.

4. S. M. Chair. Web engineering. *SIGWEB Newsletter* **8**(3):28–32, 1999.

5. A. Cockburn. *Agile Software Development.* Longman Publishing Co., Boston, MA, 2002.

6. Community. *Firefox Feature Brainstorming,* 2006.

7. Mozilla Community. *MozTorrent Plugin,* 2006.

8. S. Decker and M. R. Frank. The networked semantic desktop. In C. Bussler, S. Decker, D. Schwabe, O. Pastor, editors. *Proceedings of the WWW2004 Workshop on Application*

Design, Development and Implementation issues in the Semantic Web, CEUR Workshop Proceedings, 2002.

9. Browser development community. *Web Hypertext Application Technology Working Group,* 2006.

10. M. Gaedke and J. Rehse. Supporting compositional reuse in component-based web engineering. In *Proceedings of the 2000 ACM Symposium on Applied Computing (SAC '00),* pages 927–933. ACM Press, New York, 2000.

11. M. Gaedke, C. Segor, and H.-W. Gellersen. WCML: Paving the way for reuse in object-oriented web engineering. In *Proceedings of the 2000 ACM Symposium on Applied Computing (SAC '00),* pages 748–755. ACM Press, New York, 2000.

12. A. Ginige and S. Murugesan. Guest editors' introduction: Web engineering an introduction. *IEEE MultiMedia* 8(1):14–18, 2001.

13. S. Golder and B. A. Huberman. The structure of collaborative tagging systems. *Journal of Information Science* 32(2):198–208, 2006.

14. M. Y. Ivory and R. Megraw. Evolution of web site design patterns. *ACM Transactions on Information Systems* 23(4):463–497, 2005.

15. R. Khare and T. Çelik. Microformate: A pragmatic path to the semantic web. In *Proceedings of the 15th International Conference on World Wide Web (WWW '06),* pages 865–866. ACM Press, New York, 2006.

16. L. Lamport. *Specifying Systems: The TLA+ Language and Tools for Hardware and Software Engineers.* Longman Publishing Co., Boston, MA, 2002.

17. C. Marlow, M. Naaman, D. Boyd, and M. Davis. Position Paper. Tagging, taxonomy, flickr, article, toRead. In *Proceedings of the 17th ACM Conference on Hypertext and Hypermedia (HYPERTEXT 2006),* pages 31–40, 2006.

18. C. Mesnage and M. Jazayeri. Specifying the collaborative tagging system. In *Proceedings of the 1st Semantic Authoring and Annotation Workshop (SAW '06),* 2006.

19. T. N. Nguyen. Model-based version and configuration management for a web engineering lifecycle. In *Proceedings of the 15th International Conference on World Wide Web (WWW '06),* pages 437–446. ACM Press, New York, 2006.

20. D. Oberle, S. Staab, R. Studer, and R. Volz. Supporting application development in the semantic Web. *ACM Transactions on Internet Technology* 5(2):328–358, 2005.

21. V. Perrone, D. Bolchini, and P. Paolini. A stakeholders centered approach for conceptual modeling of communication-intensive applications. In *Proceedings of the 23rd Annual International Conference on Design of Communication (SIGDOC '05),* pages 25–33. ACM Press, New York, 2005.

22. T. Reenskaug. Models–views–controllers. Technical Note, Xerox PARC, 1979.

23. L. Rutledge, L. Aroyo, and N. Stash. Determining user interests about museum collections. In *Proceedings of the 15th International Conference on World Wide Web (WWW '06),* pages 855–856. ACM Press, New York, 2006.

24. L. Sauermann, A. Bernardi, and A. Dengel. Overview and outlook on the semantic desktop. In *Proceedings of the 1st Workshop on The Semantic Desktop at the ISWC 2005 Conference,* 2005.

25. L. Sauermann, G. A. Grimnes, M. Kiesel, C. Fluit, H. Maus, D. Heim, D. Nadeem, B. Horak, and A. Dengel. Semantic desktop 2.0: The Gnowsis experience. In *Proceedings of the*

5th International Semantic Web Conference (ISWC 2006), LCNS 4273, pages 887–900. Springer, Berlin, 2006.

26. P. Sinclair, P. Lewis, K. Martinez, M. Addis, and D. Prideaux. Semantic Web integration of cultural heritage sources. In *Proceeding of the 15th International Conference on World Wide Web (WWW '06)*, pages 1047–1048. ACM Press, New York, 2006.

27. D. Thomas, C. Fowler, and A. Hunt. *Ruby: The Pragmatic Programmer's Guide*, second edition. The Pragmatic Programmers, Raleigh, North Carolina, Dallas, Texas, 2006.

28. D. Thomas, D. H. Hansson, A. Schwarz, T. Fuchs, L. Breedt, and M. Clark. *Agile Web Development with Rails: A Pragmatic Guide*, second edition. The Pragmatic Programmers, 2006.

29. M. Völkel, M. Krötzsch, D. Vrandecic, H. Haller, and R. Studer. Semantic wikipedia. In *Proceedings of the 15th International Conference on World Wide Web (WWW '06)*, pages 585–594, ACM Press, New York, 2006.

30. L. von Ahn. *Human Computation*. Ph.D. thesis, School of Computer Science, Carnegie Mellon University, Pittsburgh PA, 2005.

PART III

TECHNOLOGIES FOR SOFTWARE EVOLUTION

8

MIGRATING TO WEB SERVICES

Harry M. Sneed

8.1. FORCES DRIVING MIGRATION

In principle, IT users are in a constant state of migration. Hardly have they succeeded in moving to a new technical environment before that environment has become obsolete, and they are faced with the necessity of moving again. There are two driving forces in this migration movement:

- One is the constantly changing IT technology.
- The other one is the constantly changing business world.

There is, of course, an intricate relationship between the two issues, making it difficult to deal with them separately, but this separation of concerns is essential to understanding their interdependence (3).

8.1.1. Technology Change

The IT technology is changing at a rate of once every five years. Earlier in the 1970s and 1980s, the rate of change was every 10 years. The reason for this shortening of the technology life cycle is not only to provide the users with more functionality, but also to satisfy

Emerging Methods, Technologies, and Process Management in Software Engineering. Edited by
De Lucia, Ferrucci, Tortora, and Tucci
Copyright © 2008 John Wiley & Sons, Inc.

the capital market. Software technology vendors are under extreme pressure from their stockholders to increase their sales and to raise their corporate profits. Until now, the only way to do that was by introducing new products and convincing users to buy them (16).

The software vendors, supported by the technology freaks from the academic world, have cultivated a mania that anything new is beautiful and that everything old is ugly. To be regarded by his peers or by other IT users, one has to be on the leading edge of technology. Those who remain true to an older technology are treated with disdain and even ridiculed. This applies to individuals as well as to organizations. Both are being manipulated by vendor marketing and the need to keep up with their neighbors. Whether the new technology really improves their performance is open to question. Nicholas Carr and other experts from the business world have their doubts (10).

The fact is that IT users feel compelled to move to a new technology even without evidence that it will lower their costs or increase their productivity. Like limericks, they are herded together and pushed into an unknown future, blindly confident that they are on the right path. No self-respecting IT user would even consider straying away from the herd for fear of being isolated and considered exotic. They seem to accept the fact that migration is inevitable.

With increasing sophistication of new technology, the benefits of using it have become increasingly blurred. The advantages of the new technology over the previous one have become less and less obvious, so that the vendors have to spend more and more money on marketing to convince the users that the change is good for them. The notion of return of investment (ROI) has become a key issue in introducing new technologies, but more often the calculation is manipulated in favor of the new technology (40).

In the early days of computing, migration was driven by hardware change. The software and the programming languages were more or less dependent on the hardware they were running on. The costs of the software were low compared to the other costs. Fortran and COBOL programs could run in both batch and dialogue modus and could process punch cards as well as magnetic tapes and removable disc units. In recent times, technology change has become more of a software issue. The programming languages and the middleware are now the driving forces for migration.

This shift of emphasis began in the 1990s with the move to client–server systems. Here, the change was both hardware and software. Every user department wanted to have its own local computer with its own terminal work stations, but still the local computer should be connected to a central host computer somewhere, with a global database. Connecting the many nodes in a client–server environment became a major problem and lead to a market for middleware. In this distributed hardware environment, it became necessary to also distribute the software, and this made it necessary to shift the programming paradigm from procedural to object-oriented (11).

The primary costs of the client–server migration were software costs. The existing mainframe programs had to be converted or rewritten. Many had to be downsized to even fit into the storage of local servers (35).

The migration from the mainframe to client–server systems entailed many complicated techniques such as scrapping of user interfaces, hierarchical to relational database conversion, program downsizing, and procedural to object-oriented language transformation (37). Many compromises had to be made in order to push the migration through in an acceptable time with acceptable costs. Often good software had to be perverted in order to satisfy the requirements of the new distributed hardware environment. Much effort was spent on objectifying the systems—that is, transforming procedural programs into object-oriented components. This was an extremely difficult task, which was never really satisfactory solved despite the fact that a lot of research went into it (26).

Most users were content in the end to reimplement their user interfaces and to convert their data to relational databases. Very few users ever succeeded in redeveloping their old applications in a truly object-oriented way. This is because they were never able to recapture how the legacy systems operated in detail. The costs of redocumenting a legacy system down to the level of elementary operations and then reimplementing in a different architecture were prohibitive. Thus, in moving to the client–server technology, the quality of the existing software in the business applications actually degenerated as a result of architectural mismatch (15).

No sooner had the IT-user community completed the migration of its software to a client–server architecture, then the next wave came along in form of the Internet. This migration negated many of the aspects of the client/server migration. Now it was important to have all of the components on one common machine, so that they could be readily accessed by all the internet users. This often meant moving the distributed software back to a single host computer. The object-oriented nature of programs remained, but the methods now had to be directly accessible from outside. This destroyed the purpose of many a class hierarchy. Besides that, the client user interfaces, implemented with some graphic user interface (GUI) tool kit had to be replaced by Web pages in HTML. What is more, the distributed data had to be collected again in a common generally accessible database (12).

Most of the IT users had yet to complete the migration from client or server to the Internet when the latest technology, namely service-oriented architecture, came along. Now it became necessary to break the software up into service components stored on network servers with a standardized Web service interface. The client software should be replaced by business process procedures programmed in some kind of Business Process Execution Language (BPEL) which steers the process, displays and accepts data via cascaded style sheets, and invokes the Web services. Now every local process has to maintain its own state as well as its own data, since the Web services should be stateless and without access to their users own database. Service-oriented architecture (SOA) requires a radical break with past technologies and a complete revamp of the enterprise applications (5).

SOA is now the third major technology paradigm change in the last 15 years, changes driven by the software industry's insatiable need for new revenues. The IT users are actually victims of a volatile IT industry, intent on using them to sustain revenues by constantly introducing new technologies. If a user is to keep up with the ever-changing technology, then he must be in a constant state of migration. In fact, technical migration already has a permanent status in most large corporations, having established organizational units just for that purpose, not to mention the many software houses, including those new ones in India, which thrive on such technical migrations (4).

8.1.2. Business Change

Besides the pressure for technology change, there are also those forces driving business change, Organizations have gone from the classical deep hierarchical structures of the 1970s to the distributed business units of the 1990s to the now lean, process-oriented and fully computer-dependent, networked organizations of today. Of course, the changes to the business side are tightly coupled to the changes in IT technology. Without the Internet, it would not be possible to distribute business processes across the globe, just as it was not possible to break up businesses into individual business units without having them connected via common database servers in a client–server hierarchy. In this respect, technology and business changes complement one another (1).

Business change is driven by the desire to make organizations more cost effective. The business reengineering revolution propagated by Hammers and Champy had the goal of structuring the business according to the business processes (18). Rather than splitting up the responsibility for a particular process, such as order processing among several different units, each with a different specialty, one unit was to be responsible for the whole process from beginning to end. This is best illustrated by the handling of passengers for an air flight. Earlier, there was one employee outside to check you in. Another employee was inside to put you on the plane. Today, there is one employee who checks you in and who accompanies you to the plane. This employee is responsible for the whole boarding process. The parallel process of handling the baggage is the responsibility of others.

By fixing responsibility for a business process to one unit or individual, it is easier to ensure accountability and to measure performance. It is obvious that the business unit responsible for a local process does not want to be dependent upon a global IT department to accomplish their job. The responsible manager wants to have his own local IT that he can control. The distributed systems architecture offered this solution. In the end, each business unit had its own local server and its own team of IT specialists that could be used on demand. Although productivity of the individual business units went up, so too did the total costs of ownership. The costs of maintaining different solutions for each separate activity became, in the end, greater than the costs of sharing common resources (36).

The concept of a service-oriented IT promises to remedy this problem. It is an attempt to unite the business concept of distributed, independent business units, each managing a different process, with the concept of using common IT resources, which can be applied to many processes. SOA is in fact more of a business issue than a technical one. Today's business world requires extreme flexibility. The business processes must be continually adapted to satisfy changing customer requirements. There is no longer time to initiate extensive and costly development projects. Even if they are agile, they still require time to deliver a workable product and the outcome is still uncertain. Useful software requires time to ripen, time that most struggling business units no longer have. There is a pressing need for software on demand. This means that the basic functionality should be available before it is even required. The business users need only select from a large catalog of software services (the Universal Description, Discovery and Integration (UDDI)) those functions that they require for their latest business process and to prepare the control procedures for invoking and linking the ready-made services, using a business process language (21).

8.2. THE EMERGENCE OF WEB SERVICES

This changes the role of the company IT from a software producer to a software broker. It is the task of the IT to see that the required services (i.e., the software components behind the service) are available when they are needed. This means setting up a warehouse of reusable software components, a perennial vision of the software world that began with the FORTRAN common subroutine libraries in the 1960s, progressed to the PL/I build-in functions and the macro libraries of the 1970s, continued with the reusable business modules of the 1980s, and cumulated in the class libraries of the 1990s.

It has always been a goal of the software industry to reuse as much as possible of its proven components. This has less to do with the costs of development than with the high costs of testing. It requires an enormous effort to detect and remove all of the faults that a piece of software might have and to demonstrate that the software does what it is supposed to. For that the software has to go through a long ripening process. It would be irrational not to want to reuse that which is already proven. In this respect, Web services are just another variant of the reoccurring reuse theme (24).

What is different about Web services is that they can be physically located anywhere in the World Wide Web, that they have a standard accessing interface, and that their implementation is independent of the environment they are operating in. Earlier reusable components such as the classes in a common class library had to be compatible with the classes using or inheriting them. The same applied to standard business modules. With Web services, this is no longer the case. They can be implemented in any language, even in basic Assembler language and in any operating system as long as they are able to service their interface.

The use of a message-oriented interface with XML and SOAP makes the implementation of the service software independent of the clients. The Web Service Definition Language (WSDL) is an XML-based language for interpreting the messages that are passed between the service and the clients. The service software must only be able to read and write the WSDL messages. That the Web services can be located in any node of the network is made possible by the HTTP addressing mechanisms. Each service has its own unique address and can receive messages from any other node in the network which has access to that address (39).

Other than these Internet-specific features, there is no real difference between Web services and the standard subroutines of the 1960s. They process a set of arguments they receive to produce one or more results that they return. If they are stateless, they will have no own memory, meaning that whatever intermediate data they have collected will be forgotten when they are finished. That puts the burden of maintaining the correct processing state on the client. If they retain the data state, they become much more complicated, because in that case they have to distinguish between their clients and keep their data separated. This too is a reoccurring problem. It existed as well for the teleprocessing monitors of the 1980s such as CICS and IMS-DC and has been solved in many different ways (30).

The problem with Web services is the same as it has always been with reusable standard modules, and that is the question of granularity. How much functionality should one Web service provide. For example, the Web service could be for maintaining a bank account with all of the functions that go along with that: opening the account, making deposits, making withdrawals, transferring funds, computing interest, creating balance notices, checking credit limits, and closing the account. This will, of course, require a highly complex interface. On the other hand, the Web service could be restricted to simply computing interest. That would lead to a very simple interface (19).

The business users would prefer the latter solution—the smallest granularity— because it gives them the maximum flexibility. The IT department would prefer to offer the first solution, because it is easier to manage. Having many messages also puts a big load on the network since the many messages have to be passed back and forth between the Web clients and Web servers. This was not the case with standard sub-routines or base classes running in the same address space as their users. That leaves two problems to solve:

- The problem of maintaining state
- The problem of determining granularity.

The research community has to deal with these two issues and come up with viable sol-utions for Web services to be adapted in industry. Not only must state be maintained, but it must also be secured. The proper level of granularity is context-dependent and must be determined for every particular situation. There is no global solution. It will not be easy to find proper solutions to these problems.

A third problem is how to come up with the Web services in the first place. Unlike babies, they will not be brought by the stork and deposited at the front door. They have to either be purchased, rented, borrowed, recovered, or built. These are the five basic alternatives to providing Web services to be discussed here.

8.3. PROVIDING WEB SERVICES

The five sources of Web services are, as mentioned above:

- To be purchased
- To be rented
- To be borrowed
- To be built
- To be recovered

8.3.1. Purchasing Web Services

Web services can be bought from a software vendor. Most of the classical ERP software package dealers also offer their components as Web services, so any IT user can buy them. This applies not only to commercial business software but also to engineering and scientific software, which can be purchased off the shelf. The advantages of such ready-made off-the-shelf Web services are:

- They are readily available.
- They are well-tested and relatively reliable.
- They are supported by the vendor (22).

The second and third advantages should not be underestimated. It requires a significant amount of effort to test even a simple Web service in all the variations of its usage. It is also comforting to know that the Web service will be maintained on a regular basis, that it will be updated and that the customer does not have to deal with these issues.

The disadvantages of off the shelf Web services are as follows:

- They are usually very expensive.
- They are restricted in their functionality.
- The user has no possibility of altering them.
- They are most often too big and monolithic.

The biggest disadvantage is the lack of flexibility. Using large, monolithic Web services such as a ready-made billing system or a credit checking package is like building with prefabricated walls. The IT user has to build his business processes around the purchased Web services. As such, the Web services determine how his business processes are structured. The user is not only purchasing software but the whole business process as well.

For some IT users, this may be a blessing. They don't have to spend time and effort in designing business processes, but they also lose the main advantage of Web services, which is flexibility. They might as well buy the whole business process, as they have done in the past. There is no sense in moving to a service-oriented architecture. For other IT users keen on customizing the business processes, this is an intolerable restriction. What will become of competition if every competitor is using the same business process?

8.3.2. Renting Web Services

An alternative to buying Web services is to rent them. Many ready-made software vendors such as SAP and Oracle are now working out plans to make their services available on a rental basis. Rather than having to purchase the software packages and install them in his environment, the IT user has the option of using only those functions he requires, when he requires them (i.e., on demand). He then pays only for actual usage. This business scheme has many advantages over the purchasing scheme:

- The user is not obliged to install and update the Web service on his site.
- The user is always working with the latest updated version.
- The user only pays for what he really uses.

Owning software is not always advantageous to the software user. He has to deal with the total costs of ownership. Not only does he have to install and test the software in his environment, but he also has to install and test the new releases. Maintaining the software in his environment has a high price. The advantage is that he can customize the software to satisfy his particular requirements. The user is not obliged to adjust his business process to fit the standard software, which is the case when he is only renting.

The same applies to Web services. If he buys them, he can adapt them. If, however, they are rented, he must use them as they are. If the granularity of the services is small enough, this will not be too great a problem for him. He can build them into his business processes like gravel stones in a cement wall, but if they are built like slabs of ready-made concrete, then he has to adapt his construction plans to fit them in. On the other hand, the user is free from having to constantly install and test new releases (25).

8.3.3. Borrowing Web Services

Taking Web services from the open source community is equivalent to borrowing them. Proponents of open source are those who would prefer to let others do their work for them and then to take it over with or without changes. On the one hand, they don't want to pay for it; on the other hand, they don't want to develop it. Open source Web services are seen as public property that anyone can use.

There are two issues here: one moral and the other legal. The moral issue is that software, including Web services, is intellectual property. Someone has sacrificed his or her valuable time to construct a solution to a pressing problem. If this solution happens to be valuable to someone else, then that person should be willing to pay for it. Otherwise, he is violating the principles of a free market economy. So in this respect, the use of open source Web services is questionable and not in tune with the society in which we live.

The legal issue is the question of liability. Who is liable for what the borrowed service performs? Of course, it cannot be the authors, since they are oblivious to where and how their intellectual property is being used. Therefore, it can only be the user of the borrowed good. In taking Web services from the open source community, the user is free to adapt the source to his own particular needs, but then he also must assume responsibility for its correctness and its quality, meaning to test it thoroughly for all possible usages. Most persons do not realize that testing software is equivalent in time and cost to developing it. And, if the source is unfamiliar to the persons who must adapt and correct it, it may be even more expensive than if they were able to write the software themselves. This way they would at least be familiar with the code. Numerous studies in the software maintenance community have proven that the greatest effect in maintaining software is the effect spent on trying to comprehend it (41).

Code comprehension is the biggest barrier to using open source code. So, users should think twice before they start borrowing Web services from the open source community. This could turn out to be a Trojan horse.

8.3.4. Building Web Services

Web Services can, like other software packages, be developed by the user organization itself or by a contractor working for him. The difference with regard to conventional software applications is that Web services, if they are defined correctly, should be much smaller and easier to build. The other difference is that Web services are common property of the enterprise that provides them; that is, they belong to all of the departments of that enterprise. That is a serious break with the past tradition of how software in an enterprise is financed.

In the past the IT Department has been considered to be an internal software house with the mission of providing services to the various user departments. If the marketing department wants a new customer relationship system, it commissions the IT Department to develop or buy one for them. If the logistics department wants a new order entry system, it commissions the IT Department to build it for them. It is the user departments that have the power over the purse and that are only prepared to pay for something that has a direct benefit to them.

In the case of Web services, it is not clear to whom they belong. Anyone within the organizational network can access them. So who should pay for them? The fact is that it takes a lot of effort to plan, develop, and test good Web services. They should be more stable and reliable than the restricted use systems of the past, and they should also be reusable for different purposes within different contexts. Like other user systems, Web services will cost three times more than ordinary single-user systems. User departments are very reluctant to fund projects that are not dedicated to their requirements and that promise only a long-term benefit. If they have a problem to be solved, they want it to be solved immediately and directly, that is, it should be customized to fulfill their particular requirements and nothing else.

Developing Web services is a long-term investment (6). It will take at least two years before enough services of sufficient quality can be made available to the user business processes. It is questionable if the users are willing to wait so long. The benefits of using self-developed Web services will only become visible after some years. In the meantime, the IT Department must sustain the continuity of the existing systems. This puts a double burden on the organization. For this and other reasons, developing one's own Web services may not be an attractive alternative. The biggest barrier is the time required. The second is the question of financing.

8.3.5. Recovering Web Services

The fifth and final alternative is to recover Web services from the existing software applications. It is true that the existing software may be old, out of date, and difficult to manage, but it works. Not only does it work, but it is also adapted to the local organization. It fits to the data and the environment of the organization. So why not reuse it. The goal should be not to use the existing applications as a whole, since they would probably not fit into the new business processes, but to extract certain parts from them. These parts could be methods, procedures, modules, or components. The important thing is that they are independently executable. For that they have to be wrapped. Wrapping technology is the key to reusing existing software. It is not so important what language the existing software is written in, so long as it is executable in the server environment (2).

Since requests to Web services can be redirected, it is perfectly legitimate to have different hosting servers for the different language types. Thus, one could have COBOL and PL/I services on one server and $C/C++$ services on another. What matters is that the extracted components are equipped with a standard WSDL interface that converts the data in the requests to local data in the program and that converts the outputs of the program to data in the requests. Creating such interfaces can be done automatically so there is no additional effort required here other than that of testing the interface (32). The service itself will have been tested through years of productive use. The low costs and the short time in which recovered Web services can be made available is the biggest advantage of this approach.

The major disadvantages are as follows:

- The software is old and not easily comprehensible.
- The conversion of the data from an external to an internal format reduces performance.
- There may not be programmers available familiar with the legacy languages.

An additional problem is that of maintaining data state from one transaction to another if the software was not originally designed to be reentrant. Reentrancy will have to be retrofitted into the software. Then the question of how to maintain the states of the many users comes up, but this is not a specific problem of recovered Web services. It applies to them all.

8.4. WEB SERVICE MINING

The main focus of this contribution is on how to recover Web services from existing applications, also referred to as Web service mining. Much of the business functionality of an organization has already been implemented at one time or another. The problem is that it is not readily accessible. The functionality is buried in legacy software systems (9).

To make this functionality available for reuse as Web services, it has to be extracted from the context in which it has been implemented and adapted to the technical requirements of a service-oriented architecture. This involves four different activities:

- Discovering
- Evaluating
- Extracting
- Adapting

8.4.1. Discovering Potential Web Services

In principle, every application function performed by the legacy code is a potential Web service. Here one should note that a great portion of legacy code is dedicated to performing some technical function or to serving some obsolete data storage or data communication technology. Studies have shown that this amounts to almost two-thirds of the total code. That leaves only one-third of the code for achieving the application objectives. It is that code which is of interest for recovering. The problem is that the application focused code is highly intertwined with the technical code. Within one block of code, i.e. method, module or procedure, there may be both statements for setting up a data display mask and statements for computing the value added tax. In searching through the code, the analyzer tool must recognize these statements which provide the business value (33).

On the other hand, not all business functions are correct. Many will have become obsolete over the years. So, not only must the application functions of the code be identified, they must also be checked for being currently of value. This leads to two research issues here:

1. How to identify code performing an application function
2. How to determine if that function is still of current value to the user

Both issues will require some form of rule-based decision making. The important thing is that the user is able to adjust the rules to his needs, meaning that the analysis tools have to be highly customizable. They also have to be very fast, since they will be scanning through several million lines of code to identify which portions of that code are potential Web services. So what is required here is actually a sophisticated search machine for processing source code. It will probably not be possible to select potential Web services without the help of a human being. So there will also have to be some user interaction build into the tool to give the user the opportunity to intervene in the search and to make decisions that the tool cannot. Such interactive source mining tools is a major research topic.

The key to discovering potential Web services in existing code has been described by this author in a previous paper on the recovery of business rules (34). The approach is to identify the names of the essential data results and to trace how they are produced. This is achieved via an inverse data flow analysis. The data flow trace may pass through several methods or procedures in different classes or modules. It is necessary to identify all of them. An example is a credit rating. The essential result is the credit rate, but several modules or classes may be involved in producing that result. Therefore all of them must be combined to produce one single Web service—that is, compute credit rating. This problem is associated with the problem of impact analysis in software maintenance.

8.4.2. Evaluating Potential Web Services

Another research issue in connection with the discovery of potential Web services is the assessment of those code fragments selected as potential Web services. Here the owner of the code must determine whether or not it is even worth extracting the code fragments from the systems in which they reside. This is a question of reusability. Metrics have to be developed which will signal whether the code is reusable or not. The author has dealt with this problem before and published a paper on it (28). The key metric is that of reusability. A piece of software is reusable if it can be readily separated from the code around it. It has few functional links (i.e., calls to functions in the surrounding code), and it shares little data with the other procedures. Thus, one must count foreign calls and other branches outside of the code block in question as well as the nonlocal data—that is, data declared outside of that code block. These must then be related to the size of the code block or blocks in statements.

This may be a good starting point, but it is not enough. There are also the questions of code quality and business value. The question is whether the code is good enough and valuable enough to migrate over into the new architecture. For this, many of the existing quality metrics can be used. The business value must be measured in terms of how valuable the results produced by this particular piece of code are. There is very little research on this. Finally, it must also be calculated what it will cost to extract the code relative to the benefits of reuse. For this, metrics are needed to measure the maintainability, testability, interoperability, and reusability of the code as well as the business value of the functionality performed by that code.

The evaluation of potential Web services is not a trivial matter and will require proven metrics to master. This is where the measurement community is called upon to provide a sound set of metrics to guide the decision whether to reuse or not.

8.4.3. Extracting the Web Service Code

Once a code fragment has been identified as being a potential Web service, the next step is to extract it from the system in which it is embedded. This can become a highly intricate task, especially when the code is not a separately compilable unit. Procedural modules may share global data with other modules in main storage. They may also call other modules. All of these dependencies must be capped in order for the procedural code to be extracted from its environment. Object-oriented code is generally easier to extract than procedural code, but there are also problems here. A particular class may inherit from higher-level classes, which one does not want to extract with it. The class may also invoke methods in foreign classes which return essential results. These dependencies have to be eliminated either by class flattening or by method inclusion. However, none of these solutions are simple. Research is needed to determine the best means of extracting both procedures and classes.

A particularly difficult problem in extracting code from legacy systems is that of extracting features (17). Particularly in object-oriented software, functionality is often dispersed through many classes contained in various components. A feature is a chain of distributed methods triggered by an event and resulting in a predefined output, such as the answer to a query or a computed result—for instance, a price or a credit rating. To produce this result, different methods in different classes must be executed in a given sequence. A proposed Web service will most likely correspond to a feature. Extracting features from components poses a difficult challenge to the software research community. It is questionable whether it is possible to extract only those methods traversed by the feature, since those methods use class attributes which may affect other methods. On the other hand, extracting whole classes will result in very large Web services containing a lot of code not relevant to the task of the Web service at hand. Solving this problem, if it is at all solvable, will require a significant effort on the part of the research community.

8.4.4. Adapting the Web Service Code

The final research issue is that of adapting the extracted code units to be reused as Web services. This entails supplying them with a WSDL interface. The input arguments that they received before either from a parameter list, a user interface mask, an input file, or some other means of data input must be reassigned as arguments within the WSDL request. That means converting them from XML and moving them from the incoming SOAP message to the internal storage of the Web service. The output results that they returned before as output masks, return values, output files, reports or other means of data output must be reassigned as results of the WSDL response. That implies moving them from the internal storage of the Web service to the outgoing SOAP message and converting them into XML character format (7).

All of these steps can be automated. In fact, code adaptation is the activity which lends itself best to automation. Yet, there is a still need for finding the best ways of doing this. Research is required on adaptation tool development. The remainder of this chapter describes the author's approach to automating the adaptation of potential Web services.

8.5. APPLYING WRAPPING TECHNIQUES

There is no universally best way to wrap application programs. The choice of a wrapping technique depends on the program type. In the domain of business data processing, there are three basic program types:

Online transaction programs

Batch processing programs

General subprograms (35)

No matter what language is used—whether Assembler, PL/I, or COBOL—all of the programs of the same type have common features.

Online transactional programs are driven by a teleprocessing monitor such as IMS/DC, CICS, or Tuxedo. Their structure is dependent on the transaction monitor type. In some cases, the application program has the control and calls on the transaction monitor to perform services for it. In other cases (e.g., with CICS), the application is a subprogram of the transaction monitor and performs its functions when called by the monitor. It is event-driven. All of the communication data are managed by the teleprocessing monitor. The application program is provided with pointers to address it, which are kept in a common communication area.

In both cases, online programs are never just COBOL or PL/I programs. They are full of language features imposed on them by the teleprocessing monitor in the form of either extended instructions, macros, or special call interfaces. CICS imposes its EXEC CICS macros on the host program, so that they are embedded in the body of the code. IMS imposes special data structures and parameters on the host program. The parser of such an online program must recognize and parse these special language constructs, just as it deals with the statements of the host language.

When wrapping an online program, it is necessary to switch off all of those operations that are communicating with the environment, whereas other operations that are allocating storage or handling error messages have to be left on. The requirement here is to replace the masks with their fixed fields and attributes with an XML-type document, while leaving the logic of the program as it was. As described later, online programs can also be converted to subprograms with a linkage interface; however, this entails altering the program structure. In either case, the task of wrapping is to provide data to the online program, and this can be done best by rendering the program stateless (30).

Batch programs are driven by the input files they process. These can be transaction files or parameter files. Normally a batch program will read sequentially through one or more input files or message queues processing one or more records or messages at a time until it has reached the end. The result could be a database update, an output message stream, an output file, or a report. The state of the input domain determines what is to be done.

The basic structure of a batch program is that of nested loops, one for each semantic level of the data as was recognized by Michael Jackson long ago (20). Loops are terminated by control group transitions. What distinguishes a batch program from an online program is that it cannot be interrupted and that it is dedicated to one task. Therefore it has a memory that it itself transforms from one state to the next.

The key to wrapping a batch program is to replace one input media by another—for example, to substitute a sequential file of fixed formatted records by a message queue of XML documents. The logic of the program remains untouched. The input data content remains the same. Only the form is altered.

Subprograms are driven by their parameters. Depending on the arguments, certain results are computed and returned. The logic of a subprogram is already that of a server performing requests from a client—the caller. Each call should be dealt with, independently of the others. If a subprogram does retain state, it is done so for a specific purpose—that is, to resume processing at a specific point, as is the case with program inversion (15).

This makes the wrapping of subprograms relatively easy. One need only emulate the interface. The module behavior remains invariant. Even the call by reference can be satisfied by storing the parameters in the wrapper and passing their address references to the target procedure. If another interface type is used, such as an XML document in lieu of a COBOL data structure, the new interface will have to be converted to the old one prior to invoking the subprogram. Upon returning, the old interface (e.g., the COBOL structure) is reconverted back into the new one (i.e., the XML document). Here standard API techniques are applicable (42).

8.5.1. Wrapping Online Programs with an XML Interface

Online programs respond to synchronous requests from a client website, meaning that the client fills out a Web page, submits it, and waits for a response. The server software should react quickly to prevent the client from having to wait too long, implying that it should have short transaction paths and be free of unnecessary operations and data. The process for wrapping online programs must be tuned to meet these requirements. The *SoftWrap* process described here consists of five steps, each of which builds upon the state left by its predecessor.

- First, the program is stripped of all existing TP-Monitor operations, these being removed or replaced by standard COBOL calls to the wrapper.
- Second, the program is stripped of all code blocks not required to execute the transactions designated by the user.
- Third, all data previously belonging to the input/output maps or made accessible to the program via common storage areas are transferred to a single data structure in the linkage section.
- Fourth, the usage of the data in the linkage section is analyzed to determine whether it is input, output, or both.
- Fifth, the linkage data structure is converted to an XML data description table for extracting data values from an incoming XML form and converting them to a COBOL data structure and for generating an outgoing XML document from the fields used as outputs.

The reason for stripping the CICS or IMS-DC operations is to eliminate the map processing and to make the program independent of a proprietary TP Monitor. Programs that were under CICS event-driven now become data-driven (27).

The rationale behind the stripping of unnecessary code is to remove redundancy. Much of the code in online transaction processing programs is devoted to housekeeping purposes for the sake of the teleprocessing monitor. Much of it, if not all, can be removed without affecting the business logic. The technique for code removal is procedural slicing. The user marks which functions—paragraphs or sections—he wants to retain. By means of a recursive call analysis, all paragraphs and sections used by these are also marked. After that all unmarked code blocks—paragraphs and/or sections—are stripped from the code. Procedural slicing and its application to code stripping have been well covered in the literature (14).

Collecting data items for restructuring as parameters is necessary since maps are no longer being provided by the TP Monitor. The input data are now being passed as a parameter to the wrapped program. In turn the output data are being passed back to the caller as output parameters. That means that data elements previously contained in the maps must now be transferred to the linkage section, but not all. Maps also contained a number of control fields—for instance, attribute bytes and length words which are no longer necessary. They are deleted from the data structure. In addition, all housekeeping data not relevant to the business task at hand are also removed, leaving only that data which is really referenced by the new reduced program. Experience has shown that this leads to an over 50% reduction in the size of the program's data division (13).

The wrapped online program is left with three parameters—a method id, a return code, and a data structure—corresponding to the connecting XML document.

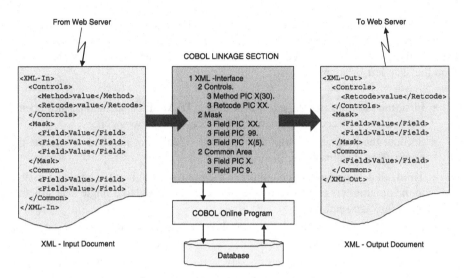

Figure 8.1. Wrapping online programs.

The method id is required, if the user wants to invoke a particular function in the program without going through the others. If it is not set, the whole program is executed. The return code is required to pass back an error condition to the client, if something goes wrong. Exception handling is left to either the client or the wrapper (see Fig. 8.1).

The data structure contains both the arguments from the client website and the results produced by the server. If the arguments have not already been edited by the client, they should be checked again here in accordance with a set of plausibility rules—the pre-conditions—before being processed. The results of the server program too should be verified against a set of post conditions prior to returning to the caller (23).

In order to distinguish between arguments and results, a data usage analysis of the procedural code is made. The data are marked as either input, output, or in/out. It was decided against creating two separate data structures—one for input and one for output—because there are many parameters that are both, and this would have led to name conflicts in the code. It proved to be better to have a single data structure but to anno-tate the elementary data items according to their usage. This allows the same data structure to be used both for input and output. Of course, there are still two separate XML docu-ments, one from which the COBOL data structure is initialized and one which is generated from the COBOL data structure. The procedure for creating an XML data description table is common to both online and batch and is described later in a separate section.

Upon completing the five-step process, there is a wrapped version of the previous online program that can be compiled and loaded for execution in the internet environ-ment. The original version remains unchanged in the CICS or IMS environment. If a logical change occurs to the original program, then the derived Internet version has to be regenerated. It is for this reason that the wrapping process has to be fully automated. The responsible programmer need only initiate the automated job to generate, compile, and link the Internet version.

8.5.2. Wrapping the Subprograms with an XML Interface

Subprograms within an online transaction processing environment are more susceptible to wrapping since they already have a parameter interface and are data driven. The only task here is to separate the input parameters, (i.e., arguments), from the output parameters (i.e., results). If a parameter is both input and output, it has to be marked accordingly. If a parameter is marked as an input, it will be set from the attributes in the input document. If a parameter is marked as an output, it will be extracted and inserted in the output document. If a parameter is both, it will be set from the input document and inserted into the output document (see Fig. 8.2).

Thus there are only two steps involved in the process of wrapping a subprogram:

- First, to identify how the linkage parameters are used by analyzing their sets and uses.
- Second, to generate an XML data description for initializing and extracting the parameters.

It is the task of the wrapper to invoke the XMLIN stub routine for the entire linkage section, which is then initialized from an XML input document. After control has been returned from the subprogram, the XMLOUT stub routine is invoked to generate

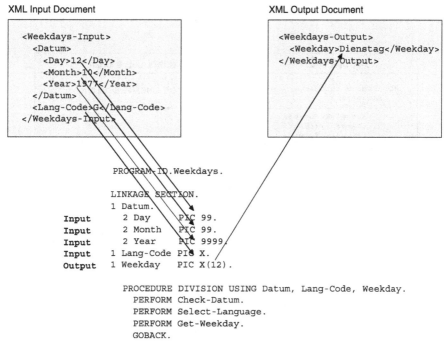

Figure 8.2. Wrapping subprograms.

an XML output document from the output fields in the linkage section. There exists a standard wrapper program—XMLWrap—for this purpose.

8.5.3. Converting XML to COBOL and Vice Versa

The key to converting XML-data to COBOL-data is the XML data description table generated from the COBOL data description. For each COBOL structure an aggregate entry is created with a beginning and end tag. For each elementary COBOL field a <Field> tag is created with six attributes (see Fig. 8.3):

<level>	:=	2-digit level number
<name>	:=	30-character COBOL-name
<type>	:=	1-character COBOL data type
<pos>	:=	field position in bytes from start
<lng>	:=	field length in characters
<occurs>	:=	number of field occurrences
<defines>	:=	field which this field may redefine
<usage>	:=	field usage in/out/inout

When converting XML data to COBOL, the data description table is first checked against the document type definition to ensure that the structure of the data is correct (43). If not, the document is rejected. Otherwise the data description table is then read into an internal table by the stub module and a storage space is allocated as large as the last position plus the last length. Then, the XML content file is read; each item is

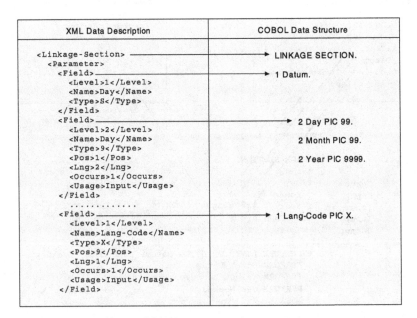

Figure 8.3. XML / COBOL data conversion.

checked against the internal table, its value converted and set to the appropriate position within the storage space allocated, provided that its usage is input or inout. Data fields not referenced in the XML document are set to a default value such as spaces or zeros.

When converting COBOL data to XML, the internal data description table is created and an XML document initialized with header and style sheet. Then the data description table is serially processed to locate all fields marked as output or inout. For each output field the value at the position indicated in the table is converted from the type indicated in the data description table and inserted as a character value with the appropriate name tag in the XML output document. This output document is then transferred back to the client.

The hierarchical COBOL data structures fit well to the hierarchical XML data structures and, since COBOL uses fixed field formats, it is rather simple to convert them to and from tagged ASCII character strings. COBOL and XML data structures are totally compatible. In fact, it appears as if COBOL data structures and XML data structures would have a common origin (8).

8.5.4. The SoftLink Process

The SoftLink process developed by the author for linking legacy components to the Web consists of seven steps:

- Step 1 is the function mining step. Functions to be reused are marked and extracted from the existing program together with the data they use.
- Step 2 is the wrapping step. A new interface is created for each of the extracted functions.
- Step 3 is the XMI generation step. From the interface description in the original language of the program, an XML subschema is generated.
- Step 4 is the generation of the server stubs for parsing the incoming XML messages and for marshaling the outgoing messages.
- Step 5 is the client transformation step. From the XML subschema the Java classes are generated to send and receive the XML messages.
- Step 6 is the server linking step. The stubs are linked together with their server functions on the host to create dlls.
- Step 7 is the client build. The generated Java classes are built into the Java interface component for connecting the website to the Web services on the host (see Fig. 8.4).

Function Mining. In the function mining step, the tool *SoftWrap* displays the source of the legacy program from which functions are to be extracted for reuse as Web services. In the case of Assembler the user may select individual CSECTS or labels. In the case of PL/I the user may select internal procedures or nested blocks. In the case of COBOL the user may select sections or paragraphs. In the case of C the user may select functions or procedures. In all cases the code unit selected is extracted together with all of its subordinate units—that is, subroutines referenced by that unit.

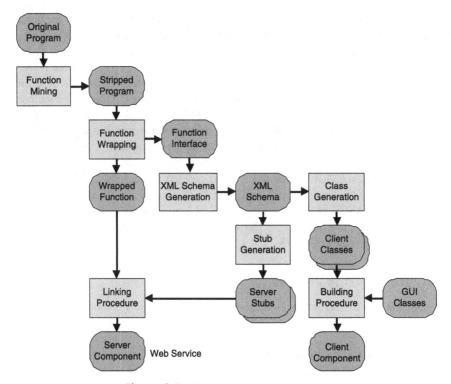

Figure 8.4. Web service creation process.

Since the subroutines may themselves refer to other subroutines, the process of attaching dependant code is repeated until no more subroutines are found. This corresponds to procedural slicing and is a recursive algorithm for collecting nodes of a procedural graph which has been presented in a previous paper (31). If too many subroutines are collected, the perspective Web service may become too large and have to be discarded. Therefore, it is best to study the impact domain of a selected function before extracting it. It is also necessary to cap the GO TO's branching out of the domain selected to ensure that the function can be executed independently.

Function Wrapping. Once a function is extracted from the existing source, together with all of its subfunctions, the next step is to wrap it. This is done automatically by the tool *SoftWrap*, which creates an entry and an interface to that function. The interface creation is proceeded by a data flow analysis that identifies all of the variables referenced either directly or indirectly by the function. This includes overlaying data structures and indexed arrays. If an elementary item in a structure is referenced, then the whole structure is included in the interface.

In the end, all of the data used by the wrapped function become part of its interface. If the function is small, the interface will be narrow. If, however, the function is large, the interface can become very wide. It is up to the user to narrow the scope of the functions. In any case, the functions are stateless components, They do not contain any static data. Having this feature makes them reentrant for use in multithreaded processing. The data belong to the task. The code is now sharable.

XML Schema Creation. Following the wrapping of the selected reusable functions and the creation of new functional interfaces, the next step is to transform those interfaces into an XML schema while, at the same time, generating server stubs to process XML messages based on that schema. When the functions are wrapped, their interfaces are created in the original language, be it Assembler, PL/I, COBOL, or C. They become either Assembler macros, PL/I includes, COBOL copies, or C header files. This way the interfaces are independent of the middleware. They could be translated either into CORBA-IDL or into XML. To this end, they are preserved in a macro library on the mainframe.

For the purpose of connecting the extracted functions to the Web, the interfaces are converted to XML. Each interface is essentially a structure that is defined to be a complex type in XML. Its attributes are its name and type and its name space. If there are substructures within the structure, they also become complex types. In case of repeating groups, the maximum number of occurrences is given.

The individual parameters are elements with the standard attributes foreseen by XMI—name, type, href, occurs, and so on. In addition, there are the following extended attributes assigned to facilitate the data transformation to EBCDIC data types on the host. These are:

- **Pos** := displacement of the data field within the host data structure
- **Lng**:= length of the host data field in bytes
- **Pic** := COBOL or PL/I edit type pattern, e.g. S999.99
- **Use** := computational, packed decimal, display, and so on.

These attributes enable the parser to place the input data at the proper position, with the proper length and in the proper format within the message buffer containing the parameters of the called function. Inversely, the output data may be extracted from the message buffer to be placed in an outgoing XML document. This XML schema is the basis for all further processing. Upon generation, it is stored in the XML repository.

Server Stub Generation. The parsers for processing the incoming XML messages from the clients and for marshaling the XML messages back to the clients are generated in this fourth step from the XML schemas. For the sake of compatibility with the run-time system the target functions are running in, the parser stubs are created in the same language as that of the functional modules. In the case of COBOL, they are made in COBOL. In the case of PL/I, they are made in PL/I. In the case of C, they are made in C. This avoids any problems arising from translingual connections.

When a session is started, the XML schema is read in from the XML repository and an internal data description table created with an entry for each parameter. The entry contains the name, type, picture, usage, displacement, length, and occurrence. Then when the target function is invoked, it calls the input stub to give it the incoming message. The stub reads the next XML document from the input queue, picks out the data values from the document, and converts them over into host data types. The converted values are then assigned to the corresponding fields in the address space of the wrapped program.

The output stub is triggered whenever a map, record, or report line is to be written out, or when there is an exit from the wrapped function. In any case, the stub takes the output data results from the address space of the wrapped program, converts them to ASCII character values, and inserts them into an XML output document to be forwarded back to the client. By keeping the internal data description table in the server cache, the XML schema need only be interpreted once, at the beginning of each session.

Client Class Generation. he same XML schemas which are the basis for the generation of the server stubs are also used to generate the client classes. For each server function (i.e. Web service), two Java classes are generated, one for creating the request to the server function and one for interpreting the result returning from the server. The class methods are invoked by the user interface classes that are processing the user's Web page.

These two generated classes have a twofold purpose. On the one hand, they save the client programmers the trouble of having to write them themselves and, on the other hand, they ensure that the XML interfaces are always made in a uniform fashion.

Web Service Binding. In the final step, the server functions are linked together with their stubs into individual dynamic link load modules to be made available on the

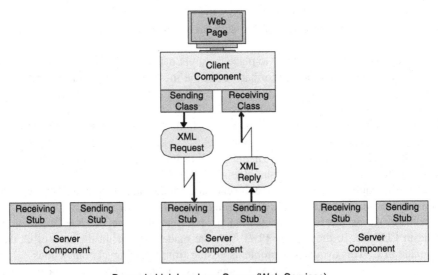

Dynamic Link Loads on Server (Web Services)

Figure 8.5. Web service architecture.

host under either *WebLogic* or *WebSphere*. These dll modules function in the same way as Web services and can be made available to *DotNet* as well. They can be invoked from any Web browser anywhere in the internet. The invoking client component need only include the classes for sending and receiving the XML interfaces to the server functions. Of course for *DotNet* the classes would have to be generated in C# for compatibility reasons.

The important difference to the Web services proposed by MicroSoft is the fact that these services are automatically generated out of existing legacy programs with no manual intervention. This also distinguishes them from the usual reverse engineering approaches. It represents a significant savings in design, coding, and testing effort. Furthermore, it fulfills the long-standing requirement of reusing legacy functionality without having to reprogram it. The existing application functions are made accessible to the Internet just as Tibbetts and Bernstein envisioned it (see Fig. 8.5) (38).

8.6. EXPERIENCE IN THE FIELD

The method described above has been applied to a large-scale bank application, written in COBOL and running under IMS-DC with a relational DB/2 database. The system contained 92 COBOL modules plus 11 Assembler modules and accessed some 65 DB/2 tables. The purpose of the application was to process transactions coming in from an Automated Teller Machine (ATM). The goal of the project was to make the COBOL system executable under CICS as well as the IBM object framework *WebSphere*. To achieve this, the IMS-DC operations were removed and replaced by a wrapper that builds up a queue of incoming ATM transactions and feeds them sequentially to the underlying business functions which in turn invoke the underlying DB/2 access routines. In this way the bulk of the COBOL code could be preserved, although the system itself was now encapsulated as an object in a distributed architecture.

Besides being invokable as a single large object, individual modules could also be called from foreign systems since such a module received its own standard interface in which its data and functions are specified. When completed, this experimental project demonstrated the feasibility of wrapping even large online transaction processing systems for migration to a new environment. The performance was dependent on *WebSphere*, but this system performed insignificantly less well than the other *WebSphere* applications of the bank (29).

8.7. CONCLUSION

This contribution has outlined different strategies for supplying Web services to a service-oriented architecture. As pointed out, they can be bought, rented, borrowed, developed, or recovered. There are advantages and disadvantages of each approach. The cheapest and quickest means of supplying Web services, other than borrowing them from the open source community, is to recover them from the existing applications in the ownership of the user.

There is a pressing need for more research in this area of code recovery. First, techniques are required to identify the code based on the results produced. Second, metrics are required to evaluate the reusability of the code identified. Third, tools are needed to extract chains of interconnected code blocks—that is, code features from the environment in which the code resides. Finally, tools are needed to automatically wrap the extracted code and adapt it as a Web service. All of these steps are subject to automation; however, in order to automate them, the optimal and most reliable means of performing these tasks must be investigated and different techniques compared. In this respect, the researches community can make a valuable contribution to the migration process.

REFERENCES

1. P. Andriole. The colaborale integrate business technoogy strategy. *Communications of the ACM* **49**(5):85–90, 2006.

2. L. Aversano, G. Canfora, A. Cimitile, and A. De Lucia. Migrating legacy systems to the Web is an experience report. In *Proceedings of the 5th European Conference on Software Maintenance and Reengineering (CSMR 2001)*, IEEE Computer Society Press, Lisbon, pages 148–157, 2001.

3. J. Benamati and A. Lederer. Coping with rapid changes in IT. *Communications of the ACM* **44**(8):83–88, 2001.

4. P. Bharati. India's IT service industry is a competetive analysis. *IEEE Computer* **38**(1):71–75, 2005.

5. M. Bichler and L. Kwei-Jay. Service-oriented computing. *IEEE Computer* **39**(3):99–101, 2006.

6. J. Bishop and N. Horspool. Cross-platform development—Software that lasts. *IEEE Computer* **39**(10):26–35, 2006.

7. T. Bodhuin, E. Guardabascio, and M. Tortorella. Migrating COBOL systems to the WEB by using the SOAP. In *Proceedings of the 9th Working Conference on Reverse Engineering (WCRE-2002)*, IEEE Computer Society Press, Richmond, pages 329–388, 2002.

8. N. Bradley. *The XML Companion—Document Modelling.* Addison-Wesley, Harlow, G.B., pages 71–89, 2000.

9. G. Canfora, A. R. Fasolino, G. Frattolillo, and P. Tramontana. Migrating interactive legacy system to Web services. *Proceedings of the 10th European Conference on Software Maintenance and Reengineering*, IEEE Computer Society Press, Bari, pages 24–36, 2006.

10. N. Carr. Software as a commodity. *Harvard Business Review* **51**(5), May 2003.

11. P. Duchessi and I. Chengalur-Smith. Client/server benefits, problems, best practices. *Communications of the ACM* **41**(5):87–94, 1998.

12. R. Evaristo, K. Desouza, and K. Hollister. Centralization Momentum—The pendulum swings back again. *Communications of the ACM* **48**(2):67–71, 2005.

13. R. Fanta and V. Rajlich. Removing clones from the code. *Journal of Software Maintenance* **11**(4):223–244, 1999.

14. K. B. Gallagher and J. R. Lyle. Using program slicing in software maintenance. *IEEE Transactions on Software Engineering* **17**(8):751–761, 1991.

15. D. Garlan, R. Allen, and J. Ockerbloom. Architectural mismatch—Why reuse is so hard. *IEEE Software* **12**(6):17–26, 1995.

16. R. Glass. The realities of software technology payoffs. *Communications of the ACM* **42**(2):74–79, 1999.

17. O. Greevy, S. Ducasse, and T. Girba. Analyzing software evolution through feature views. *Journal of Software Maintenance & Evolution* **18**(6):425–456, 2006.

18. M. Hammer and J. Champy. *Reengineering the corporation—A manifest for business revolution.* Harpers Business, New York, 1993.

19. E. Horowitz. Migrating software to the World Wide Web. *IEEE Software* **15**(3):18–21, 1998.

20. M. A. Jackson. *Principles of Program Design.* Academic Press, London, pages 67–82, 1975.

21. D. Krafzig, K. Banke, and D. Schama. *Enterprise SOA,* Coad Series, Prentice-Hall, Upper Saddle River, NJ, 2004.

22. G. Larsen. Component-based enterprise frameworks, *Communications of the ACM,* **43**(10):24–26, 2000.

23. B. Meyer. Applying design by contract. *IEEE Computer* **25**(10):40–51, 1992.

24. H. Q. Nguyen, B. Johnson, and M. Hackett. *Testing Applications on the Web.* John Wiley & Sons, Indianapolis, 2003.

25. P. Pak-Lok and A. Lau. The present B2C implementation framework. *Communications of the ACM* **49**(2):96–103, 2006.

26. R. Seacord, D. Plakosh, and G. Lewis. *Modernizing Legacy Systems.* Addison-Wesley, Reading, MA, 2003.

27. A. Sellink, C. Verhoef, and H. M. Sneed. Restructuring of COBOL/CICS legacy systems. In *Proceedings of the 3rd European Maintenance and Reengineering (CSMR 1999),* IEEE Press, Amsterdam, pages 72–82, 1999.

28. H. Sneed. Measuring reusability of legacy software systems. *Software Process* **4**(1):43–48, 1998.

29. H. M. Sneed. *Objektorientierte Softwaremigration,* Addison-Wesley, Bonn, pages 1–29, 1999.

30. H. M. Sneed. Generation of stateless components from procedural programs for reuse in a distributed system. In *Proceedings of the 4th European Maintenance and Reengineering (CSMR 1999),* IEEE Press, Zürich, pages 183–188, 2000.

31. H. Sneed. Extracting business logic from existing COBOL programs as a basis for reuse. In *Proceedings of the 9th International Workshop on Program Comprehension (IWPC 2001),* IEEE Computer Society, Toronto, pages 167–175, 2001.

32. H. Sneed. Wrapping Legacy COBOL Programs behind an XML Interface. In *Proceedings of the 8th Working Conference on Reverse Engineering (WCRE 2001),* IEEE Computer Society Press, Stuttgart, pages 189–197, 2001.

33. H. Sneed. Integrating legacy software into a service oriented architecture. In *Proceedings of the 10th European Conference on Software Maintenance and Reengineering (CSMR 2006),* IEEE Computer Society Press, Bari, pages 3–14, 2006.

34. H. Sneed and K. Erdos. Extracting business rules from source code. In *Proceedings of the 4th International Workshop on Program Comprehension (IWPC'96),* IEEE Computer Society Press, Berlin, pages 240–247, 1996.

35. H. M. Sneed and E. Nyâry. Downsizing large application programs. *Journal of Software Maintenance* **6**(5):235–247, 1994.

36. P. Strassman. The total cost of software ownership. *IT Cutter Journal* **11**(8):2, 1998.

37. A. Terekhov and C. Verhoef. The realities of language conversion. *IEEE Software* **12**(6):111–124, 2000.

38. J. Tibbetts and B. Bernstein. Legacy applications on the web. *American Programmer* **9**(12):18–24,1996.

39. S. Tilley, J. Gerdes, T. Hamilton, S. Huang, H. Muller, D. Smith, and K. Wong. On the business value and technical challenges of adapting Web services. *Journal of Software Maintenance & Evolution* **16**(1–2):31–50, 2004.

40. S. Tockey. *Return on Software*. Addison-Wesley, Boston, 2005.

41. A. von Mayrhauser and A. M. Vans. Identification of dynamic comprehension processes during large scale maintenance. *IEEE Trans. on Software Engineering* **22**(6):424–437, 1996.

42. D. W. Wall. Processing online transactions via program inversion. In *Communications of the ACM* **30**(12):1000–1010, 1987.

43. R. Westphal. Strong tagging Der Ausweg aus der Interface-Versionshölle. *Objektspektrum* **4**:24–29, 2000.

9

SOFTWARE EVOLUTION ANALYSIS AND VISUALIZATION

Martin Pinzger, Harald Gall, and Michael Fischer

9.1. INTRODUCTION

Software evolution analysis is concerned with analyzing software changes, their causes, and their effects. It includes the retrospective analysis of the data stored in software repositories. Such data comprises the release history with all the source code and change information, bug reporting data, and data that are extracted from the execution traces. In particular, the analysis of release and bug reporting data has gained importance because they store a wealth of information valuable for analyzing the evolution of software systems.

Software visualization is a means to support the analysis of different aspects of a software system with graphical views. In this chapter we present four different visualization techniques with the focus on visualizing *evolutionary* aspects of software systems. In particular, aspects concern the evolution of source code units (*Multiple Evolution Metrics View*), the evolution of features (*Feature Evolution View*), the developer contributions (*Developer Contribution View*), and the change coupling between source code units (*Change Coupling View*). Each technique allows the user to create different views with the objective to speed up the analysis and understanding of the software system under study. For instance, views show the as-implemented structure of the system enriched with evolutionary metrics information that highlight areas of interest. Such areas that we call hot spots refer to unstable implementation units, shortcomings

Emerging Methods, Technologies, and Process Management in Software Engineering. Edited by De Lucia, Ferrucci, Tortora, and Tucci

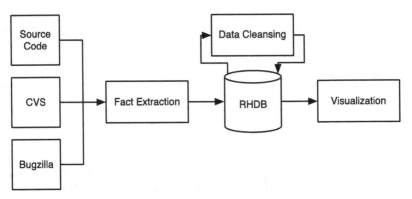

Figure 9.1. Software evolution analysis and visualization process with the data extraction steps (left), the RHDB and data cleansing step (center), and the visualization approaches (right).

in the implementation of certain features, or shortcomings in the design and team structure. Pointing out these shortcomings and providing means to improve the current design, implementation, and team collaboration structure is our primary objective.

The main data source used by the four presented visualization techniques is the release history database (RHDB) (7). This database integrates the facts extracted from several source code releases, feature data, versioning (i.e., CVS), and bug tracking (i.e., Bugzilla) data.

Figure 9.1 depicts an overview of our general software evolution analysis and visualization process. The left-hand side shows the different data sources from which the raw data are retrieved. Currently, our techniques use multiple source code releases, execution traces, versioning data from CVS repositories, and bug reporting data from Bugzilla repositories. The facts extracted from the different data sources are stored into the RHDB. In a data cleansing step the facts of the different data sources are linked, allowing us to navigate from bugs to the modified source code entities and to features affected by the change and vice versa. Furthermore, we consider multiple releases and establish such links between the releases to navigate the different versions of an entity.

For each source file we then measure the evolution metrics comprising size, program complexity, various numbers of reported bugs, number of modifications, and so on. Regarding the dependency relationships between source files, the strength of the dependency is measured such as the number of method calls, number of attribute accesses, or number of common commits of two files. The so-obtained new data are stored into the RHDB and from there they can be retrieved by our visualization techniques.

9.2. MULTIPLE EVOLUTION METRICS VIEW

In this section we present an approach to create different higher-level views on the source code. These views visualize the software modules and their dependency relationships. Software modules stem from the decomposition of a system into manageable implementation units. Such units, for instance, are source code directories, source files, or classes. Dependency relationships refer to *uses* or *inheritance* dependencies. The uses-dependencies are further detailed into dependency relationships on the source code level namely file includes, method calls, variable accesses, and type dependencies.

The objective of the Multiple Evolution Metrics View is to point out implementation-specific aspects of *one* and *multiple* source code releases—for instance, highlighting modules that are exceptionally large, complex, and exhibit strong dependency relationships to other modules. Furthermore, modules with a strong increase in size and complexity, or modules that have become unstable, are highlighted. Such views can be used by software engineers—for instance, to (a) get a clue of the implemented design and its evolution, (b) to spot the important modules implementing the key functionality of a software system, (c) to spot the heavily coupled modules, and (d) to identify critical evolution trends. The basic ideas and underlying concepts of Multiple Evolution Metrics View have been developed in the work of Pinzger et al. (20).

9.2.1. Source Code Data

For the Multiple Evolution Metrics View the input data comprises structural source code information and metrics data extracted from a number of source code releases. Source code metrics quantify the size, program complexity, and coupling of modules and the strength of dependency relationships. Typical module size metrics are lines of code, number of methods, number of attributes, and so on. Program complexity metrics, for instance, are McCabe Cyclomatic Complexity (18), Halstead Intelligent Content, Halstead Mental Effort, and Halstead Program Difficulty (10). The strength of dependency relationships, for instance, is given in number of static method calls or attribute accesses between two modules.

The extraction and computation of the dependency relationships and the metric values are done using parsing and metrics tools. In our case studies with the Mozilla open source web browser we used the tool Imagix-4D[1] for C/C++ parsing and metric computation for a selected set of source code releases. Metric values of each module and dependency relationship are assigned to a feature vector. Feature vectors are tracked over the selected n releases and composed to the evolution matrix E. The values in the matrix quantify the evolution of a module or dependency relationship:

$$E_{i \times n} = \begin{pmatrix} m'_1 & m''_1 & .. & m^n_1 \\ m'_2 & m''_2 & .. & m^n_2 \\ . & . & ... & . \\ . & . & ... & . \\ m'_i & m''_i & .. & m^n_i \end{pmatrix}$$

[1]http://www.imagix.com

It contains n feature vectors with measures of i metrics. Evolution matrices are computed for each module and dependency relationship. They form the basic input to our ArchView visualization approach.

9.2.2. Visualizing Multiple Metric Values of One Release

The ArchView approach is an extension of the Polymetric Views technique presented by Lanza et al. (16). Instead of using graphical shapes limited in the number of representable metrics ArchView uses *Kiviat* diagrams also known as *Radar* diagrams. These diagrams are suited to present multiple metric values available for a module as described next.

Figure 9.2 shows an example of a Kiviat diagram representing measures of six metrics $M_1, M_2, \ldots, M_6$ of one release of the implementation unit `moduleA`. The underlying data is from the following evolution matrix E:

$$E_{6\times1} = \begin{pmatrix} m'_1 \\ . \\ . \\ . \\ m'_6 \end{pmatrix}$$

In a Kiviat diagram the metric values are arranged in a circle. For each metric there is an axis in the diagram. The size of the diagram is fixed and each metric value is normalized according to it. In the examples presented in this section we use the following normalization:

$$l(m'_i) = \frac{m'_i * cl}{\max(m'_i)}$$

where cl denotes the size of the Kiviat diagrams and $\max(m'_i)$ is the maximum value for a metric m'_i across all modules to be visualized. With the normalized value and the angle

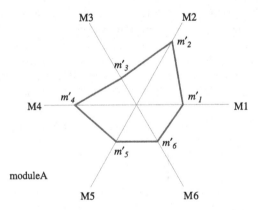

Figure 9.2. Kiviat diagram of moduleA representing measures of six source code metrics $M_1, M_2, \ldots, M_6$ of one release.

of the straight line denoting the metric, the drawing position of the point on the line is computed. To make the metric values visible in the diagram, adjacent metric values are connected, thereby forming a polygon such as shown in Fig. 9.2.

Kiviat diagrams are the nodes in a graph representing modules. These nodes can be connected by edges denoting, for instance, uses–dependency relationships between modules. Edges typically are drawn as arcs indicating the direction of relationships. The Polymetric Views principle is also applied to edges by mapping the number of underlying dependency relationships such as the number of static method calls between two modules to the width of an arc.

The set of metrics and their arrangement in the diagram can be configured. The same holds for the types of dependency relationships and the metric that is mapped to the width of arcs. This allows the user to create *different* views on the implementation highlighting particular aspects. For instance, Fig. 9.3 shows a view on four content and layout modules of the Mozilla source base of release 1.7.

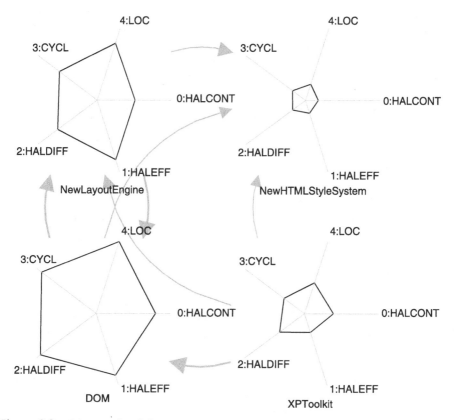

Figure 9.3. Kiviat graph of four Mozilla content (DOM) and layout (NewLayoutEngine, NewHTMLStyleSystem, XPToolkit) modules showing program complexity, lines of code, and strong include (arcs) of release 1.7.

The aspects visualized in this graph concern the highlighting of the large and complex modules as well as the strong include dependency relationships between them. Kiviat diagrams represent the four modules, and arcs between them represent the include dependency relationships. In the Kiviat diagrams the size of a module is represented with lines of code (LOC), program complexity with Halstead (HALCONT, HALEFF, HALDIFF), and McCabe Cyclomatic Complexity (CCMPLX) metrics. The width of arcs represents the strength of the include dependency relationships whereas the number of include relationships crossing module boundaries are counted. Large and complex modules are pointed out by large polygons. Strong include dependencies are represented by thick arcs.

Using this mapping, the view clearly shows that NewLayoutEngine and DOM (Document Object Model) are large and complex. Compared to them, NewHTMLStyleSystem is a rather small module. The module view also shows the strong include dependencies between the four modules. Interesting is that DOM, which implements content functionality, includes a high number of files from the NewLayoutEngine and NewHTMLStyleSystem module which provide functionality for the layout of Web pages and not the other way round as we have expected. Furthermore, there is a strong bidirectional include dependency between the NewLayoutEngine and the DOM modules. Both potential shortcomings should be discussed with the developers because they hinder separate maintenance and evolution of these three modules.

9.2.3. Visualizing Multiple Metric Values of Multiple Releases

When visualizing the metric values for a number of subsequent releases, our main focus is on highlighting the change between metric values. Typically, increases in values indicate the addition and decreases the removal of functionality. The addition of functionality is a usual sign of evolving software systems, so it represents no problem. In contrast, the removal of functionality often indicates changes in the design. For instance, methods are moved to a different class to resolve a bidirectional dependency relationship and improve separation of concerns, or methods are deleted because of removal of dead code (i.e., code that is not used anymore).

To highlight the changes in metric values, we use the Kiviat diagrams as described before. The n values of each metric obtained from the multiple releases are drawn on the same axis. Again the adjacent metric values of the same release are connected by a line forming a polygon for each release. Then the emerging area between two polygons of two subsequent releases are filled with different colors. Each color indicates and highlights the change between the metric values of two releases. The larger the change the larger the polygon.

Figure 9.4 depicts the same four Mozilla modules as before, but this time with metrics data of three subsequent releases 0.92, 1.3a, and 1.7. Light gray polygons denote changes between the releases 1.3a and 1.7.

The view shows strong changes in the two modules DOM and NewHTMLStyle System. In the latter module the two Halstead metric values HALCONT and HALDIFF decreased between the previous and the last release remarkably, though the

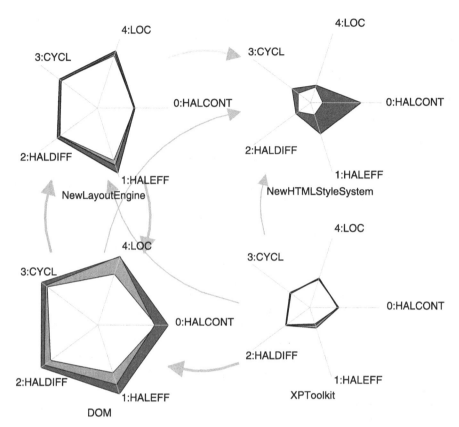

Figure 9.4. Kiviat graph of four Mozilla content and layout modules showing program complexity, lines of code metrics, and strong include (arcs) of three subsequent releases 0.92, 1.3a, and 1.7.

size (LOC) did not change a lot. Apparently the source code of these modules got refactored. The metric values of the DOM module first increased and then in the last release decreased again. First, functionality was added to the module which during the implementation of the last release was refactored. In comparison to these two modules, the metric values of the other modules indicate only minor changes in size and program complexity; hence they are stable. Based on the assumption that modules that changed in past release will be likely to change in future releases the two modules DOM and NewHTMLStyleSystem are the candidates that should be taken care of.

9.3. FEATURE EVOLUTION VIEW

Features are a way to view software systems from the perspective of the user. According to Kang et al., (12) a feature is *a prominent or distinctive aspect, quality, or characteristic of a software system or systems.* Since features are used in communication of users and developers, it is important to know which features are affected by the functional modifications of a software system. The feature visualization technique presented in this section focuses on creating higher-level views on features and their implementation in source code as well as their dependencies according modifications and bugs. The basic ideas and underlying concepts of Feature Evolution Views have been developed in the work of Fischer and Gall (5).

9.3.1. Feature, Modification, and Bug Data

The input data for our visualization is selected from the RHDB. Modification reports are obtained from versioning systems such as CVS. They contain information about *who* changed *which* source file *when*. Bug reports are obtained from bug tracking systems such as Bugzilla. Among other reports, they contain information about the date the bug was reported, the component affected, a short problem description, the priority and severity of a bug, and comments and patches for solving it.

Concerning the extraction of feature data we use the software reconnaissance technique presented by Wilde and Scully (25). We execute different usage scenarios such as loading a website in Mozilla and track the execution traces using a profiling tool (e.g., GNU gprof). The execution traces contain the sequence of functions (i.e., call graph) executed for each user scenario. The execution traces obtained for the different scenarios then are abstracted to the level of source files and mapped to concepts that represent features. The set of functions and source files implementing a feature then are stored to the RHDB.

Modification reports and feature data are linked by source files. The linkage of modification and bug report data is either provided by the versioning and bug tracking system or has to be reconstructed. For CVS and Bugzilla it is the latter case. Links are reconstructed done by querying the modification description (i.e., CVS commit messages) for references to bug reports (e.g., bug #2345). Whenever such a reference is found a link between the modification and corresponding bug report is stored to the RHDB. For more details on the feature data extraction and data integration algorithms we refer the reader to the work of Fischer et al. (5, 6).

9.3.2. Project View—Projecting Bug Reports onto Directory Structure

The Project View visualizes the implementation of features by source files and their coupling via bug reports using graphs. Nodes represent source code directories, and dashed gray edges denote the directory hierarchy (project tree). Features are represented as rectangles attached to directory nodes containing the source files implementing them. Gray solid arcs in the graph denote the coupling between features via bug reports. Figure 9.5 depicts an example of such a view on three Mozilla features.

Formally, two nodes v_i and v_j of the graph are connected if two directories contain source files sharing a bug report (i.e., were modified to fix a bug). The weights for the edges between nodes are computed by the equation below. n specifies the current

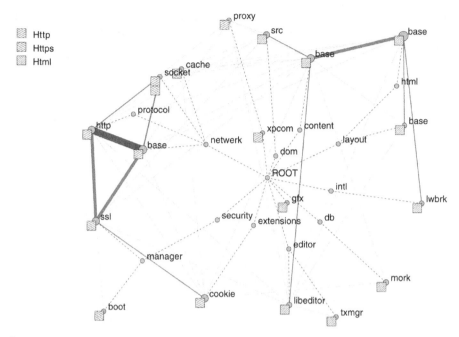

Figure 9.5. Implementation and coupling relationships of Mozilla features Http, Https, and Html via bug reports (5).

number of connections between the two nodes and n_{max} the (global) maximum number of connections between any two nodes of the graph:

$$\text{weight } (v_i, v_j) = (-1)\left(\frac{n}{n_{max}}\right)^k + o$$

For an offset $o = 1$, all weights are mapped onto a range of $[0...1]$, where 0 means the closest distance (k controls the distance generation between closely related nodes). In the resulting graph, thicker lines and a darker coloring means that the number of bug reports that the two nodes have in common is higher. We use the tool Xgvis (22) (which implements the multidimensional scaling algorithm) to layout the graph.

A critical step in the graph generation process is the selection of parameters for the weights since this has a direct impact on the final layout. We used a ratio of at least $20:1$ for project-tree edges and bug report edges. This scheme gives more emphasis to the directory structure than to connections introduced by bug reports. In the first step of the data generation process, the objects of the directory tree are assigned to their respective nodes of the graph. The minimum child size (minchild) specifies which nodes remain expanded or will be collapsed. Collapsing means that objects from the subtree are moved up to the next higher level until the size criterion is met, but not higher than the first level below the "ROOT" node. Unreferenced directories are filtered out. In the second step it is possible to move fewer referenced nodes to a higher level to obtain a more compact representation. The effect on the graph is that unreferenced leafs are suppressed, although they contain enough objects to meet the minchild criterion. This further reduces the amount of information to be visualized improving understandability of resulting graphs.

In the following subsections we show two examples of project views as created in a case study with the open source project Mozilla.

9.3.3. Bug Report Coupling Between Mozilla Features Http, Https, and Html

The three features Http, Https, and Html are depicted in Fig. 9.5. As input data we selected all bug reports for these features with the exception of bug reports classified as "enhancements" from the start of the project until the freeze date (2002-12-10). For the visualization we configured our algorithm with *minchild* = 10 (the number of artifacts, i.e., files in a subtree) and *compact* = 1 (the number of bug reports referenced by a node).

For the optimization process, we weighted the edges of the project-tree with 20, whereas an edge introduced through a single bug report was weighted with 1. The factors $k = 0.2$ and $o = 0.2$ for the weight function were used to emphasize the spreading between nodes for visualization purposes.

The overall amount of bug reports detected for a node is indicated via the diameter of a node and features "hosted" by a node are attached as boxes. Easy to recognize is the placement of nodes belonging to the Html feature on the right-hand side, and Http, Https on the left-hand side of Fig. 9.5. The nodes netwerk/base, netwerk/ protocol/http, and security/manager/ssl are interesting since they are coupled via 90 bug reports for base-http and 40 bug reports for each of the other two edges. This indicates a high degree of coupling between the features Http and Https.

Another interesting aspect is the spreading of the Html feature over 10 different nodes. Modifications may be hard to track since several files in different directories contribute to a single feature. The two nodes content/base and layout/ html/base are remarkable since they are coupled via 35 bug reports, although only four and three files are located in their respective directories.

As a result, Fig. 9.5 shows strong change dependencies for the involved features across different directories and points to architectural deterioration distilled from the evolution data:

1. Features spread across the project-tree may indicate the involvement of large amounts of the code base for their realization and thus the change impact can be big.
2. Dependencies across branches of the project-tree may indicate that there exist dependencies such as invocation, access, inheritance, or association.
3. Frequently reported bugs concerning certain source code locations of features can point to implementation or design problems.

9.3.4. Bug Report Coupling Between Mozilla Features and Mozilla core

The `core` feature (ambiguously assignable source files) and all other investigated features are depicted in Fig. 9.6 on a coarse-grained level (edges that represent less than five references are omitted). For this configuration we selected all reports which were rated "major" or "critical." We also set the minimum subtree size to 250 (minchild) entities and the minimum number of BR references to 50 (compact). This resulted in a graph with 37 nodes and 315 edges induced by bug reports. By changing the values for minchild and compact, it is possible to generate an arbitrarily detailed graph of the whole project. Since Mozilla has more than 2500 subdirectories, a complete graph representation of the whole project tree is far beyond the illustration capabilities of this medium. It is intuitive that the most critical subsystems in Mozilla are connected in the visualization, which is also supported by our findings.

The nodes with the highest density in major and critical bug reports are `content` (with 608 references), `layout/html` (444), `layout/xul/base` (223), and `layout` (212). Another interesting aspect is the spreading of edges. In total 343 connections between nodes are depicted. If we select only those edges representing at least 10 references, then we can find the following ranking: node `content` with 19 edges, `layout/html` with 10, `docshell` with 9, `dom` with 5, and `layout/xul/base`, `netwerk` and `uriloader` with 4 edges each. The other nodes have

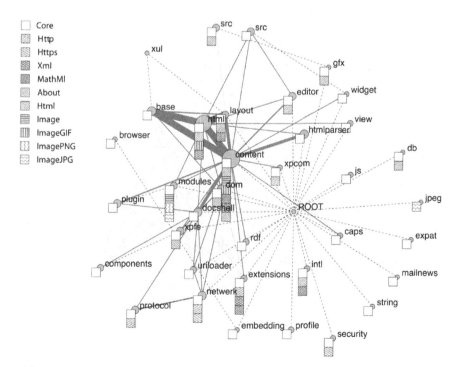

Figure 9.6. Implementation relation between Mozilla features and Mozilla core (5).

three or less edges with such a weight. In total, 23 nodes share edges with other nodes with at least 10 references, but 19 of them are connected with content. This confirms the exceptional position of content, which is also indicated by the six different features located there.

As a result, pictures such as Fig. 9.6 allow an analyst to draw the following conclusions:

1. Nodes with frequent changes appear larger than others and can be spotted easily.
2. Unstable parts of a system such as content are located near the center of the graph and they are highly coupled with other nodes.
3. Features that have a common code base are attached to particular nodes and placed close to each other (e.g., MathMl and Xml).
4. Specific feature sets (e.g., the Image feature) that are scattered over several nodes can be easily spotted (e.g., nodes jpeg, modules, layout/html, content).

As a consequence, locations of intensive change history and scattering of features point to software parts that should be considered for further investigation in terms of eliminating high complexity or architectural deterioration.

9.4. DEVELOPER CONTRIBUTION VIEW

In this section we concentrate on visualizing the efforts spent by developers for fixing bugs and evolving software systems. The primary objective of this visualization is to provide insights into how many times a source code unit has been changed and who did the changes. Resulting views show patterns that allow us to reason about the change behavior of source code units, such as if there is a central developer or many developers doing the changes. The basic ideas and underlying concepts of Fractal Views have been developed in the work of D'Ambros et al. (2).

9.4.1. Modification Data

As in the previous approach, we obtain the modification reports from the RHDB and for each author and source file we count the number of commits. For instance, Table 9.1 shows the developers who worked on the Mozilla source file nsTextHelper.cpp and, for each of them, the number of commits performed.

9.4.2. Fractal Views

Fractal Views visualize the development effort of each author spent on source code units. For this view, source code units refer to source files. Each module is represented by a Fractal Figure drawn as a rectangle that is itself composed of a set of filled

TABLE 9.1. Authors and number of commits of the Mozilla source file nsTextHelper.cpp (2)

Author	Commits
warren@netscape.com	5
gerv@gerv.net	2
dcone@netscape.com	2
dbaron@fas.harvard.edu	1
cltbld@netscape.com	1
pierre@netscape.com	1
dmose@mozilla.org	1
jaggernaut@netscape.com	1
8 developers	14 commits

rectangles having different sizes and colors. Each rectangle, and thus each color, is mapped to an author who worked on the file. Using the principle of measurement mapping, the area of the rectangle is proportional to the percentage of development effort spent by the author over the whole effort. Consequently, the more effort a developer spent on a particular module, the larger is the corresponding rectangle. The effort is given as the number of commits but not limited to this. Other measures such as the number of added and deleted lines can also be used.

The following example with the file `nsTextHelper.cpp` depicted in Fig. 9.7 explains the construction process of Fractal Views. The data are taken from Table 9.1.

The first dark gray rectangle on the left-hand side represents the author having the highest number of commits, namely `warren@netscape.com`. The area of the rectangle is 5/14 of the total area since the number of commits performed by `warren@netscape.com` is 5 while the total number is 14. All the other rectangles are rendered in the same way, changing the direction of the longer side each time.

The drawing direction is changed to improve scalability of our visualization technique. Even when there are hundreds of authors, Fractal Figures will convey that the development is highly fragmented.

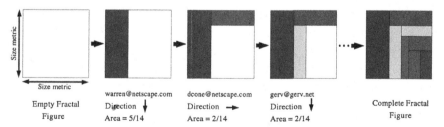

Figure 9.7. Principle for creating the fractal figure for the Mozilla source file nsTextHelper. cpp (2). © 2005 IEEE.

9.4.3. Classifying Source Files with Fractal Views

Fractal Views are used to reason about the development effort of entities from the authors point of view. We can compare entities looking at their figures and classify them according to development patterns. We distinguish four major development patterns as shown in Fig. 9.8: only one developer (a); only few developers and balanced effort (b); many developers but unbalanced effort—one performed half of the work, all the others performed the second half together (c); and many developers performing roughly the same amount of work (d).

Fractal Views can also be used on higher-level source code units such as source code directories. For this the measures of contained entities (i.e., source files) are aggregated. For instance, the number of revisions of a directory is the sum of the numbers of revisions of all contained source files. In addition, the expressiveness of Fractal Views is

(a) One developer

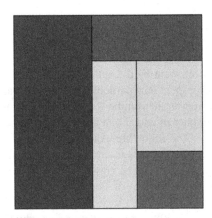

(b) Few balanced developers

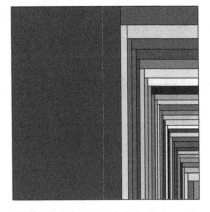

(c) One major and many minor developers

(d) Many balanced developers

Figure 9.8. Development patterns based on the Gestalt of Fractal Figures (2). © 2005 IEEE.

extended by mapping measures to the size of rectangles. This allows us to categorize those higher-level entities in terms of development effort and distribution.

For instance, Fig. 9.9 shows the `webshell` directory hierarchy of Mozilla. The Fractal Figures represent directories including at least one source file, while gray figures are associated with container directories—that is, directories containing only sub-directories. As size metric we use the number of files. The figure marked as 1 represents the largest directory—that is, the directory containing the highest number of source files. It exhibits a "Many balanced developers" development pattern.

The set of figures marked as 2 is characterized by the following: (1) The figures belong to the same hierarchical structure; (2) they exhibit a one-developer, or mainly one-developer, pattern; (3) some of them contain a great amount of files.

Another example taken from the Mozilla case study is given by Fig. 9.10. The Fractal View is on the `editor/libeditor/html` directory. Fractal Figures represent source files (left-hand side) and directories (right-top corner). We use number of revisions for the size of rectangles.

The Fractal Figures representing the source files point out one file (marked as 1) that is frequently modified by multiple developers. The development pattern of this file indicates many balanced developers. The rectangles marked as 2 are also interesting because they show similar change behavior. They are likely to be change coupled (frequently changed together) because (1) they have the same development pattern and a similar

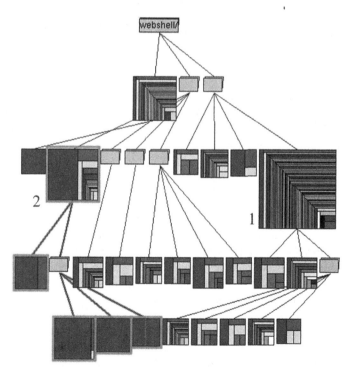

Figure 9.9. Developer contributions to the webshell hierarchy of Mozilla (2). © 2005 IEEE.

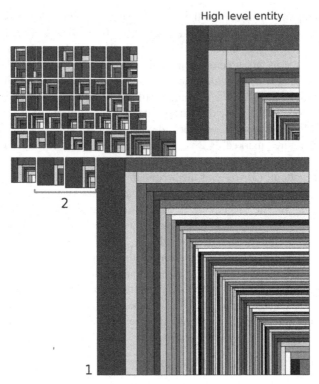

High level entity

Figure 9.10. Developer contributions to the editor/libeditor/html directory of Mozilla (2).
© 2005 IEEE.

appearance and (2) their development pattern are different from that characterizing the directory. The Fractal Figure representing the directory reflects the patterns of contained source files: There are many balanced developers with major contributions from two developers and brown developers.

9.5. CHANGE COUPLING VIEW

Change coupling occurs when two or more software modules are changed by the same author at about the same time. In this section we introduce the EvoLens visualization technique that focuses on highlighting this change coupling between source files and software modules. Software modules refer to directories in the project tree. The basic ideas and underlying concepts of the Change Coupling Views have been developed in the work of Ratzinger et al. (21).

The objective of the Change Coupling Views is to highlight source files and modules that are changed together most frequently. This knowledge then, for instance, can be used as starting points to detect shortcomings in the design and to assess the impact of changes (e.g., when changing this module, also these other modules have to be changed).

9.5.1. Change Coupling Data

The data for Change Coupling Views are obtained from the RHDB. It comprises the source code directory information, the number of commits per source file, and the change coupling relationships between files. Currently, the database is built from CVS data. Because CVS does not support commit transactions, change coupling relationships between source files have to be reconstructed. For the reconstruction of these relationships we use the author, data, and commit message information. Basically, modification reports from the same author with the same commit message and approximately the same time-stamp $t \pm \epsilon$ are grouped into a transaction. Between each such group of files, change coupling relationships are established and stored into the RHDB.

9.5.2. EvoLens Views

EvoLens approach is an interactive graph-based visualization technique that represents the directory structure and source files as nested graphs. Source files are represented by ellipses and surrounding directories as rectangles. Change coupling dependencies between source files are visualized as straight lines between nodes.

EvoLens also follows the measurement mapping principle described before. For source files the growth rate in lines of code added or deleted is mapped to the color of nodes. Basically, a light color denotes minimum and an intensive color denotes maximum growth. Concerning the change coupling, the number of common commits between two files is mapped to the width of arcs: The greater the number of common commits that two source files share, the thicker the arc between the two corresponding nodes. In the following we explain the different visualization concepts with examples taken from a case-study with a picture archiving system.

9.5.3. Nested Graph Visualization

When analyzing a large software system, a top-down approach starting with a coarse grained picture is recommended. EvoLens follows this top-down approach by using nested graphs. Modules are visulaized on the top-level, submodules on the next level, followed by source files, which are visualized on the lowest level. A *focal point* is used to focus the analysis on the change-coupling relationships of a specific entity. Entities not change coupled with the entity in focus are left out, leading to simpler and better understandable graphs. The focal point is set by the user to always focus on the entity of interest. Figure 9.11 depicts an example of an Evolution View showing the change couplings between module and submodules with the focal point set on the module jvision.

Nodes are drawn as rectangles and represent the modules and submodules. The nesting of modules and submodules is expressed by the nesting of nodes. For instance, the node in the center shows that the module jvision consists of 10 submodules.

EvoLens draws the intra- as well as the intermodule coupling relationships. The width of the line denotes the strength of the coupling in terms of number of common commits. On the module and submodule level this number is the sum of underlying

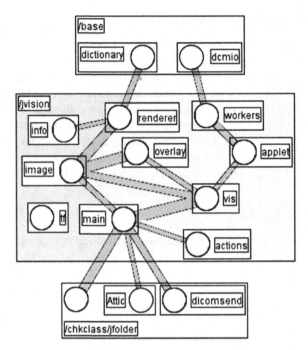

Figure 9.11. Nested graph visualization of module jvision (21). © 2005 IEEE.

change couplings between source files of module pairs. The graph of Fig. 9.11 depicts the change couplings between the submodules of jvision. Within this module the submodules image, main, renderer, overlay, and vis are frequently changed together as indicated by thick lines drawn between corresponding graph nodes. The submodule main causes the intermodule coupling with the jfolder and therefore is a primary candidate to refactor.

Zooming in and out in the graph can be done by expanding and collapsing the module and submodule nodes. In addition to this traditional zooming mechanism, EvoLens provides a filter mechanism with configurable thresholds. It allows the user to focus on the entities with strong coupling and filter out the other entities with weak couplings. In addition to the focal point, this further reduces the amount of information to be visualized in graphs.

For instance, Fig. 9.12 describes the zoom-in into submodule jvision/main. The focal point is moved to the submodule main, and its contents is unfolded and drawn in a rectangle. In this example the contained nodes are source files as indicated by the ellipses. The ellipses show different colors denoting the growth of the file. The two files MainFrame2 and SeqPanel2 increased most as highlighted by the denser color of the corresponding ellipses.

The modules and submodules change coupled with the submodule main are drawn as extra rectangles in the graph. In the example these modules are jvision with the source files VisDisplay2 and Vis2 and the module chkclass with the two source files SendPanel and CHKFolderPanel. Files with lower change coupling

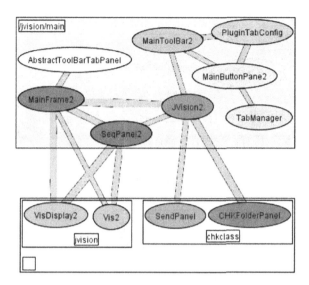

Figure 9.12. Zoom of the module hierarchy of jvision (21). © 2005 IEEE.

are filtered. Discussing this view with the developers, we found out that the main class is implemented in JVision2. This fact partially justifies the change coupling because during start-up initializations of other parts are usually made. However, a detailed inspection of the source code yielded that JVision2 exposes access to many parts of the system through static member variables. This should be improved.

9.5.4. Selective Change Coupling

Since module boundaries are sometimes too restrictive for in-depth inspections, EvoLens incorporates the visualization of individually selected sets of files. The user can choose the set of files during the inspection of the software using the mouse and let EvoLens show the change couplings for this selected set of files.

For instance, in the graph depicted in Fig. 9.13 we selected the four files: MainFrame2, VisDisplay2, ImgView2, and Localizer. These classes are the ones that are responsible for the strong change couplings between the submodules main and vis, and image and overlay of module jvision. The selected files are grouped in a rectangle, and all nonselected modules are folded. The change coupling within the group of files as well as with folded modules is shown.

The graph in Fig. 9.13 shows that all four selected files are change coupled with files of jvision. Furthermore, MainFrame2 has weak change coupling with classes of module chkclass. With the help of this feature the user can select and group different sets of modules, submodules, and files and analyze their change coupling with the rest of the system.

Change couplings are measured on a time-window basis: the number of common commits of two files during a given observation period. Such an observation period,

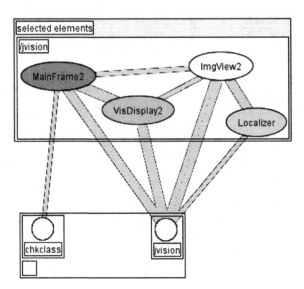

Figure 9.13. Selective Coupling of files MainFrame2, VisDisplay2, ImgView2, and Localizer (21). © 2005 IEEE.

for instance, can be from the very beginning of the project or the last six months. The observation period is user-configurable by setting the begin and end time. When the period is changed, EvoLens interactively responds by recomputing the change coupling relationships and redrawing the graph.

Figure 9.14 shows the change-coupled submodules and source files of module jvision within the entire 18 months of the inspection period (a) and the first 9 months (b). The graph on the left-hand side shows, for instance, a change coupling between the two source files MainFrame2 and VisDisplay2 that did not occur

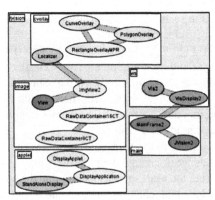

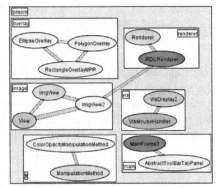

(a) Change coupling of jvision within entire history.

(b) Change coupling of jvision within first nine months.

Figure 9.14. Sliding time window in EvoLens (21). © 2005 IEEE.

in the first 9 months as shown in the graph on the the right-hand side. Consequently, the coupling between the two files was introduced through later development activities.

The coloring of the ellipses provides additional hints about the evolution of source files. For instance, the change coupling and coloring of View and ImgView2 is striking. Both modules have a strong change coupling, but the file View grew by more than 300 lines of code whereas ImgView2 remained almost constant at 150 lines of code but is continuously modified. Apparently the class implemented in file ImgView desires a more clean and stable interface to reduce the change impact when modifying related files.

9.6. RELATED WORK

A number of visualization techniques and tools have been developed in the area of reverse engineering and program understanding. Tools such as the Bookshelf of Finnigan et al. (4), Dali of Kazman and Carriére (13), Bauhaus[2] of Koschke et al., Rigi of Müller and Klashinsky, and Creole[3] of Storey et al. use graph-like visualization techniques to create views of *one* particular source code release. Nodes typically represent source code entities, and edges represent the dependency relationships between them. Similar commercial reverse engineering and program understanding tools such as Imagix4D, Sotograph, and Cast exist. Our visualization techniques are based on these techniques but also include data about the evolution and multiple source code releases. Another extension to these approaches is the use of Polymetric Views.

Polymetric Views as used by our visualization techniques have been introduced by Lanza and Ducasse (16) for visualizing source code with graphs enriched with metric values. They integrated a number of predefined views in the CodeCrawler tool (15) facilitating coarse and fine-grained software visualization. Views follow the principle of measurement mapping in that larger metric values lead to larger glyphs in a graph. Using the concepts of Polymetric Views and taking into account different revisions of classes, Lanza et al. then presented the Evolution Matrix (14). Based on size metrics tracked over a number of releases, they defined a specific vocabulary to categorize classes (e.g., Pulsar, Supernova, White Dwarf, etc.). Similarly, Gîrba et al. described an approach that based on summarizing source code metric values of several releases identifies change prone classes (9). Source Viewer 3D (sv3D) is a tool that uses a 3D metaphor to represent software systems and analysis data (17). The 3D representation is based on the SeeSoft pixel metaphor (1) and extends it by rendering the visualizations in a 3D space.

In addition to source code visualization, a number of approaches have been developed that concentrate on visualizing the revision and change history of software systems. For instance, Riva et al. analyzed the stability of the architecture (8, 11) by using colors to depict the changes over a period of releases. Similar to Riva, Wu et al. describe an Evolution Spectrograph (26) that visualizes a historical sequence of software releases. Rysselberghe and Demeyer used a simple visualization based on information in

[2]http://www.iste.uni-stuttgart.de/ps/bauhaus

[3]http://www.thechiselgroup.org/creole

version control systems to provide an overview of the evolution of systems (23). Voinea et al. presented the CVSscan approach. It allows the user to interactively investigate the version and change information from CVS repositories with a line-oriented display. The four visualization techniques presented in this chapter complement existing techniques and provide additional means, such as Kiviat diagrams or fractal figures, to analyze the evolution of software systems.

9.7. RESUME

Analyzing the evolution of software systems is a look back in the history of releases, changes, and bugs. Software repositories such as the CVS and the Bugzilla provide data about the release history, changes, and bugs as well as the different source code releases that can be retrieved from them and measured. The amount of data for software evolution analysis is multiplied by the number of releases and, hence, is huge. To handle this amount of data, multiple views and effective visualization techniques are a key.

In this chapter we presented four visualization techniques, each focusing on a different aspect of software evolution. The *Multiple Evolution Metrics View* concentrates on visualizing implementation specific aspects of one- and multiple-source code releases. For instance, it can be used to visualize the growth of modules in size and complexity highlighting the modules that have become unstable. The *Feature Evolution View* allows the developers to locate the implementation of features in the source code and to assess the impact of functional modifications in a software system. It can be used for communication of users and developers. Regarding the analysis of the change behavior of software modules, the *Developer Contribution View* can be used. It visualizes the efforts for fixing bugs and evolving a software system. Four evolution patterns characterizing the module change behavior have been identified, such as modules having few balanced or many unbalanced developers. Finally, the *Change Coupling View* highlights source files and modules that frequently are changed together. Visualizing these hidden coupling dependencies can be used to detect shortcomings in the design (e.g., changes should be local to a module) and to assess the impact of changes.

For all four visualization techniques, we presented examples from case studies with the Mozilla open source project as well as an industrial software system. They clearly show the usefulness of our approaches and strengthen the fact that different visualization techniques are needed to analyze the different evolutionary aspects of software systems.

ACKNOWLEDGMENTS

The authors would like to thank Jacek Ratzinger, Marco D'Ambros, and Michele Lanza for their contributions to this work.

The presented work was supported in part by the Swiss National Science Foundation (SNF) under the grant for the project "Controlling Software Evolution" (COSE) and the Hasler Foundation, Switzerland under the grant for the project "EvoSpaces—Multi-dimensional Navigation Spaces for Software Evolution."

REFERENCES

1. T. Ball and S. G. Eick. Software visualization in the large. *IEEE Computer* **29**(4):33–43, 1996.

2. M. D'Ambros, M. Lanza, and H. Gall. Fractal figures: Visualizing development effort for cvs entities. In *Proceedings of the 3rd International Workshop on Visualizing Software for Understanding and Analysis*, IEEE CS Press, Washington, DC, pages 46–51, 2005.

3. N. E. Fenton and S. L. Pfleeger, editors. *Software Metrics: A Rigorous and Practical Approach*, 2nd edition. International Thomson Computer Press, Boston, 1996.

4. P. Finnigan, R. C. Holt, I. Kallas, S. Kerr, K. Kontogiannis, H. A. Müller, J. Mylopoulos, S. G. Perelgut, M. Stanley, and K. Wong. The software bookshelf. *IBM Systems Journal* **36**(4):564–593, 1997.

5. M. Fischer and H. Gall. Visualizing feature evolution of large-scale software based on problem and modification report data. *Journal of Software Maintenance and Evolution: Research and Practice* **16**(6):385–403, 2004.

6. M. Fischer, M. Pinzger, and H. Gall. Analyzing and relating bug report data for feature tracking. In *Proceedings of the 10th Working Conference on Reverse Engineering*, Victoria, BC, Canada. IEEE Computer Society Press, Washington, DC, pages 90–99, 2003.

7. M. Fischer, M. Pinzger, and H. Gall. Populating a release history database from version control and bug tracking systems. In *Proceedings of the International Conference on Software Maintenance,* Amsterdam, Netherlands. IEEE Computer Society Press, Washington DC, pages 23–32, 2003.

8. H. Gall, M. Jazayeri, and C. Riva. Visualizing software release histories: The use of color and third dimension. In *Proceedings of the International Conference on Software Maintenance,* Oxford, UK. IEEE Computer Society Press, Washington, DC, pages 99–108, 1999.

9. T. Gîrba, S. Ducasse, and M. Lanza. Yesterday's weather: Guiding early reverse engineering efforts by summarizing the evolution of changes. In *Proceedings of the International Conference on Software Maintenance,* Chicago, Illinois. IEEE Computer Society Press, Washington, DC, pages 40–49, 2004.

10. M. H. Halstead. *Elements of Software Science (Operating, and Programming Systems Series).* Elsevier Science Inc., New York, 1977.

11. M. Jazayeri. On architectural stability and evolution. In *Proceedings of the Reliable Software Technlogies-Ada-Europe,* Vienna, Austria. Springer Verlag, New York, pages 13–23, 2002.

12. K. Kang, S. Cohen, J. Hess, W. Novak, and A. Peterson. Feature-oriented domain analysis (foda) feasibility study. Technical report, Software Engineering Institute, Carnegie Mellon University, 1990.

13. R. Kazman and S. J. Carriére. Playing detective: Reconstructing software architecture from available evidence. *Automated Software Engineering* **6**(2):107–138, 1999.

14. M. Lanza. The evolution matrix: Recovering software evolution using software visualization techniques. In *Proceedings of the International Workshop on Principles of Software Evolution,* Vienna, Austria. ACM Press, New York, pages 37–42, 2001.

15. M. Lanza. Codecrawler—Polymetric views in action. In *Proceedings of the 19th IEEE International Conference on Automated Software Engineering (ASE),* Linz, Austria. IEEE Computer Society Press, Washington, DC, pages 394–395, 2004.

16. M. Lanza and S. Ducasse. Polymetric views—a lightweight visual approach to reverse engineering. *IEEE Transactions on Software Engineering* **29**(9):782–795, 2003.

17. J. I. Maletic, A. Marcus, and L. Feng. Source viewer 3d (sv3d): A framework for software visualization. In *Proceedings of the 25th International Conference on Software Engineering*, Portland, Oregon. IEEE Computer Society Press, Washington, DC, pages 812–813, 2003.

18. T. J. McCabe. A complexity measure. *IEEE Transactions on Software Engineering* **2**(4):308–320, 1976.

19. H. A. Müller and K. Klashinsky. Rigi—A system for programming-in-the-large. In *Proceedings of the 10th International Conference on Software Engineering,* Singapore. IEEE Computer Society Press, Washington, DC, pages 80–86, 1988.

20. M. Pinzger, H. Gall, M. Fischer, and M. Lanza. Visualizing multiple evolution metrics. In *Proceedings of the ACM Symposium on Software Visualization,* St. Louis, Missouri. ACM Press, New York, pages 67–75, 2005.

21. J. Ratzinger, M. Fischer, and H. Gall. Evolens: Lens-view visualizations of evolution data. In *Proceedings of the International Workshop on Principles of Software Evolution*, Lisbon, Portugal. IEEE Computer Society Press, Washington, DC, pages 103–112, 2005.

22. D. F. Swayne, D. Cook, and A. Buja. Xgobi: Interactive dynamic data visualization in the x window system. *Journal of Computational and Graphical Statistics* **7**(1):113–130, 1998.

23. F. Van Rysselberghe and S. Demeyer. Studying software evolution information by visualizing the change history. In *Proceedings of the 20th International Conference on Software Maintenance,* Chicago, Illinois. IEEE Computer Society Press, Washington, DC, pages 328–337, 2004.

24. L. Voinea, A. Telea, and J. J. van Wijk. Cvsscan: Visualization of code evolution. In *SoftVis '05: Proceedings of the 2005 ACM Symposium on Software Visualization*. ACM Press, New York, pages 47–56, 2005.

25. N. Wilde and M. C. Scully. Software reconnaissance: mapping program features to code. *Journal of Software Maintenance* **7**(1):49–62, 1995.

26. J. Wu, C. W. Spitzer, A. E. Hassan, and R. C. Holt. Evolution spectrographs: Visualizing punctuated change in software evolution. In *Proceedings of the 7th International Workshop on Principles of Software Evolution*. IEEE Computer Society Press, Washington, DC, pages 57–66, 2004.

PART IV

PROCESS MANAGEMENT

10

EMPIRICAL EXPERIMENTATION IN SOFTWARE ENGINEERING

Giuseppe Visaggio

10.1. INTRODUCTION

For at least 30 years in the software engineering community, researchers have been asking practitioners to use their research results for transforming them in innovative practices or use the practices that have already been developed in research laboratories for innovating software products and processes, whereas practitioners have been asking for practices that can be used for innovating processes and products supported by evidence in order to assess their value and the risks that must be managed during their institutionalization.

Unfortunately, researchers often point out the technical benefits of a new method or tool, disregarding their usefulness and transferability in practice. Consequently, practitioners dispose of a catalogue of research results, often not transformed in practices (20, 33). Also, the available practices are not always supported by evidence needed for assuring their efficacy in real processes or their transferability within and toward business processes.

Research can help face and overcome this dystonia by developing Software Engineering as a science and removing it from those demonstrations that have made it seem closer to art (33). In fact, scientific development requires validation of theories, principles, and practices that make up the scientific knowledge. Also, empirical studies can produce evidence to demonstrate when and why it is important to apply a new principle or technology (i.e., innovation). Finally, empirical studies can contribute

Emerging Methods, Technologies, and Process Management in Software Engineering. Edited by
De Lucia, Ferrucci, Tortora, and Tucci
Copyright © 2008 John Wiley & Sons, Inc.

to build the competences that must be transferred in the innovation. In summary, empirical studies can help to make the software engineering body of knowledge a science, transform it in innovation, and diffuse it to others.

This chapter gives a synthesis of the knowledge collected in literature on the design and execution of empirical investigations (EI) merged with experience collected in research projects carried out under the author's supervision in the Software Engineering Research Laboratory (SERLAB) at the University of Bari.

The chapter is intended for Software Engineer researchers and students that desire to understand the role of empirical research in carrying out their activities and in socializing their research results. In particular, it is an important contribution in Software Engineering education for understanding the role of empirical research in deciding when and where to introduce a new technology or innovate an existing one with another. The reader is requested knowledge of Software Engineering methods, processes, techniques and practices.

Furthermore, this chapter on Software Engineering continues with the following sections: *Empirical Studies* gives an overview of (a) empirical studies and their role in building and confirming theories, (b) characterization of different types of EI that can be carried out, and (c) guidelines for designing and carrying out effective EI without defects. After outlining the main aspects of investigations, the chapter analyzes the use of such investigations in order to attribute Software Engineering with an imprint of science. The risks and the threats of an EI are critical for its correct execution and data interpretation. In this sense, the chapter contains a specific section on *Validity Risks and Threats*, which summarizes the most relevant risks and includes guidelines for executing experiments in order to mitigate them. Moreover, the section *Empirical Studies for Software Engineering Science* gives (a) an overview of the development paths in software engineering and of the need for replication, (b) analysis of problems encountered during replications and guidelines to overcome them, and (c) details of specific types of replications useable for extracting knowledge and known as Families of Experiments. The section *Empirical Investigation for Innovation Acceptance* describes (a) some experiments executed in SERLAB on the suitability of empirical studies in contributing to acceptance and (b) institutionalization of a new technology. Finally, *Building Competence through Empirical Investigation* supports the idea that, as for other sciences, EI in software engineering must contribute to extend its competences. In this sense, the section summarizes how competences on Extraordinary Maintenance have been extended in 10 years of empirical research on the topic. The section *Conclusions* closes the chapter with considerations that point out open issues following what has been presented in the previous sections.

10.2. EMPIRICAL STUDIES

10.2.1. Overview

Scientific development begins with (a) the observation of an event and aims to formulate one or more universally valid laws and (b) their abstraction in a theory. An *empirical investigation*, synonym of *empirical study*, in a broad sense, is a process that aims to discover something unknown or to validate hypotheses that can be transformed in generally valid laws. A researcher is involved in extracting and collecting data that quantify the *observations*. An observation can be made up of a subjective ascertainment; generally, observations are made using all of researcher senses. Instruments such as sensors allow us to make observations without using senses. They are often electronic and empower a researcher's observation capability.

Some observations are accidental; others are recurrent. A researcher is usually interested in the latter type of observations. His/her research aims to discover the causes that determine the observed effects on events. Moreover, if the events are positive, the causes that produce them must be known in order to repeat them. If they are negative, the causes must, once again, be known in order to avoid such events.

At first, the causes that determine the observed events determine the *hypothesis*. A hypothesis can be tentatively accepted when it is supported by a rationale that can be considered acceptable, given the current knowledge on the domain on behalf of the scientific community. Some researchers can disapprove the hypothesis. Until a hypothesis is accepted by many researchers, it is called *conjecture*. Once a hypothesis/conjecture is formulated, those favorable to it carry out an EI to support and confirm it. On the contrary, the researchers that do not share it carry out an EI to deny it.

In some cases the cause–effect relation asserted by a hypothesis/conjecture, although not supported by any or little evidence, occurs in many real cases. This experience is communicated among practitioners as practices that achieve satisfactory objectives. In this case the conjecture or hypothesis is called *heuristic*.

The hypothesis becomes a *law* when it is supported by solid empirical evidence. When a hypothesis is not confirmed by enough evidence to be considered universally valid, it is said to lead to a *principle* rather than to a law. The law/principle abstracts the collected knowledge from researchers during EI and is the means for transferring such knowledge to business processes. So, data collected from the observation are analyzed in order to confirm, support, or contradict the theory that withholds the hypothesis (24).

A law explains how, under certain conditions, an event occurs, but it does not explain the reason for such event. The reason why certain events occur in specific conditions is explained by a *theory*. Sometimes the theory exists before the law; in this case it can forecast laws and observations. However, the researcher must confirm the theory through observations and EI.

An example can be given with reference to Parnas' law on information hiding (32). Parnas *observed* that the work of Philips developers applied a conventional *heuristic* for software design: Each designed module was of small dimensions, able to be understood and coded independently from its designer; the interfaces were simple enough to be specified in their scope and designed independently from the designer. Parnas hypothesized that in order to improve maintainability of software systems, the implementation of each module was to be independent from the other ones and that a module's interface had to show the least possible information concerning its implementation. To achieve this scope, the suggested technique was the following: Given the list of project decisions, each decision was to be hidden in a module; the decisions with higher probability of change were to be implemented in modules having low relations with other modules of the system. This technique no longer considers the system performances of primary importance. Performances must be verified, after software production, through a specific test and, if violated, the designer must make new decisions, hidden in new modules, that change the previous release of the software system. This knowledge is abstracted in what is commonly known as *Parnas Law: Only what is hidden can be changed without risk.*

Parnas did not carry out any empirical studies to validate this law. Many researchers have used it but have neither replicated nor published significant results for proving the universal validity of this law. So, it is more correct to call it a *principle* rather than a law.

The *theory* that lays beneath this law can be enounced as follows. Given the following precautions, hide software project decisions in a module and design modules so that (a) their content is independent from one another and (b) their interfaces do not depend on the changes of the module contents. The generated effects are as follows: Each requirement modification corresponds to a change in one or more decisions and therefore in one or more modules; traceability between decisions and modules allows us to identify the primary impact of the modification; interface stability assures that modification of each changing module does not impact the other modules it is related to; independence of contents between modules requires that the developer only knows the content of the changing module. Thanks to this limited amount of required knowledge, maintenance is more rapid (the modification can be carried out parallel by as many developers as modules to be modified without their work interfering with one another), cost effective (the primary impact of the modification is proportional to the scope or the required change and the secondary impact is limited), and reliable (the modules being modified are identified by specific change requests).

From the viewpoint of the EI, the central aspect is the hypothesis that can be seen as a proposition that expresses a *cause–effect* relation between two theoretic constructs: *cause construct* that express the generating causes and the *effect construct* that describes the deriving effects. The theory relates hypotheses with constructs (44) as shown in Fig. 10.1.

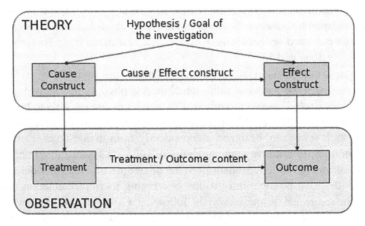

Figure 10.1. Basic concepts of empirical investigation and their relationships.

A EI observes the effect of change on one or more *factors*. The observations that are carried out with an investigation are consequence of *treatments*; each treatment is attributed to particular values of each factor. These are expressed through *independent variables*. The values that the independent variables can assume are called *levels*. The execution of the activities that make up an investigation generates one or more effects expressed through *dependent variables* that make up the *results* of the investigation. The EI must be executed in a *context* that is described by a set of characteristics that must not vary during the investigation; these are called *parameters*. When one or more factors probably have an effect on the response, which we are not interested in, their value is blocked; such variables are called *blocking factors*. Within a group or block we consider the persons with the same value of a blocking factor, so that we can study only the effect of treatment on a block. If we have more blocks with different values of the same blocking factor, the effect between the blocks cannot be studied. The tasks during the investigation are carried out by developers identified as *experimental subjects*. The object of the investigation goal makes up the *experimental unit*.

For example, suppose we investigate if a new design method produces software with higher quality than the previously used design method. An experiment is carried out with the *design method* having a factor with two levels: the *new and the old design method*. Each level is a treatment. The experimental subjects are *designers with predefined experience*. The parameters can be the variables that express the *experience as designer* of experimental subjects. The experimental unit is the *software development process* in the context of *Company XYZ*. The dependent variable can be the *number of faults* found in development. If some of the designers have already used one of the design methods (i.e., object-oriented design), they can be grouped into two groups, with experience as blocking factor, one with experience in this method and one without, in order to minimize the effect of such experience.

10.2.2. Strategies for Empirical Investigations

In an EI a researcher has control over some of the conditions of the execution and over the independent variables that must be studied. According to the context where the investigation is being carried out, it can be called either *in vivo* if it is executed on production processes of ongoing projects or *in vitro* if it is carried out in an isolated laboratory environment.

According to the level of control on variables, investigations can be classified as follows: Survey; Postmortem Analysis, also known as Ex Post or Retrospective analysis; Project Investigation; or Controlled Experiment, also known as Experiment.

A *Survey* is an empirical study that collects data from experimental subjects through questionnaires or interviews. Either it can be retrospective, on experiences collected by people that have already used instruments, methods, or processes that are object of investigation, or it can be explorative, that is, it collects opinions of innovations being investigated *a priori*.

As example, it is meaningful to show a survey on student satisfaction of a software engineering course, carried out in the Department of Informatics of the University of Bari. The survey was carried out by distributing a questionnaire to students of the course once they had taken the exam. They answered according to the experience and knowledge acquired during the course. Data analysis of the answers highlighted whether the changes made during the course were positively acknowledged by the students, or if they had comments to make. In the following, only numerical data are reported; the questionnaire also included text comments that motivated the answers. For space reasons, comments are not reported. To better understand the questionnaire, it is important to point out that during the course students carried out a project work that they chose among a set of proposals. Some project works were proposed by industrial partners and had contents not directly referable to the course content, but to the competences acquired during the course. They are called Industrial project work. Other project proposals were suggested by the team of teachers, and their content were directly referred to the course contents. They are called Didactic project works. Table 10.1 shows the questionnaire, while Table 10.2 illustrates the results after distributing the questionnaire.

The student opinions suggest the team of teachers to improve course contents and how they are provided. From Table 10.2 it can be seen that following to improvements suggested by the students, the satisfaction level is kept constant.

A *Postmortem/Ex Post/Retrospective Investigation* consists of analyzing data collected *in vivo*, with different aims from those of the investigation, on already executed projects. This type of investigation is used to confirm or deny one or more hypotheses by investigating on data collected in executed projects able to emulate investigation variables. It has low risks and costs and assures low empirical validity. Statistical instruments are usually historical series analysis and data mining.

An example is a retrospective investigation about the Multiview Framework for goal-oriented measurement plan design. Here we provide the essential contents of the investigation; interested readers can refer to reference 5. In spite of evidence of successful application of goal-oriented measurement programs in industrial contexts, there are still many open issues: dimensions of a measurement plan, complexity of interpretations, dependencies between goals, and time points for measurement activities. Our theory is to structure the measurement program so that the goals have a high internal coherence, in terms of number and scope of metrics, and low interrelation with each other in order to manage interpretation complexity. To make this theory operative, we propose the Multiview Framework (MF) approach that provides support in designing a structured large industrial measurement plan. Essentially, MF analyses goals are classified as follows: **Process goals**—aimed at evaluating the quality factor of interest with respect to a process or activity; **Product goals**—aimed at evaluating the quality of interest with respect to a deliverable or artefact; **Project Management (PM) goals**—aimed at evaluating those activities needed to plan and control the project execution; **Fitness of Investment goals (FI)**—evaluate aspects such as cost–benefit ratio and possible risks. Each of these aspects is identified as a view.

The measurement plan structure is validated by tracing the goals in a Goal-View cross-reference table. It is defined by placing the goals in the rows and placing the views in the columns (Table 10.3). So, for example, each "X" entry in an (i, j) cell of the table means that the ith goal has metrics that relate to the jth view.

TABLE 10.1. Questionnaire

1.	What is your opinion on the course content?	☐ it is well-balanced
		☐ it is not balanced
	Which topics should be faced with more detail?:	
2.	What case study did you carry out?	☐ Industrial Case Study
		☐ Didactic Case Study
3.	In your opinion, which is the most efficient choice for the course? (multiple answers are possible)	☐ Didactic case study
		☐ Industrial case study
		☐ Laboratory exercises
		☐ Classroom exercises
		☐ Written questions
		☐ Other
	Specify in case of other:	
4.	What is your opinion on the Industrial Case Study? (multiple answers are possible)	☐ It improves professionalism
		☐ It requires too much effort
		☐ It is a negative experience
	Motivate your answer:	
5.	Overall, do you consider the course (multiple answers are possible)	☐ Hard work
		☐ Useful
	Motivate your answer:	
6.	Describe three benefits of the course: 1. ___ 2. ___ 3. ___	
7.	Describe three weaknesses of the course: 1. ___ 2. ___ 3. ___	

The table is validated through two indicators: # Dependencies, increases as the number of views that a goal takes into account increases. This indicator is calculated with the following formula:

$$\# \text{Dependencies} = \sum_{i=1}^{k} (N_i - 1)$$

where k is the total number of rows of the cross-reference table, and, N_i is the number of X in the cross-reference table, with reference to the ith row.

TABLE 10.2. Survey Results

Number of Distributed Questionnaires		143 2002–2003		76 2003–2004		63 2004–2005		50 2005–2006	
Questions	Answer	Value	Variance	Value	Variance	Value	Variance	Value	Variance
1. The course contents	It is wellbalanced	88.11%	—	93.42%	0.05	87.30%	−0.07	84.00%	−0.04
	It is not wellbalanced	11.89%	—	6.58%	−0.8	12.70%	0.48	16.00%	0.2
2. The case study carried out is	Industrial case study	93.71%	—	88.16%	−0.06	92.06%	0.04	98.00%	0.06
	Didactic case study	6.29%	—	11.84%	0.46	7.94%	−0.5	2.00%	−2.97
3. The most efficient choice for the course is: (multiple answers possible)	Didactic case study	21.68%	—	19.74%	−0.09	15.87%	−0.24	18.00%	0.12
	Industrial case study	90.91%	—	86.84%	−0.05	93.65%	0.72	86.00%	−0.08
	Laboratory exercises	10.49%	—	17.11%	0.38	6.35%	−1.69	18.00%	0.65
	Classroom exercises	20.28%	—	23.68%	0.14	15.87%	−0.5	10.00%	−0.6
	Written questions	9.79%	—	10.53%	0.07	4.76%	−1.21	12.00%	0.6
	Other	0.00%	NA	0.00%	NA	0.00%	NA	0.00%	NA
4. Opinion on industrial case study (multiple answers possible)	It improves professionalism	97.90%	—	98.68%	0.008	92.06%	−0.72	98.00%	0.06
	It requires too much effort	56.64%	—	53.95%	−0.05	55.56%	0.03	72.00%	0.23
	It is a negative experience	1.40%	—	0%	NA	6.35%	NA	6.00%	−0.06
5. Overall, the course is (multiple answers possible)	Hard work	72.73%	—	63.16%	−0.15	68.25%	0.07	76.00%	0.10
	Useful	98.60%	—	100.00%	0.014	95.24%	−0.05	88.00%	−0.08

TABLE 10.3. Goal View Cross-Reference

Goals	Process				Product			PM	FI
	p1	p2	p3	d0	d1	d2	d3		
G1	X				X				
G2		X							
G3					X				
G4								X	X
G5			X				X		

The second indicator, Density of Dependencies, evaluates how strong the dependencies are; it is calculated with the following formula:

$$\text{Density of Dependencies} = \frac{\#\text{ Dependencies}}{(\#\text{ Columns}^* \#\text{ Rows}) - \#\text{ Goals}}$$

A well-designed measurement plan must minimize both indicators.

In order to validate MF, an existing measurement plan was considered, the plan was defined within an executed project, and then the proposed approach was applied to it. The validation was based on analysis of how the structure of the measurement plan would have been if the MF approach were used to design it. First the cross-validation was carried out. To this end, the comparison between the goal-view cross-reference tables of the old, Not Structured, measurement plan (NS-Plan) and the new, Structured plan (S-Plan) with MF are presented respectively in Tables 10.4 and 10.5.

As can be seen in Table 10.6, although the overall number of goals is greater in the S-Plan, the average interpretation complexity is less. This is due to the lower number of

TABLE 10.4. Cross Reference of NS-Plan

Goals	Process				Product			PM	FI
	Test Case Design	System Test	Defect Correction	Execution	Test of System	System Execution			
G_1		X	X	X	X				
G_2								X	
G_3					X	X			
G_4	X	X				X			
G_5					X	X			
G_6		X						X	X
G_7					X			X	X
G_8				X	X				

TABLE 10.5. Cross Reference of S-Plan

Goals	Process				Product			
	Test Case Design	System Test	Defect Correction	Execution	Test of System	System Execution	PM	FI
$G^{TestCaseDesign}$	X							
$G^{SystemTest}$		X						
$G^{DefectCorrec}$			X					
$G^{Exec, 1}$				X				
$G^{Exec, 2}$				X				
$G^{TestSyst}$					X			
$G^{SystExec, 1}$						X		
$G^{Syst.Exec, 2}$						X		
$G^{ProjectManag}$							X	
$G^{FitnessOfInv, 1}$								X
$G^{FitnessOfInv, 2}$								X

metrics for each goal, achieved as a consequence to applying the Multiview Framework to the NS-Plan. # Dependencies and Density of Dependencies are zero. So, this retrospective investigation is a first, positive validation of MF.

Project Investigations are carried out *in vivo* for developing, introducing, or evaluating new applications, methods, techniques, or tools. They are costly and have high risks because they require professional developers that have to work conformal to the investigation design; it requires that the investigation design be carried out respecting the conditions and collecting the measures required by the design. Thus, the time requested for carrying out the project is usually greater than expected. Also, worse performances than those expected without the treatment can occur. To summarize, this type of study is expensive and risky for product quality and for execution times of the experimental project. According to the execution conditions, a project investigation can be classified as appears in Table 10.7.

TABLE 10.6. Dependent Variable

Data Collected	NS-Plan	S-Plan
# Goals	8	11
# Measures	168	168
# Measures per goal (average)	32.75	20.18
# Dependencies	24	0
Density of dependencies	0.27	0

TABLE 10.7. Classification of Project Investigations

Number of Projects for Carrying Out the Investigation	Dependent Variables of the Investigation	
	Defined *a priori*	Defined During the Investigation
One	Investigation case	Explorative investigation
More than one	On-field investigation	On-field explorative investigation

In order to validate the effectiveness of a treatment, two projects can be compared: one applying the treatment and one as a control project carried out in ordinary conditions without applying any treatment. Seldom an enterprise is willing to carry out two projects with the same scope, considering that one is carried out solely for experimental purposes without production purposes. Also, it is difficult to produce the same context for two projects, one carried out with the treatment and one in normal conditions. In this way, the data collected on one of the projects is not comparable with the data collected on the second project. Often historical series such as $O_1, O_2, \ldots, O_n, X_1, O_1, O_2, \ldots, O_n, X_2, \ldots$ are used, where O_i are observations for collecting data and X_j are the treatments. The time between two successive observations is constant and is referred to as sample time (24). The statistical instruments used in this case also include historical series analysis. It must be verified that the trend of observations before the treatment is different from that after the treatment, and that the difference between trends is attributable to the treatment.

As example, we will consider the experience of a company that was facing the problem of reducing maintenance requests of its enterprise applications and reducing waiting times in order to improve the satisfaction rate. Details of the example are in reference 40.

The hypothesized theory is that a generalization of the application capabilities may satisfy a wider range of users. Thus, when new customers are added or the use of the application changes in time for existing customers, most of their requests are forecasted by the application, and consequently, the number of maintenance requests is reduced. If the application can be tailored to the customer requirements without modifying the software, it can be adapted in a short time. If the application has a modular structure and low complexity not damaged by previous maintenance requests, then maintenance times are expected to not worsen in time.

To fulfill such theory, a company developed a new application analysis model referring to an abstract user profile that generalizes actual customer requests; each customer requests a set of capabilities. Also, it developed a new design method combined with modular and parametric patterns able to assure software reuse, low complexity of the structure, and specialization of the application behavior by assigning values to a set of parameters. Finally, a maintenance process called Iterative Enhancement (IE) able to maintain the modularity and traceability of software was defined. To validate these technologies, they were applied to a company's applications in the Bank sector, but not to the Local Public Administration (LPA) or to the Health sectors. In the last two, the technologies remained the same. Data were collected on a trimester basis; the treatments in the

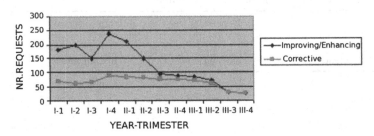

Figure 10.2. Trends of the maintenance interventions requested by Banks.

Bank sector began to have an effect in year 1; in year 2 the legacy applications of the same sector that renewed to the patterns and to the modular structures of the new applications were put into effect. Figures 10.2 and 10.3 show the maintenance requests in the sector being treated and in the two without the treatment. Figures 10.4 and 10.5 show the average waiting times for requests classified by the applications in the sectors.

Figure 10.2 shows that the treatments have relevant influence on Improving and Enhancement of software. In fact, the trend significantly decreases after the treatment. This result is confirmed in Fig. 10.3: in the two sectors that are not subject to the treatment, the trend of number of modifications is high and increases in time. There are no significant changes for corrective maintenance; thus, this treatment does not positively influence fault dissemination in programs.

Figure 10.4 points out that the waiting time for satisfying a request decreases after the treatment; once again, this is confirmed by observing that it decreases when modularization of programs is also extended to legacy systems. It is important to note that the trend in Fig. 10.4 tends toward an asymptote, while Fig. 10.5 tends to continuously increase. This indicates that the treatment of the IE reduces software degradation. Finally, note that for corrective maintenance the trend is decreasing for those applications that have been produced by processes subject to the treatment. This means that the obtained software product is more maintainable.

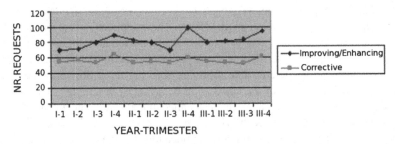

Figure 10.3. Trends of the maintenance interventions requested by the Local Public Administration and Organizations in the Health sector.

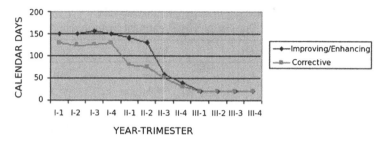

Figure 10.4. Trends of the waiting time for the maintenance interventions requested by Banks.

Experiment/Controlled Experiment is carried out *in vitro* (i.e., with controlled factors) for achieving new knowledge. In particular, the researcher wishes to prove that the treatment planned in the experiment has a cause relation on the dependent variable(s). The conceptual hypothesis to validate is divided into two operative ones:

- *Null Hypothesis, H_0*: specifies what the researcher hopes that is not true for the sample population. The intention is to reject this hypothesis with the highest possible significance;
- *Alternative Hypothesis, H_1/H_a*: specifies the assertion in favor of the rejected null hypothesis.

The experiment is characterized by a design that applies the treatments to the subjects in order to observe the effects. For example, if the factor is 1 (programming language) with two treatments (Java and C++) and *n* experimental subjects, each subject is subjected to each treatment in two experimental runs according to Table 10.8.

The assignment of each subject to a combination of the two runs is random, so the experimental subjects are equally distributed between the two treatments.

When the number of factors and the number of levels for each factor lead to a high number of combinations, the experimental project is designed with a reduced factorial technique. Table 10.9 shows an example with three factors (maintenance method,

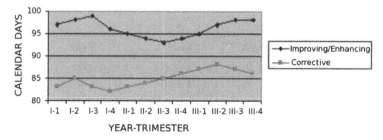

Figure 10.5. Trends of the waiting time for the maintenance interventions requested by the Local Public Administration and Organizations in the Health sector.

TABLE 10.8. Example of Experimental Subjects
Distribution in a One-Factor Two-Treatment Investigation

Experimental Subjects	Run1	Run2
S_1	C++	Java
S_2	Java	C++
S_3	Java	C++
S_4	C++	Java
. . .	. . .	. . .
S_n	Java	C++

language, type of maintenance), each with two possible levels Quick Fix (Q.F.) and Iterative Enhancement (I.E.), Java and C++, Corrective (Cor) and Evolutional (Ev) maintenance.

There are a number of different statistical tests described in the literature that can be used to evaluate the outcome of an experiment. Testing hypothesis involves different risks that are referred to as Type I Error and Type II Error. A *Type I Error* occurs when a statistical test has indicated a pattern relationship even if there actually is no pattern: reject H_0 when H_0 is true. A *Type II Error* occurs when a statistical test has not indicated a pattern relationship even if there actually is a pattern: Do not reject H_0 when H_0 is false. For completeness, the *Power* of a statistical test is the probability that the test rejects H_0 when H_0 is false. It is also the complement to 1 of the probability of Type II Error.

All statistical tests divide the sample space into two complementary parts: an area for accepting H_0 and an area for rejecting H_0. In an experiment, if the statistical value of test, falls in the first area, the null hypothesis is accepted; if it falls in the second area, the null hypothesis is rejected in favor of the acceptance of the alternative hypothesis. All the statistical tests divide the space so that the first area is wider than the second in order to avoid erroneous conclusions—that is, accepting the H_1 hypothesis when it is

TABLE 10.9. Example of Experimental Subject
Distribution in a Three-Factor (Each with Two Treatments)
Investigation

Experimental Subject	Run1	Run2
S_1	I.E., Java, Cor	Q.F., C++, Ev
S_2	Q.F., J, Cor	I.E.; C++, Ev
S_3	I.E.; C++, Ev	Q.F., J, Cor
S_4	Q.F., C++, Cor	I.E., Java, Ev
. . .	. . .	. . .
S_n	Q.F., Java, Cor	I.E., C++, Ev

actually not true (24, 25, 44). In other words, when a test is carried out, it is in many cases possible to calculate the lowest possible significance of rejecting the null hypothesis: the *p-value*. When the *p*-value is not grater then 0.05, H_0 is rejected; the lower the *p*-value, the more significant the rejection.

Statistics offers many types of tests. They can be classified into parametric and nonparametric. *Parametric tests* are based on a model that involves a specific distribution. *Nonparametric tests* do not make the same type of assumptions concerning the distribution of parameters. Table 10.10 is an overview of parametric or nonparametric tests for different experiment designs; for further details refer to references (24, 25), and (44).

As an example, we present an overview of a controlled experiment on the comprehensibility and efficiency of a Measurement Plan Design produced using MF illustrated earlier in this chapter. For further information, interested readers can refer to reference 7. The context of the experiment is a Software Engineering course at the University of Bari. Two research goals were formulated to assess, respectively, efficiency and comprehensibility of the S-Plan compared to the NS-Plan:

H_0^{RG1}: There is no difference in efficiency (effort spent for interpretation) between interpretations made in the S-Plan and the NS-Plan.

H_1^{RG1}: There is difference in efficiency between the S-Plan and the NS-Plan.

H_0^{RG2}: There is difference in comprehensibility (error proneness of interpretation) between the S- and the NS-Plan.

H_1^{RG2}: There is no difference in comprehensibility between the S-Plan and the NS-Plan.

The dependent variables are: *effort spent*, i.e. the difference between the start and end time for carrying out the interpretation of the entire measurement plan (S-Plan or NS-Plan); *error proneness*, i.e. number of incorrect conclusions made in interpreting the goals of the measurement plan (S-Plan or NS-Plan). The experimental subjects were graduate students taking the software engineering course. The sample was made up of a total of 34 subjects randomly assigned to two equal groups of 17 persons, identified as "Group A" and "Group B." All of the students were trained in the same manner, therefore they had the same experience and knowledge. The experiment design was one

TABLE 10.10. Overview of Statistical Tests

Design	Parametric	Nonparametric
One factor, one treatment		Chi-2 Binomial Test
One factor, two treatments, completely randomized design	*t*-Test *F*-Test	Mann–Whitney Chi-2
One factor, more than two treatments	ANOVA	Kruskal–Waills Chi-2
More than one factor	ANOVA	

TABLE 10.11. Experiment Design

Group/Run	RUN 1	RUN 2
Group A	S-GQM	NS-GQM
Group B	NS-GQM	S-GQM

factor (Plan quality model), two treatments (NS-Plan and S-Plan), organized in two experimental runs (Run1 and Run2) carried out in two days, described in Table 10.11.

Tables 10.12 and 10.13 summarize the results that validate the efficacy and effectiveness of the measurement plans through MF.

10.2.3. Validity Risks and Threats

With reference to Fig. 10.1 from the theory to observation or vice versa, the researcher has to do many steps, one for each arrow; in each step there are risks about the validity of results. As in reference 44, some details for a list of essential risks are presented. They can be further considered in reference 16.

Conclusion Validity refers to the relationship between the treatment and the outcome. The risk is that the researchers do not draw the correct conclusion about relations between the treatment and the outcome of an experiment. Some details on the risks belonging to this class are:

- *Low Statistical Power*: The test may reveal a pattern in the data that is not true.
- *Violated Assumption of Statistical Test*: Use of a statistical test on data lacking the characteristics that assure a proper execution.
- *Reliability of Measures*: Bad instrumentation or bad instrument layout can produce bad data.
- *Reliability of Treatment Implementation*: The implementation of a treatment is not similar between different persons or occasions.
- *Random Elements in Experimental Setting*: External elements (event or situations) can disturb the results.
- *Random Heterogeneity of Subjects*: The results are more dependent upon individual differences than upon the treatments.

TABLE 10.12. *p*-Level Values of the Mann–Whitney Test for Effort

Experimental Run	*p*-Value Effort	Results
Run 1 (Group A vs. Group B)	0.00001	Reject H_0^{RG1} and accept H_1^{RG1}
Run 2 (Group A vs. Group B)	0.00002	Reject H_0^{RG1} and accept H_1^{RG1}

TABLE 10.13. p-Level Values of the Mann–Whitney U
Test for Error Proneness

Experimental Run	p-Value Error Proneness	Results
Run 1 (Group A vs. Group B)	0.00721	Reject H_0^{RG2} and accept H_1^{RG2}
Run 2 (Group A vs. Group B)	0.04938	Reject H_0^{RG2} and accept H_1^{RG2}

Internal Validity is also concerned with the relationship between treatment and outcome. The risk is that the results may indicate a casual relationship, although there is none. In this case, the risk is better called threat. Technically, a *threat* is an event that interferes with the effects of the treatment and generates a cause–effect relation that actually does not exist. In the following, some details on threats belonging to this class are presented:

- *History* may occur when many treatments are applied to the same subject, because in a treatment the subject's behavior is impacted by the effect of previous treatments or by the combination of treatments.
- *Maturation* may occur when the subject can modify his/her behavior as the time passes. Typically they are tiredness, boredom, or learning. This risk is complex to manage because different subjects mature at different speed.
- *Testing* may be verified when many tests are done with the same subjects because subjects modify their behavior since they know how the test is performed. It is a sort of maturation.
- *Instrumentation* is the impact that the deliverables and the tools used during the investigation can have.
- *Selection* is the impact of natural variation on human performance and how results can be impacted by the selection rule of subjects. It may be risky to select volunteers or select the top ten of a previous experiment or the best expert in a discipline.
- *Mortality* may occur when some subjects drop out from the experiment because they can be representative for the experimental sample.
- *Diffusion or imitation* occurs when a control group learns or imitates the behavior of the group in the study.
- *Compensatory rivalry* may occur when a subject tests a less desirable treatment because he/she is motivated to reduce or reverse the expected outcome.
- *Resentful demoralization* that is the opposite of the previous. A subject that tests less desirable treatments may give up and not perform as good as he/she generally does.

Construct Validity is concerned with the relationship between theory and observation. The risk refers to the extent to which the experiment setting actually reflects the construct under investigation. The risks are as follows: The treatment does not reflect the cause construct well, or the outcome does not reflect the effect construct well. It is generated by weaknesses in the statistical analysis that lead to the cause–effect relation between treatment and results. In the following, some details on threats belonging to this class are illustrated:

- *Inadequate preoperational explication of construct* may be generated when the constructs are not sufficiently defined because they are translated in not efficacious measures and treatments.
- *Mono bias* may be generated when the study has only one independent variable, one case, one subject, one treatment, or one measure. In such case, the investigation may underrepresent the construct because it is not possible to cross-check an independent variable, case, subject, treatment, or measure against each other.
- *Confounding factors with the levels of factors* may be generated when a factor (i.e., experience) does not have the significant number of levels because the effect of the treatments can be revealed by different levels of a factor. For example, relevant difference in experience is between 2 and 3 years, or between 3 or 6 years; while 4 or 5 years of experience do not have a relevant effect, so the levels of experience must be 2, 3, 6, or more years. It would be incorrect to define two levels: less than or equal to 2, greater than 3.

External Validity is concerned with generalization. The risks are: wrong experimental subject, wrong environment and performances, and wrong timing so that the results are affected from changed characteristics of the original experiment. Following are some details on threats belonging to this class:

- *Population* may be generated when the subjects selected for replications are not representative of the population. Thus, it is not possible to generalize the investigation results.
- *Setting* may be generated when the setting or material used in replications are not representative of the context, making it senseless to generalize results.
- *Period* may be generated when the results of a study are biased by the specific period of operation.

10.2.4. Guidelines for Experiments

When the experimental design is poor, conclusions are not reliable and they most likely do not abstract from experimental data. Many researchers have faced this problem with the aim of producing guidelines for improving design and execution of an experiment (1–3, 13, 18, 19, 23, 28, 34, 37, 43). It is useful to analyze some critical aspects of an experiment and give some suggestions for each of them. The main sources of the following remarks are reference 28 and the author's experience.

The *Experiment Context* must be defined *a priori* and, in particular, the entities involved, the attributes, and the measures to carry out for formalizing the context characterization must be identified. For example, the factors that can be characterized are: the environment where the project is carried out (in house; independent software house; university work groups, ...); the competences and the experiences of involved personnel; the type of software used (design tools, compilers, test tools, ...), and the software process used (standard development process for an enterprise, quality assurance process, configuration process, ...). Unfortunately, in software processes many context variables are complex to define. Much research must be done to improve our definition capabilities. A relevant example, in this context, is reported by Kitchenham et al. (27), which outlines an ontology for defining context characterization factors of software maintenance.

The research/investigation hypothesis to test must be clearly defined *a priori*. More precisely, the hypothesis must be connected to an underlying theory that must be validated. When this traceability does not exist, the result of the investigation does not contribute to extend the current body of knowledge. In software engineering, results of experiments that aim to prove a same hypotheses are often contradictory. If hypothesis and theory are not traceable, it is difficult to explain the results and their contradictions, as well as use them. The hypotheses we refer to are assertions (statements) that must be proven through an experiment, previously indicated with H_0/H_1. In order to avoid confusion, some authors refer to them as *research/investigation questions* or *research/investigation goals* rather than hypotheses. For example, an experiment willing to prove the following assertion would be senseless: The cyclomatic number of a module is related to the number of faults found. Some experiments have pointed out that the number of faults reduces as the cyclomatic number increases and that the two variables are not correlated. Other experiments have shown how the number of faults decreases with a relevant correlation among the two variables, as the cyclomatic number decreases. To explain this last finding, it has been hypothesized that when the cyclomatic number is high, the developers pay more attention to writing code, and therefore they introduce less faults. This knowledge is not supported by empirical evidence in software engineering development. A better explanation can be given if we refer to Parnas' theory; the correlation between cyclomatic complexity of a module and the identified faults should be related to the efficacy of the learning effort that the developer must sustain to understand the module content and its behavior.

The *experiment design* should be defined so that experimental subjects and instruments are representative of the investigation context. Also, it must define *a priori* how the experimental subjects will be selected and how they will be subject to each treatment. The schema resulting from the design must either eliminate, as much as possible, the causes that may lead to threats of experimental results or forecast how to measure their effect on the results. In defining the experimental design, it must be clear if differences between *experimental subject* and *experimental unit* exist. If so, the two concepts must be traced with one another. Often the experimenter confuses them, so, for example, if questionnaires are to be distributed, the experimental design must point out that the experimental subjects are those answering the questionnaires, while the experimental units are the enterprises where the interviewees worked. Each unit contains many subjects. When designing an experiment, it is useful to adopt *schemas* known in literature that have been adopted and are supported by evidence. This will avoid useless risks and reduce threats to validity of results. Also, the design must foresee appropriate *control levels* to prevent expectations of participants and experimenter from influencing the results in any way. In an experiment the dependent variables must clearly be defined and motivated, along with how to analyze the corresponding data. Also, the scope of dependent variables and the statistical analyses must be appropriate and avoid conceptual conflicts; otherwise interpretation of results may lead to confusion. Finally, when designing an experiment, it is better to avoid controlling subjects' behavior. More precisely, experimental subjects must not have the feeling of being observed or controlled, especially in an investigation project. In this case the subjects may be influenced in their behavior, knowing that they are controlled and would therefore act differently than in normal conditions. So, for example, it is important to not modify the measures that the enterprise is familiar to and collects on a regular basis. It is recommended to use measures that can be collected on products without developers knowing about it, or on support processes able to provide information on the investigated ones (8). However, it is not the case to consider experimental results as a technique for evaluating developer performances.

The *data* to *collect* must be preferably *objective* and formally defined. Subjective data must be rigorously defined in order to reduce the degrees of freedom of the measurer. Furthermore, collection and control modalities should also be rigorously defined.

Presentation and interpretation of results must outline how the researcher has drawn conclusions and allow other interested readers to verify them. Reference 28 explicates guidelines for producing reports on experiment results and lists many references that detail the issues faced in the publication. Once an experiment is concluded, appropriate documentation that describes the experiment should be produced so it can be transferred to other researchers. To this intent, literature presents various proposals (26, 30). For completeness, some brief guidelines for producing documentation that make up an *investigation package* are listed:

- Detailed description of the *treatments*, including all types of instructions and tools that support the execution.
- The *experimental objects* the treatments are applied to, for example code, software design, or specifications.
- *Instructions* for describing the exact behavior of the actors involved in the investigation, including the researchers.
- *Details of the* pilot *studies or* of the trial *experiments*.
- *Mechanisms for collecting and controlling experimental data*, both automated and manual.
- *Teaching materials* for preparing experimental subjects to the investigation.
- *Raw data* collected in the original experiment, when possible.
- *Description*, measures, and manners for collecting competences and capabilities of subjects, and definition of the population characteristics, the selected subjects must belong to.

- *Replication power*, according to the flaws identified in the original experiment and in other replications, in terms of number and types of subjects, data control, or statistical analysis to carry out on collected data.
- *Rationale for decision making* during design and execution of the experiment, in order to avoid that replications miss out on important aspects.
- *Cost estimation* of the investigation.
- *Cost–benefit analysis* concerning the application of results according to their value for stakeholders.

10.3. EMPIRICAL STUDIES FOR SOFTWARE ENGINEERING SCIENCE

10.3.1. Overview

EI represents an important contribution for consolidating software engineering as a science. In fact, it is used in all sciences, from natural to engineering and social. Software Engineering (33) develops from an observed problem that leads to either a negative effect or a nondesired effect and follows two alternative paths each carried out by researchers. In the first case (Fig. 10.6) the researcher defines a theory, makes it operative through methods, processes, and techniques described as *innovative technologies*, and investigates them to verify whether they solve the problem. If so, the theory and the technologies are accepted, otherwise the theory and/or the technologies are

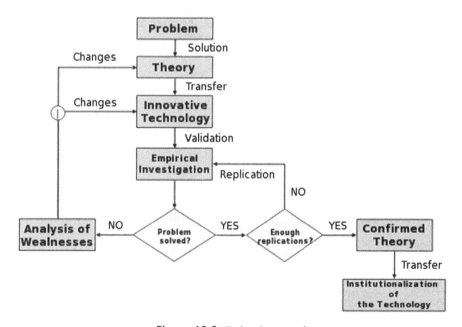

Figure 10.6. Technology pool.

modified and experimentation goes on. Alternatively (Fig. 10.7) the researcher defines new innovative technologies along with the conjecture that the new technologies are effective for solving a problem. Following to experimentation in case of positive results, the technologies are accepted and experimentation results are abstracted in a theory. Otherwise, they are modified and investigated again. For example: Information hiding is based on a theory but EI is necessary for validating the technologies that make it operational in software development processes; object-oriented paradigm is successfully used as a technology that allows us to develop higher-quality software compared to other paradigms. Once again, empirical validation on the efficacy of the OO paradigm is poor as well as the abstracting theory, which is still missing.

Software engineering along with its practices is human centered. Thus, its efficacy depends on complex factors such as motivation and experience. Effectiveness of practices is based on these factors, which are difficult to comprehend and control. Consequently, the relation between their application and the effect of product and process innovation cannot be deterministic. Such relations can be evaluated empirically (20). The results of an EI can depend on the behavior of experimental subjects, the various characteristics that the same problem can assume in different contexts and from various variables, often tacit and uncontrollable.

The above aspects of EI point out the need for *replication*. So, coherently with the modern scientific ideology, software engineering also requires that experimental results be replicable by external parts. In reference 29 the authors point out that "the use of precise repeatable experiments is the hallmark of a mature scientific or engineering discipline." A replication in software engineering, on one hand, aims at assuring that the relation between innovation, the problem it solves, and the theory that sustains such relation are generally valid; on the other hand, it aims to generalize knowledge that takes into account the large variability of explicit and tacit experimental conditions.

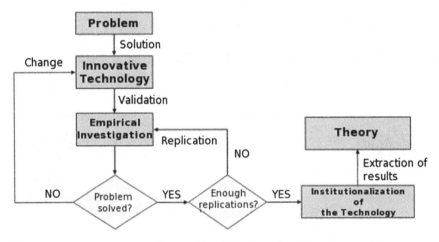

Figure 10.7. Theory pool.

10.3.2. Replication of Empirical Investigation

In an executed investigation, carried out by others, it is important to verify that it is "safe-guard against unintentional error or deception" (31). A replication can help convince potential stakeholders of the fact that adopting an innovation that supports a theory is effective. A new experimental result can be interesting and exciting, although the same result achieved in many occasions is even more convincing and therefore more accepted. Replicated investigations, carried out in different contexts, that confirm the results of the original study and the underlying theory are a manner for collecting such a body of evidence.

In replications, the researcher must control the experimental risks of validity. In fact, many times the result of a replication can be different from the original experiment due to lack of control on some risks. For example, Shneidemann et al. (39) in an experiment on usefulness of flow charts concluded that flow charts were not useful for representing and algorithm. The replication of this experiment carried out by Scanlan (38) identified a flaw in the previous experiment: Time given to subjects was not a variable of the original experiment. They could take all the time they considered necessary, whatever representation they used. In reference 38 the author shows that the flow chart representation saved time. This was proven because the time assigned was controlled. Thus, given the same time interval, the subjects using the flow chart for algorithm description obtained more complete results than with any other technique. In this case, the original experiment was impacted by a construct validity risk.

In replications, it is important that researchers quantify the costs and benefits according to the data collection instruments. These are important for producing a cost–benefit analysis of the investigation that can be useful for obtaining commitment on behalf of other experimental units willing to replicate the investigation. Note that a replication produces a body of knowledge on the costs and benefits and, consequently, increases its reliability and becomes a convincing factor for further replications.

Unfortunately, there are many aspects that make it difficult to reproduce the same conditions of the original study in a replication—that is, to carry out a *strict replication*. First, the variables that describe the context of an investigation are many, as mentioned in previous paragraphs. They can change due to time, if the replication is carried out in the same context, or due to changes in the context itself. Second, the replication of an investigation is usually carried out with different experimental subjects than the original or previous replications. So, a replication can come to conclusions that differ from the ones achieved in the original investigation and in other replications, due to diversities in competences and experiences of subjects and not to the treatment itself. For example, consider that a developer, along with his/her experience, can improve productivity up to six times. If the experimental subjects of the replication are more expert than the ones of the original investigation, the observed results may be positive, but their experience can have influenced the results more than the treatment. This second aspect adds further difficulty to a strict replication: subjects of the replication may have different expectations than the subjects involved in the original investigation. Such difference in expectations can affect results.

A replication having results that conform to the preliminary investigation aims to confirm the original findings. If the original study generates positive results with respect to a theory, its replication enforces the success; if the original study comes to negative conclusions, the replication confirms the failure. Instead, a replication that achieves results discordant from the original study motivates a further analysis aiming to identify flaws in the design and execution of the experiment.

In order for a strict replication to be considered as part of a so-called *investigation battery* (35), an appropriate package documentation describing the original experiment must be produced. The investigation package assures an adequate accuracy of the replication. Thus, when one or more replications lead to results that deny cause–effect relations validated in an original experiment, the researchers can adopt either of two initiatives. In the first case, if the efficacy of the investigated innovation is supported by heuristics, the theory it refers to must be enforced before it can be accepted. Enforcing the theory means modifying the investigation goals, the cause-construct, the effect-construct, or all of them. Consequently, the variables and the design of the original investigation are changed. After the modification the original experiment is carried out again; if the results conform to the experimenter's expectations, the investigation is repeated to achieve external validity. In the second initiative, in case of an innovation that has not proven its efficacy, the researcher should understand if the innovation or the theory must be modified according to the results obtained in the experiment and its replications. In each case, the original investigation has to be modified and executed again. Once successful results are achieved, it must be replicated for external validity. In the first case the theory is pooled by the innovation, whereas in the second case the innovation is pooled by the theory.

For completeness, it is important to define the number of ideal replications for creating an appropriate body of evidence. In case of a controlled experiment, we can refer to statistical factors (25). For all other types of investigations, a useful guideline for defining the appropriate number of replications is the *importance* attributed to an investigation. The original investigation has relevant importance; the second replication has even more relevance because it confirms the findings of the original study; the third is important for enforcing the body of evidence. As the body of evidence becomes stronger, the importance of the replications reduces. When the body of evidence is considered operatively acceptable, the importance of the replications is further reduced, so they are no longer necessary.

10.3.3. Empirical Investigations for Generating Knowledge

The actual reuse of empirical results requires they be abstracted in knowledge and packaged in an understandable format by those interested in the results. Packaged knowledge must be reusable without of the support of the researcher that produced it. Also, it must be general in order to be applied in different contexts and at the same time be tailored to the specific context of use (17). To achieve this aim, the components of the package, specified in the previous section, must be produced. More precisely, the package should contain all the necessary information for evaluating how similar or different the replicating context is to the original one.

The above considerations attribute the role of *in vivo* investigations to reuse of empirical results that continuously replicate the original experiment and generate the knowledge for improving and extending the theory confirmed by the original study and by its body of evidence. For this scope, Basili (10, 11) provides an organizational schema for collecting experiences on reuse of empirical results, for analyzing them and generalizing the knowledge contained. This schema is known as *Experience Factory (EF)*. The EF collects experiences and empirical validations on data related to development processes in various contexts: costs, benefits, risks, and improvement initiatives. For clearness, the EF shown in Fig. 10.8 is briefly described. Further details can be found in references 10 and 11 even though the schema is slightly different. Once a project begins, goals are defined; also, resources and the project context are characterized. This information allows us to extract existing *Experience Packages* from the *Experience Base*, which are explicated in *products, lessons learned*, and *models*. Either with or without support, the Project Manager defines the process he/ she intends to use and derives the project execution plans. During project execution, data collected by the *analyzer* are registered in the project database. They are synthesized in order to search for other experience packages that can improve project execution with respect to the project goals. At the end of the project, the data collected are compared to those of existing experience packages and formalized to provide further validation to the package or to extend their content. Following a project, the new empirical evidences can be integrated with the ones existing in the experience base and eventually lead to generalization of knowledge. In this way the experience base represents assets of knowledge to diffuse and socialize.

In order to abstract knowledge for empirical results, it is possible to consider the replications that make up the so-called *Families of Experiments* (12). Each experiment in the family replicates other experiments in the same family, changing the context settings. This requires a framework that explicates the various models used in the investigations of the family, able to document the key decisions made during design. The framework must allow us to identify the pivot of an investigation that should remain invariant together with the factors that vary in each study of the family so that the

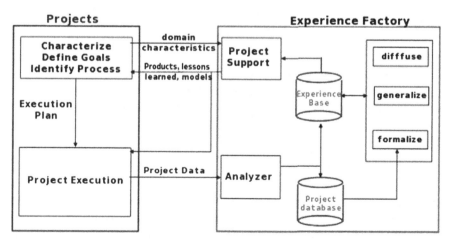

Figure 10.8. Experience factory.

results can be generalized in a unifying theory that explains all the research goals of the experiments.

The framework this chapter refers to is the Goal Question Metrics (GQM) proposed by Basili and Rombach (9) and adapted for rigorously defining a research goal. In the following the details of the adapted framework, following the improvements made by the author, are described.

The research goal is defined through five parameters:

1. *Object of Study*: Process, product, or any other experience model.
2. *Purpose*: To characterize/explore (what is?), evaluate (is it good?), predict (can I estimate something in the future?), control (can I manipulate events?), improve (can I improve events?).
3. *Focus*: Model aimed at viewing the aspect of the object of study that is of interest—for example, effect on reliability of a product, on defect detention/prevention, and on capability of the process/accuracy of the cost model.
4. *Point of view*: What aspect of the effect do we intend capturing? For example, the point of view of the researcher who is trying to gain some knowledge about the focus.
5. *Context*: Models aimed at describing the environment in which the measurement is taken; (e.g., students/practitioners, novice/experts, *in vivo/in vitro*); projects to execute during the investigation/already executed projects.

To further clarify the parameters of the research goal, the values they assume in the investigation should be declared. The *object of study* may be a process that requires technical competences for carrying out specific tasks (technique), or a process that describes how to manage the application of techniques for achieving a goal (method), or processes that describe the entire development of software (lifecycle). The *purpose* of the investigation is commonly to *evaluate* something. The researcher tends to study a technology for evaluating its effect on a development phase. The most frequent viewpoints are those of the researcher or knowledge-builder. Project investigations usually also include the manager's viewpoint, interested in evaluating the effects of a technology on effort, schedule, and return of investments. When the object of study is a technology, the *focus* most likely evaluates the effect of the technology on one or more software components, whether they be process, product, or developers. The *context* includes many environmental factors. The studies can be carried out on students or experts, with or without time constraints, in well-known or yet to discover application domains.

A goal of an investigation can include multiple factors; in this case a distinct study should be designed for each combination of values that the factors can assume. Furthermore, each study will be related to a specific goal. Given this scenario, the researcher's task is to collect the results of each study and generalize them in an assertion that will make up the knowledge extracted from the family of experiments.

An example of family is provided: *Object of study* consists of two maintenance paradigms (Quick Fix (QF) and Iterative Enhancement (IE)); the *purpose* is to evaluate

QF vs. IE, with *focus* of evaluating the influence of the methods on a set of character-istics $\{Q_1, Q_2, Q_3, Q_4\}$, from the viewpoint of the process efficacy on behalf of the developer in a set of contexts $\{C_x\}$. C_x is the variable that make the previous goal a family of goals. At this point, the values they can assume must be explicated.

Q_1: *Correctness*
Modified Component Set: MCS
Expected Component Set: ECS
Correct Component Set: CCS
Correctness: $COR = \#(CCS \cap ECS)/\#ECS$

Q_2: *Completeness*
Completeness: $COM = \#(MCS \cap ECS)/\#ECS$

Q_3: *Modification Timeliness*
Time for designing a modification: T_{des}
Time for coding the designed modification: T_{cod}
Time for carrying out the maintenance: $T = T_{des} + T_{cod}$

Q_4: *Traceability*
\# experimental subjects that have safeguarded traceability: N_s
\# experimental subjects: N
Traceability: $TR = N_s/N * 100$

C_1: *University Students* (Un.St.) that manage an *Impact of Modification Low*
C_2: *University Students* that manage an *Impact of Modification High*
C_3: *Professionals* (Prof) that manage an *Impact of Modification Low*
C_4: *Professionals* that manage an *Impact of Modification High*

For space reasons, descriptions of the experiment process and execution will not be provided. Table 10.14 reports a summary of the results. For clearness, given a specific Paradigm P_i, a "+" sign before the paradigm name means that it gives more value than its competitor; a "++" sign indicates a significant increase of value compared to the competitor paradigm investigated in the study.

To summarize, the efficiency of each maintenance paradigm is expressed by T, and the effectiveness is expressed by the set of other quality parameters measured. So, the knowledge that can be abstracted from the analysis of results reported in Table 10.14 is the following: IE is more efficient than QF; IE is generally more effective than QF

TABLE 10.14. Summary of Experiment Results

Experiment Site	Number of Replications	Context		COR	COM	T	TR
		Expertise	Impact of Modification				
Un. Bari	3	Un. St.	Low	+IE	+IE	+QF	+IE
Un. Bari	3	Un. St.	High	+IE	+IE	+IE	++IE
P.A.	1	Prof	Low	+IE	++IE	+Q.F.	+IE
P.A.	1	Prof	High	+IE	++IE	+IE.	++IE

which gains in efficiency compared to IE only for small modifications. However, it has large risks of traceability and therefore most likely leads to a qualitative decrease of the software application. This empirical knowledge denies previous heuristics that, according to developers, QF is more efficient than IE. Results also point out that the heuristic neglects the low efficiency of QF for what concerns quality assurance of the software system. Furthermore, experience point out that the maintenance paradigm is more efficient with IE on professionals than with students. Finally, the heuristic stating that QF is more efficient is verified only when the modification impact is low.

10.4. EMPIRICAL INVESTIGATION FOR INNOVATION ACCEPTANCE

Being software engineering human-centered, an innovation can be introduced and diffused in real processes if it is accepted by the developers involved in the processes. The following theory can be conjectured: Knowledge on the use and in the advantages that an innovation can bring to software development is necessary conditions, although not sufficient, for the innovation to be accepted on behalf of developers because it depends on social and economic factors of the experimentation. Acceptance is the basic factor for socializing the innovation and therefore acquiring it. In order to carry out the cause construct of the previous theory, a useful treatment is to involve the developers that must acquire the innovation as experimental subjects. The expected outcome is that the participants internalize the new knowledge, and then they socialize it and favor its diffusion and institutionalization.

The author has used his experience to carry out EI in enterprises for verifying the previous theory. In this chapter, for space reasons, the details have not been reported. However, interested readers can refer to references 4 and 41 as references on acquired experience that can be useful to other researchers either for selecting the most appropriate investigation or for emphasizing the previous theory.

Each analyzed study has been classified in one of the listed categories and rated with respect to organizational and technical factors, described in Table 10.15, on an ordinal scale (H = high, L = low). Table 10.16 reports the results of the experimentations. Some considerations can be made.

In a *Retrospective investigation*, developers that have participated in executed projects are involved as unaware experimental subjects. In this sense, they can learn and

TABLE 10.15. Characterizing Factors

Parameters for Organizational Factor	Investment	Investment made by the organization for introducing the innovation	High (H) when technology transfer occurs in more than 6 months. It is difficult to forecast the impacts of the innovation on the organization's production processes.
	ROI	Return on investments obtained by the organization after introducing the innovation	High (H) when it is at least three times the investment in two years' time.
	MANAG Imp	Improvement perceived by the management	Subjective evaluation expressed by personal considerations and answers to interviews and questionnaires.
Parameters for Technical Factor	DEV_Imp	Improvement perceived by the technical staff using the new technology	Subjective evaluation expressed by personal considerations and answers to interviews and questionnaires.
	Diff_QM_Def	Difficulty encountered by innovators for defining the quality model used to evaluated innovation efficacy and effectiveness	High (H) when at least three major releases of the quality model were produced during the investigation before obtaining a final version.
	Diff_QM_Acc	Difficulty encountered by stakeholders in accepting the quality model	High (H) when at least three other meetings were requested by stakeholders for further explanations on the quality model and its application.

share only the validity of measures used and their interpretations; that is, they perceive the benefits of the innovation. They are not involved in using the innovation. Thus, one of the primary conditions for acceptance is missing. This strategy of investigation, according to the previously mentioned theory, does not impose conditions for accepting an innovation. Empirical experience confirms this deduction: Developers, including the ones that executed the projects, do not internalize the innovation.

TABLE 10.16. Ranking of Parameters in the Different Investigations

Characteristics	Retrospective Investigation		Pilot Case Study		Explorative Case Study		Field Study		Controlled Experiment	
			CASE STUDY						EXPERIMENT	
Experimental Units	ITALIAN BANK—X	ITALIAN BANK—Y	ITALIAN BANK—Y	FRENCH BANK	PUBLIC ADMIN.	ITALIAN SME-Z	ITALIAN SME-W	MULTINAT ENT.	UNIV & SME	UNIV
Investment	L	L	H	H	H	H	H	H	L	L
ROI	L	L	H	H	L	H	H	H	L	–
MANAG Imp	H	H	H	H	H	H	H	H	L	L
DEV Imp	–	–	L	L	L	H	H	H	L	L
Diff_QM_Def	L	L	H	H	H	L	L	L	H	H
Dif_QM_Acc	H	H	H	H	H	H	H	H	L	L

Note: H, high; L, low.

Project Investigation is evaluated according to the type of investigation. In the *Investigation Case*, the developer learns to use the innovation but is seldom convinced of its benefits, even though he/she agrees on the measures used and the interpretations given. According to the author, this is because the developer sees the experiment design as imposed from external parts and does not feel involved. An *on-field investigation* has a variant: Usually the experimental project is validated during the experimentation and involves developers that understand the results and internalize the technologies. An *Explorative Investigation* achieves the same results as the investigation case, with the difference that the experimental subject is observed and not involved. Therefore the experimented innovation seems even more extraneous to the subject. The *on-field explorative investigation* does not achieve the same effects as the on-field investigation, because subjects are observed and not involved.

In an *experiment*, if developers are appropriately motivated and impressed from the results, they foresee the benefits of the innovation. Given the short period of the experiment, developers usually do not adequately interiorize the innovation. According to the previous hypothesis, this type of investigation does not favor institutionalization of an innovation.

10.5. BUILDING COMPETENCE THROUGH EMPIRICAL INVESTIGATION

10.5.1. Overview

The importance of EI as a practice to enforce the body of knowledge in software engineering is commonly acknowledged. In particular, EI stimulates the growth of knowledge and the development of abilities required in practical cases, in order to confirm known models. Moreover, EI points out weaknesses of previous knowledge, stimulates new knowledge, and highlights the problems that arise in transforming the state-of-the-art in state-of-the-practice. Also, it validates approaches for such transformation. In the following the author briefly illustrates the competences gained in Software Extraordinary Maintenance processes in about 10 years of Empirical Investigations in SERLAB; more details are in reference 6.

For the sake of clarity, some terms used in the following are defined. *Competence* is defined as the *knowledge* and *abilities* that allow to manage available resources in order to systematically reach a predefined goal. According to reference 36, knowledge is obtained through the understanding of information, relationships among them, and their classification. We define ability as the application of knowledge to practical cases aimed at solving a task in a real environment.

The current survey of EI deals with Extraordinary Maintenance (EM). *Ordinary Maintenance* refers to interventions aimed at overcoming a behavior that is not compliant with the requirements, or aimed at making the system adequate to the application and technological domain evolution. It has been empirically proven by Lehman (21, 22) that ordinary maintenance injects degradation in system quality, maintenance becomes more onerous, and the software ages. *Extraordinary Maintenance* refers to interventions aimed at slowing down the aging and therefore preserving the economical value.

The literature provides more processes than those discussed in the following analysis. They require higher competences, although they are part of our experience. Further detail is given here:

- *Reverse Engineering* (RE), which allows us to obtain a description of a system at a higher abstraction level starting from a description given at a lower one (15).
- *Reengineering*, which allows us to obtain a new form of some artefacts, with an improved quality and the consequent improvement of their implementation (15).
- *Restoration* is added to the previous list through our experiences; it is a variant of the restructuring process that consists of restructuring the source code in order to obtain a new version satisfying the principle of structured programming based only on the structural features of code. The variant consists of also taking into account the meaning of the restructured code (41, 42).

The capabilities of the previous processes are further referred to in reference 38, while the experiences developed in industrial projects usually tempt us to answer the following questions:

Q1: When should each process be used?
Q2: Why should a certain process be used?

For improving acceptance of EM processes, further questions are usually the following:

Q3: Which are the costs and benefits related to use of the process?
Q4: Which risks are involved and how are they mitigated?

They make up a knowledge package extracted from data analysis and generalization of results collected during the EM on a system, which for convenience we will call *Italian Bank—X* (Table 10.16), running for an Italian Bank (42). All the experimental data presented in this and the next section refer to the bank's information system, except for when it is explicitly declared. They are detailed in reference 14.

The type of EI that produced the data of this and the next section consisted of a Retrospective Investigation carried out on data collected during an EM of the previously mentioned information system. The results of the investigation require further validation through replications of analogous experiments. Thus they are expressed as lessons learned.

10.5.2. Aging Symptoms

To establish the conditions for which EM processes are required, it is necessary to measure the software qualities that reveal when this is necessary. The experience of SERLAB in EM suggests that we express such quality through indicators, identified as *aging symptoms*. What follows is a nonexhaustive list that may be extended following other EIs.

Pollution. Many components of the system, both data and functions, are included in the software, although useless for the system purposes. This symptom makes maintenance activities more difficult and costly by introducing uncertainty in identifying the components impacted by a modification. Consequently, maintenance is less reliable. The metrics used for this indicator are as follows:

- *Duplicated programs*: programs that are present multiple times with different identifiers in the program libraries of the software system.
- *Unused programs*: programs in the software system libraries whose results are no longer used by users of the system.
- *Program in Libraries*: the programs belonging to the components library of a system.

Embedded Knowledge. The knowledge of the application domain is embedded within programs, as an effect of past maintenance. It emerges with the documentation that is not traceable with the software. The embedded knowledge cannot be reused by maintainers, and therefore maintenance becomes more and more unreliable because the change impacts cannot be precisely identified. The measures used for quantifying this indicator can be many and depend on the level of knowledge of the system. In our case the following have been used:

- *Number of Business Functions Used*: the number of business functions or services that users can request the system for.
- *Number of Functions Traceable in the Software*: the number of business functions or services, known by users, that are traceable within system documentation or code.
- *Poor Lexicon*: the names of data and procedures are incoherent with the meaning of corresponding variables and programs, and therefore comprehension is more difficult. This implies a higher maintenance effort.

Coupling. There are many relations among system or program components, and the resulting data and control flow are difficult to understand and manage. The literature provides many measures for coupling. In the following, *cyclomatic number* is used for measuring internal coupling of a program between procedures of a data intensive system like the one used in the experiment. For evaluating coupling between programs, the following measures have been used:

- *File Owner Program*: A program P_j belonging to a software system S is defined Owner Program of F_i if it contains the functions for modifying the content of F_i.
- *Pathological Files*: F_i is called Pathological if there are two or more programs in S able to modify the content of F_i.

When two programs are owners of the same file, they are strictly coupled because they know both the structure of the files and their content. Each modification of either structure or content impacts on all its owner programs, which can be different for each impacted program.

A system with such coupling has a high impact for each modification carried out on a pathological file. Furthermore, since the content of a pathological file is related to many programs' behavior, it is difficult to produce test cases able to examine the behavior of only one or few owner programs. In fact, each record of a pathological file impacts differently on each of the owner programs.

Poor Architecture. Often maintenance activities carried out during system life cycle have been executed according to different architectural approaches, sometimes conflicting with each other. This favors inappropriate decisions during maintenance that degrade the system architecture and consequently increase maintenance effort. The measures used to point out the consequences of such decisions and that quantify this indicator are:

- *Unused File*: files that are created, updated and deleted but never read.
- *Obsolete Files*: files that are never updated and deleted.
- *Temporary File*: files that are created/read, but never updated/deleted.
- *Semantically Redundant Data*: data whose definition domain is the same as, or is contained in, the definition domain of other data.
- *Computationally Redundant Data*: data that can be computed starting from other data of the same database.

10.5.3. Reverse Engineering

When the EM started, the average age of programs was 12 calendar years, but its core was written 23 years before. To avoid wasting effort, the first treatment applied to the system was an inspection with the aim of identifying and eliminating the causes of pollution. The results are reported in Table 10.17.

It is clear how the elimination of pollution, although manual, limits the actual software asset that should be subject to EM; it economizes on the entire EM process. Pollution can be created by ordinary maintenance. So, the first lesson learned is as follows:

- Software inspection with the aim of inventorying the software patrimony of an enterprise application intercepts and eliminates large amounts of pollution.
- If such inspection is carried out on a regular basis, it requires less effort and can be used for monitoring the software system and avoid the presence of useless components.

A first approach in finding Embedded Knowledge was carried out through a survey having maintainers and users as experimental subjects. During the interviews they were

TABLE 10.17. Values for Pollution Measures Before and After the Treatment in RE

Pollution Measures	Before Inspection	After Inspection
Duplicated programs	4.323	0
Unused programs	294	0
Programs in libraries	6.508	1.891

asked to describe the business functions they were aware of in the software system they used or maintained:

- *Number of Business Functions used*: 935;

An inspection process was adopted to analyze how many of these functions were localizable in the documentation and in the code of the software system:

- *Number of functions traceable in the software*: 25

It was not possible to identify the programs providing the remaining 910. The lesson learned is as follows:

- Extracting knowledge from programs is costly and poorly reliable. It is necessary to update documentation so that traceability with programs is always preserved. Thus, periodical inspections of traceability are necessary.

Commonly acknowledged heuristics state that RE aims at describing the system at a higher abstraction level, in order to better comprehend it. Therefore, RE was executed.

The process used two commercial tools for two critical tasks: one for RE the programs and the second for RE the database. The chosen tools were usually adopted in several environments, were up-to-date, and had a good reputation in both industrial and academic communities. Moreover, they were very costly for both buying and using. Unfortunately they turned out to be inadequate: the first tool stopped when the number of decision points in the program exceeded a given threshold; that threshold was lower than the number of decision points in the application. The second tool had very high response times (about 5 days!) when the number of data to analyze exceeded a given threshold. Also in this case the threshold was lower than the number of data to analyze.

The treatment of RE process did not reach the goal of assuring software comprehension. In fact, the obtained documentation did not help data and program comprehension, mainly because the technical quality was badly decayed and comprehension very difficult. Details of the investigation can be found in reference 42. Here only some critical aspects are summarized:

- Seventy-five percent of programs had cyclomatic values between (about) 75 and (about) 185; that is, highly over the threshold recommended by software engineering best practices.
- Many programs included strictly coupled modules. Figure 10.9 shows, for example, the relationship graph between the modules of a program (the most critical of the software system, because it was aimed at trapping users' transactions and requiring the system for the adequate services).

The lessons learned are as follows:

- RE process is effective in obtaining a higher description level, starting from a lower abstraction level, but quality of documentation strictly depends on the quality of processed components. Therefore, RE is unable to improve comprehension; instead, the goal of RE is to preserve traceability between two different abstraction levels of the system, after executing maintenance activities at the code level. For example, when a maintenance task changes code with a good structural quality and did not inject high degradation, then RE can be used to

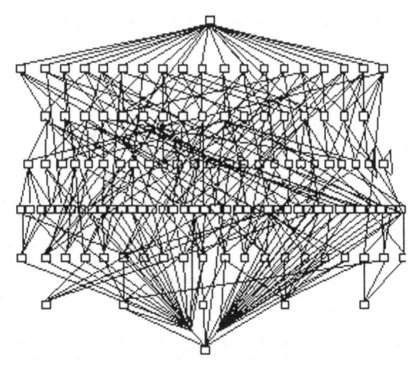

Figure 10.9. Graph of the module relationships generated for the program A0000.

rebuild the program structure after the maintenance task. Monitoring documentation comprehension is necessary, due to the degradation maintenance injects in code and therefore in comprehension of documentation (21, 22).

- RE process includes several activities, which can be formally described and therefore supported by automatic tools, so the process costs are low.
- The choice of tools is risky because they can be inadequate for the specific system; this risk should be considered also when the tools have good reputation in the market, but their efficacy is not empirically proved, for instance, through a stress test in a proper sample of real programs.

10.5.4. Restoration

A possible solution for overcoming the Embedded Knowledge consists of restructuring the legacy system before RE. This process is quite simple, and it is supported by several tools. Unfortunately, these tools do not help to solve the problem of comprehension, because they eliminate knots in program control flows, but they do not change the total amount of decision points. Thus cyclomatic value is unchanged, and situations similar to Fig. 10.9 remain unchanged; the tools move or duplicate pieces of code with the aim of eliminating the knots, and often the relative position of a piece of code in a program is meaningful. Therefore moving or duplicating code without considering the meaning can reduce program comprehension.

For these reasons, a new kind of EM process was defined and applied to the banking system: Restoration (41, 42). In detail, Restoration restructures the software according to the meaning of code. In order to improve code comprehension, it does the following:

- It removes dead data—that is, data declared, but never used.
- It removes obsolete programs—that is, programs that are included in the system and that use dead data and therefore produce unusable results.
- It removes dead instructions—that is, those never executed.
- It improves significance of data and procedural names, according to nonmeaningful ones.

After the previous improvements, the code must be restructured according to the following guidelines:

- Remove *procedural IFs*—that is, IFs dominating two code blocks, each of them with an autoconsistent meaning, which can therefore be executed autonomously. In order to eliminate the IF, each block must be called in different contexts, depending on the program state.

Table 10.18 summarizes the results of restoration. Figure 10.10 shows A0000 call graph improvement after restoration. After improving the software structure, it was possible to rename about 63% of the data and procedures, having better understood their scope. Consequently, it was possible to improve the poor lexicon. After improving

TABLE 10.18. Measures Showing the Effect of Restoration
Treatments

Measures	Before Restoration	After Restoration
Dead data	3.597	0
Total defined data	9.000	5.403
Obsolete programs	1.252	0
Programs in libraries	1.891	639
Dead instructions	270.507	0
Total instruction	1.502.734	1.232.227
Procedural IFs	435.889	217.457

program comprehension, Embedded Knowledge decreased. In fact, the *number of functions traceable in the software* increased to 852.

For sake of completeness, it allowed to improve cyclomatic values of programs (for 75% of programs it is between 5 and 15), but they are still over the threshold recommended by software engineering.

After restoration, the programs still had another type of coupling: Pathological Files. Figure 10.11 shows the distribution of ownership in a software system. It points out, for example, that seven files have a pathology encountered in 40 programs. This coupling remained the same even after restoration.

The lessons learned are as follows:

- Restoration improves Embedded Knowledge, Poor Lexicon and, partially, Coupling; the quality of architecture and design remains the same. For instance, it does not improve information hiding in the system modules.
- Effort and efficacy of the maintenance process is improved.

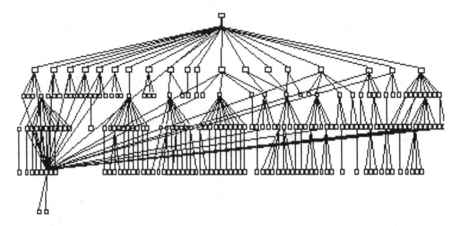

Figure 10.10. Graph of the module relationships generated for the program A0000 after restoration.

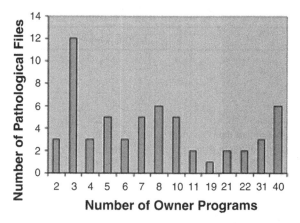

Figure 10.11. Distribution of Pathological Files.

- Restoration requires rigorous but not formalized techniques, so it cannot be supported by tools; therefore the process is person-intensive and, as an effect, it is very costly.
- Another risk is due to the specific skills that the process requires on behalf of developers.
- Formal conditions about process termination cannot be defined; its continuous application determines continuous improvement in code or in database, but this increases the process cost risk.
- The cost risk can be mitigated by defining adequate effort-slices for each component to be restored. The process stops after the end of the established effort-slice; the greater the effort-slice, the greater the quality of the restored system. Therefore the project manager will assign a higher effort-slice to more critical programs.
- The risk about developers' skills can be mitigated through adequate training.

It is the case to carry out inspections of the maintained software system on a regular basis, measuring the aging symptoms. When these are damaged beyond certain limits, restoration must be carried out. This allows us to renew the system with small restoration interventions, with low costs and few risks.

10.5.5. Reengineering

The reengineering process is necessary to remove ageing symptoms that the Restoration process was not able to remove. Its application led to the results shown in Table 10.19. Measurement analysis pointed out how reengineering allowed us to overcome all of the software system's aging symptoms.

This process is intrusive because it requires that all procedures and data be processed at the same time and it involves the entire system. So it is necessary to freeze the software system during reengineering; also, all ordinary maintenance activities should be interrupted until the process is concluded. This is impossible for an enterprise that uses the software system to be reengineered.

TABLE 10.19. Measures Before and After the Reengineering Treatment

	Before Renewal	After Renewal
Unused Files	7	0
Temporary Files	2	0
Obsolete Files	2	0
Pathological Files	58	0
Nonredundant data	3.825	4.061
Semantically redundant data	1.578	632
Computationally redundant data	946	0
Used data	5.403	4.693

The author has defined an *iterative reengineering process* (44) for overcomming this problem. It allows partitioning the system into components, and each of them is reengineered independently from the others. Coexistence between legacy and reengineered components is guaranteed during the execution of the process, so users can continue operating with the system as a whole, accessing both reengineered and legacy functions and data. The freezing time of ordinary maintenance is kept low, depending on the size of the components to be reengineered.

This process was executed for an industrial system supporting chemistry item distributors. It has, first of all, demonstrated the transferability of the reengineering process, even after the interventions to make it iterative. During the reengineering period, which took 18 calendar months, 98 maintenance interventions were requested; of these, 63 were frozen for less than 10 working days, 28 between 11 and 15 days, and only 7 between 15 and 28 working days.

The lessons learned in that experience were as follows:

- Process goals concern improvement of technical quality of architecture and detailed design, along with the updating of functional and technical capabilities; the reengineering process is effective in removing aging symptoms, which are not removed by other EM processes.
- Iterative reengineering may be executed without having to restore the system.
- Reengineering allows us to update services provided by programs, slowing down the business-value decay.
- The main risk of the process lies in identifying the components to reengineer at each iteration: An inadequate partitioning can lead to longer reengineering cycles and to a longer freezing time of ordinary maintenance requests.
- The risk can be mitigated using proper techniques (14).

10.5.6. Summary

To conclude, the results achieved during execution of EM processes and the lessons learned during the empirical investigations, described in the previous sections, are now abstracted. The abstraction of results is expressed in terms of answers to the questions previously illustrated which express the effectiveness of EM maintenance. Comments are synthesized in Table 10.20.

TABLE 10.20. Synthesis of Competence Contents

| | Software Extraordinary Maintenance Processes | | |
Competence Components	Reverse Engineering	Restoration	Reengineering
When each process is used	After a set of maintenance activities that modify the code. When the Embedded Knowledge injected by maintenance in the software system is low. When the software system is aged, inspection should be carried out to characterize the software patrimony, before applying this process.	Embedded Knowledge is high or there is Poor Lexicon, and modules are Coupled. When the software system is aged, inspection should be carried out to characterize the software assets, before applying this process.	Removes aging symptoms that the previously EM process were not able to eliminate. When the software system is aged, inspection should be carried out to characterize the software assets, before applying this process.
Why a certain process is used	Should be used to monitor the Pollution effect determined by maintenance. If carried out in the appropriate moment, it can improve Embedded Knowledge, updating documentation to preserve traceability between two different abstraction levels of the system.	Improve comprehensibility and structure of the software system so that ordinary maintenance is more cost effective, quick, and reliable.	The goals of the process involve improving the technical quality of architecture and detailed design, along with updating functional and technical capabilities.
Costs and benefits in using the process	The cost is low because almost all activities are automated; the benefit is the traceability that allows maintainers to make future changes quickly.	The costs of this process is very high; benefits consist of improvement in maintainability that reduce maintenance process costs.	It is costly but improves the maintainability and saves investments on software production because it extends the system's life.
Risks involved and how they are mitigated	Risk of tools suitability; the mitigation requires the tool supplier to provide Empirical Evidence or to elicit its suitability using the investigation about the tool behavior under Stress Test.	The risk is the termination condition: Its absence could determine long execution times and high effort. This can damage the cost–benefit balance. Mitigation actions consist of defining two thresholds: an effort-slice to spend and a software quality level to reach; when either threshold is reached, the restoration process is stopped.	The efficacious identification of components to be reengineered at each iteration. Mitigation consists of a correct use of the process in reference 44.

10.6. CONCLUSIONS

The aim of this chapter has been to introduce researchers and students interested in empirical research to the essential concepts that are available in literature considering the work of many authors and researchers. It is an introduction to issues on empirical research as a method for bringing software engineering toward science. It collects and synthesizes many published experiences and others made in SERLAB. Thus, it is aimed toward readers that intend making empirical research part of their activities. Interested readers can start from consulting the references suggested in the provided literature and go on from there in identifying further references that surely provide many more sources than the ones cited.

This chapter points out that EIs in software engineering have characteristics more similar to social sciences than to natural sciences, due to the human-centric nature of its processes. This centrality requires the following:

- Specific precautions during design and execution of an EI in order to avoid that inexistent effects are identified
- Replications for confirming complex relations that human characteristics generate in software processes
- Techniques and abilities for strictly repeating experiments or planning variations of one or more factors, in order to define a family of experiments and generalize results

Moreover, this chapter analyzes 10 years of research experience carried out in SERLAB to support and improve transfer of research results and of innovative technologies in industrial processes. It enforces how data should be collected during replications that, although not strictly necessary for confirming underlying theories, are important for calibrating cost-benefits and proving the risk and the mitigation initiatives for the institutionalization of a innovation. In this sense, the chapter has also pointed out that each type of investigation contributes differently in favoring innovation technology acquisition.

The experience presented highlights how in software engineering, as all other sciences, EI is an important factor for extending competences of any body of knowledge.

Finally, the chapter faces the following list of open issues:

- The study of methods and tools for systematizing guidelines that make investigation results accurate and reliable.
- The improvement of frameworks for packaging experiments so they can be replicated either strictly or by varying experimental factors.
- The elicitation of data that are recommended be collected during replications and that are necessary and sufficient for making an experimented innovation accepted by practitioners.

REFERENCES

1. D. Altman, S. Gore, M. Gardner, and S. Pocock. Statistical guidelines for contributors to medical journals. *British Medical Journal* **286**:1489–1493,1983.

2. D. Altman. *Guidelines for Contributors, Statistics and Practice*, S. M. Gore and D. Altman, editors. British Medical Association, London 1991.

3. D. Altman. Statistical reviewing for medical journals. *Statistics in Medicine* **17**:2661–2674,1998.

4. P. Ardimento, M. T. Baldassarre, D. Caivano, and G. Visaggio. Innovation diffusion through empirical studies. In *Proceedings of the 17th International Conference on Software Engineering and Knowledge Engineering (SEKE)*, Taipei, China, pages 701–706, 2005.

5. P. Ardimento, M. T. Baldassarre, D. Caivano, and G. Visaggio. Multiview framework for goal-oriented measurement plan design. In *Proceedings of 5th International Conference on Product Focused Software Process Improvement (PROFES)*, LNCS 3009, pages 159–173, 2004.

6. P. Ardimento, A. Bianchi, N. Boffoli, and G. Visaggio. Empirical investigation for building competences: A case for extraordinary maintenance. In *Proceedings of the 17th International conference on Software and Knowledge Engineering (SEKE)*, Taipei, China, pages 695–700, 2005.

7. M. T. Baldassarre, D. Caivano, and G. Visaggio. Comprehensibility and efficiency of multiview framework for measurement plan design. In *Proceedings of the International Symposium on Empirical Software Engineering (ISESE)*, Rome, Italy, pages 89–99, 2003.

8. M. T. Baldassarre, D. Caivano, and G. Visaggio. Noninvasive monitoring of a distributed maintenance process. In *Proceedings of IEEE Instrumentation and Measurement Technology Conference (IMTC 2006)*, Sorrento, Italy, pages 1098–1103, 2006.

9. V. R. Basili and H. D. Rombach. The TAME project towards Improvement-oriented software environments. *IEEE Transactions on Software Engineering* **13**(12):1278–1296, 1987.

10. V. R. Basili. Software development: A paradigm of the future. In *Proceedings of the International Computer Software and Applications Conference (COMPSAC)*, Orlando, FL, pages 471–485, 1989.

11. V. R. Basili, G. Caldiera, and H. D. Rombach. Experience factory, J.-J. Marciniak, editor. *Encyclopedia of Software Engineering*, Wiley, New York, pages 528–532, 1994.

12. V. R. Basili, F. Shull, and F. Lanubile. Building knowledge through families of experiments. *IEEE Transactions on Software Engineering* **25**(4):456–473, 1999.

13. C. Begg, M. Cho, E. Eastwood, R. Horton, D. Moher, I. Olkin, R. Pitkin, D. Rennie, K. F. Schultz, D. Simel, and D. F. Stroup. Improving the quality of reporting of randomized trials (the CONSORT statement). *Journal of the American Medical Association* **276**(8):637–639, 1996.

14. A. Bianchi, D. Caivano, and V. Marengo. Iterative reengineering of legacy systems. *IEEE Transactions on Software Engineering* **29**(3):225–241, 2003.

15. E. J. Chifosky and J. H. Cross II. Reverse engineering and design recovery: A taxonomy. *IEEE Software* **7**(1):13–17, 1990.

16. T. D. Cook and D. T. Campbell. *Quasi-Experimentation—Design and Analysis Issues for Filed Settings*. Houghton Mifflin Company, Boston, 1979.

17. A. Endres and H. D. Rombach. *A Handbook of Software and System Engineering Empirical Observation Laws and Theories*, Pearson Education Limited, Addison-Wesley, Reading, MA, 2003.

18. H. Fukuda and Y. Ohashi. A guideline for reporting results of statistical analysis. *Japanese Journal of Clinical Oncology* 27(3):121–127, 1997.

19. M. J. Gradner and D. G. Altman. *Statistics with Confidence*, BMJ, London, 1989.

20. R. L. Glass. *Software Conflicts Essay on the Art and Science of Software Engineering*. Yourdon Press, New York, 1991.

21. M. M. Lehman and L. A. Belady. *Program Evolution: Processes of Software Change*. Academic Press, New York, 1985.

22. M. M. Lehman, D. E. Perry, and J. F. Ramil. Implications of evolution metrics on software maintenance. In *Proceedings of the 1998 International Conference on Software Maintenance (ICSM'98)*, pages 208–217, Maryland, 1998.

23. S. M. McGuigan. The use of statistics in the British Journal of Psychiatry. *British Journal of Psychiatry* 167(5):683–688, 1995.

24. C. M. Judd, E. R. Smith, and L. H. Kidder. *Research Methods in Social Relations*, sixth edition, Harcourt Brace JovanovichOrlando, FL, 1991.

25. N. Juristo and A. M. Moreno. *Basics of Software Engineering Experimentation*. Kluwer Academic Publishers, Boston, 2001.

26. E. Kamsties and C. Lott. An empirical evaluation of there defect detection techniques. Technical report ISERN 95-02, Department of Computer Science, University of Kaiserslautern, May 1995.

27. B. A. Kitchenham, G. H. Travassos, A. Von Mayrhauser, F. Niessink, N. F. Schiedewind, J. Singer, S. Takado, R. Vehvilainen, and H. Yang. Toward an ontology of software maintenance. *Journal of Software Maintenance: Research and Practice* 11(6):365–389, 1999.

28. B. A. Kitchenham, S. L. Pflegger, L. M. Pickard, P. W. Jones, D. D. Hoaglin, K. E. Emam, and J. Rosenberg. Preliminary guidelines for empirical research in software engineering. *IEEE Transactions on Software Engineering* 28(8):721–734, 2002.

29. J. Lewis, S. Henry, D. Kafura, and R. Schulman. An empirical study of the object-oriented paradigm and software reuse. In *Proceedings of the Conference on Object Oriented Programming Systems Languages and Applications (OOPSLA)*, pages 184–196, 1991.

30. C. M. Lott and H. D. Rombach. Repeatable software engineering experiments for comparing defect-detection techniques. *Empirical Software Engineering* 1(3):241–277, 1996.

31. C. Nachmias and D. Nachmias. *Research Methods in the Social Sciences*. Edward Arnold, London, 1981.

32. D. L. Parnas. On the criteria to be used in decomposing system in modules. *Communications of the ACM* 15(12):1053–1058, 1972.

33. S. L. Pflegger. Soup or art? The role of evidential force in empirical software engineering. *IEEE Software* 20(1):66–73, 2005.

34. A. M. Porter. Measure of correlation and regression in three medical journals. *Journal of the Royal Society of Medicine* 92(3):123–128, 1999.

35. R. Rosenthal. Replication in behavioural research. *Replication Research in the Social Sciences*, J. W. Neuliep, editor. Sage Publications, Thousand Oaks, CA, 1991.

36. I. Rus and M. Lindvall. Knowledge management in software engineering. *IEEE Software*, 19(3):26–38, 2002.

37. H. S. Sacks, J. Berrier, D. Reitman, V. A. Ancona-Berk, and T. C. Chamlers. Meta-analyses of randomized control trials. *The New England Journal of Medicine* **316**(8):312–455, 1987.

38. D. A. Scanlan. Structured flowcharts outperform pseudocode: An experimental comparison. *IEEE Software* **6**(5):28–36, 1989.

39. B. Schneiderman, R. Mayer, D. McKay, and P. Heller. Experimental investigation of the utility of detailed flowcharts in programming. *Communications of the ACM* **20**(6):373–381, 1977.

40. G. Visaggio. Assessment of a renewal process experimented in the field. *The Journal of Systems and Software* **45**(1):3–17, 1999.

41. G. Visaggio. Value-based decision model for renewal processes in software maintenance. *Annals of Software Engineering*, **9**(1–4): 215–233, 2000.

42. G. Visaggio. Ageing of a data-intensive legacy system: Symptoms and remedies. *Journal of Software Maintenance and Evolution: Research and Practice* **13**(5):281–308, 2001.

43. L. Wilkinson and Task Force on Statistical Inference. Statistical methods in psychology journals: Guidelines and explanations. *American Psychologist.* **54**(8):594–604, 1999 (http://www.apa.org/journals/amp/amp548594.html).

44. C. Wohlin, P. Runeson, M. Host, M. C. Ohlsson, B. Regnell, and A. Wesslen. *Experimentation in Software Engineering: An Introduction.* Kluwer Academic Publishers, Boston, 2000.

11

FOUNDATIONS OF AGILE METHODS

Alberto Sillitti and Giancarlo Succi

11.1. INTRODUCTION

Agile Methods (AMs) are a set of development techniques designed to address some problems of modern software development (i.e., projects over budget and over schedule). Such methods do not pretend to be useful in any kind of software project or to be the solution to reduce costs and increase quality of any product. However, in specific contexts and for specific problems, AMs simply helps developers to focus on the objectives of their customers and deliver the right product for them without wasting time and effort in activities that are not able to generate value for the customer.

Traditional software development approaches (i.e., waterfall, spiral, iterative, etc.) require a deep knowledge of the application domain and of the actual needs of the customer (including the final user). However, this precise knowledge is rarely available and even in such cases the customer usually asks for changes during the development. Unfortunately, software development is characterized by uncertainty and irreversibility (5, 10); therefore, planning everything upfront is not useful in many application domains.

Uncertainty means that requirements are not stable and the customer is not able to specify them in a complete and coherent way. Often customers are not even able to tell which are the main functionalities required and they change their mind very frequently.

Emerging Methods, Technologies, and Process Management in Software Engineering. Edited by
De Lucia, Ferrucci, Tortora, and Tucci

249

Irreversibility means that even if software is intangible, some decisions cannot be changed without deeply affecting the schedule and the budget of a product. This is well understood in other disciplines such as civil engineering. The customer is aware that he cannot change the shape of a building just before adding the roof. However, in the software area, customers are often unaware that certain modifications have a comparable impact.

The main consequences of uncertainty and irreversibility are:

1. The complete knowledge required to build a system is not always available and/ or is subject to change during development.
2. Make assumptions trying some solutions and throw them away if they do not fit; this is not always applicable (waste of time and money).

Traditional software development techniques try to limit uncertainty and irreversibility through very detailed plans. They try to specify everything at the beginning in order to avoid expensive changes later in the project. However, in certain application domains and for certain problems, plans simply do not work or they are inefficient. This is true regardless the quality of the people involved in the project.

Even if plans are supposed to help organizations, many project managers acknowledge that in many kinds of projects they cannot follow them due to market needs, and often they succeed.

AMs acknowledge the difficulty of defining detailed plans at the beginning of a project and include the support to changes into the development process. In this way, requirements are collected and discussed with the customer for the entire duration of the project according to the feedback provided by the customer. The development is performed iteratively, and the product is shipped to the customer at every iteration (lasting from 2 weeks to 2 months in XP) for the evaluation.

AMs focus only on the final outcome of the development process (the code) and on the value provided to the customer. Additional artefacts (i.e., design documents, huge documentations, etc.) are considered waste, since they require time for their development and become useless and misleading if not properly maintained. A poor maintenance of the documentation is common in case of delays in the development. In such cases, all the effort is spent in coding (and testing) the code without updating the documentation properly. Since this scenario is quite common, the main idea is to reduce the time spent for the unnecessary documentation and use automated tools for reverse engineering to produce it when needed.

Often, AMs are misinterpreted. For instance, some people say that they are applying AMs because of the following:

1. They jump directly into the code without writing analysis and design documents.
2. They do not write documentation.
3. They reduce the time spent in meetings.

However, this is not AMs, this is cowboy coding. AMs provide a way to organize software development beyond plans but still with a rigorous process to follow. Often, using

AMs is more challenging than applying traditional software development methods since AMs require a higher level of commitment, higher kills, and so on. They are very diffi-cult to implement and to manage but they are designed to cope with the challenges of the modern software market (i.e., short time-to-market, high quality, etc.).

Moreover, AMs require more agility than the organizational structure of a company (i.e., new kinds of contracts, more decisions left to the team, etc.) and more flexible people with multiple skills and the ability to play several roles inside the development team. Therefore, AMs are not for everyone and they do not fit every software project.

This chapter analyzes the key concepts of the agile development and the difficulties for their effective implementation. Even if there are several AMs available (XP, Scrum, DSDM, Crystal, Agile Modelling, etc.), we focus on the first version of eXtreme Programming (XP) (2) since it is the most popular one.

11.2. AGILE METHODS

AMs are a family of development techniques designed to deliver products on time, on budget, and with high quality and customer satisfaction (1, 7). This family includes several very different methods. The most popular include:

- eXtreme Programming (XP) (2, 4)
- Scrum (16)
- Dynamic Systems Development Method (DSDM) (19)
- Adaptive Software Development (ASD) (8)
- The Crystal family (6)

The aim of these methods is to deliver products faster, with high quality, and satisfy cus-tomer needs through the application of the principles of the lean production to software development (15).

The concepts of the lean production (22) have been developed during the 1950s at Toyota (13). Such concepts involve several practices that are now part of most manufac-turing processes, such as just-in-time, total quality management, and continuous process improvement. The basic principle of lean production is the constant identification and removal of waste (*muda* in Japanese)—that is, anything that does not add value for the customer to the final product.

Since AMs are in some sense the implementation of the lean production in the soft-ware area, they focus on the following:

1. Delivering value to the customer
2. Satisfying the customer

Delivering value to the customer implies that the development team has to produce only what provides value and reduce to the minimum everything else. AMs emphasize producing and delivering to the customer only useful features (from the point of view of the customer). Producing anything that is not required is considered a mistake.

In particular, adding a feature that is not needed not only requires effort but also creates additional code, which may contain errors and make the code larger and more complex to maintain, to correct, and to improve.

To achieve such reduction of waste, AMs claim to be (1) the following:

- Adaptive rather than predictive
- People-oriented rather than process-oriented

To ensure customer satisfaction, a close collaboration between the development team and the customer is required. Thus:

- Requirements are fully identified and correctly understood.
- Final products reflects what the customer needs, no more and no less.

11.3. THE AGILE MANIFESTO

The Agile Manifesto (http://www.agilemanifesto.org/) summarizes the basic and common background of all the AMs. This document defines the aim of the AMs and it is the reference point for the entire community.

AMs emphasize the human factor in the development process and the importance of direct, face-to-face communications among stakeholders, the value of simplicity, perceived as an elimination of waste, and continuous process improvement, as the transposition to the Software Industry of Total Quality Management (15).

The Agile Manifesto defines AMs as a set of development methods sharing the following four values:

1. *Individuals and Interactions over Process and Tools*: AMs emphasize the collaboration among developers and the human role in the process and in the organization, as opposed to institutionalized processes and development tools (1).
2. *Customer Collaboration over Contracts*: AMs give more importance to the cooperation between developers and customers than to a careful and detailed definition of contracts (1). Informal communication between the team and the customer can replace most of the written documentation, even very detailed contracts.
3. *Working Software over Documentation*: One main source of waste in software development is *extra processes or documentation*. Paperwork consumes resources, slows down response time, hides quality problems, gets lost, degrades, and becomes obsolete. When paperwork is required, it is necessary to keep it short, keep it high level, and perform it offline. AMs focus on the *understanding* of the product through collaboration with the customer and delivery of working software, thus reducing the amount of documents required (9).
4. *Responding to Change over Following a Plan*: "Agility is the ability to both create and respond to change in order to profit in a turbulent business environment" (9). Changes are opportunities to help customers to address the turbulence of the marketplace rather than problems for the development.

The former two values refer to management of human resources, while the latter ones refer to process management.

From these values, there are some derived principles that are shared among all the AMs. The main principles listed in the Agile Manifesto are the following:

- *The highest priority is to satisfy the customer through early and continuous delivery of valuable software*: Developers have to ship the product incrementally starting from the most important requirements for the customer.

- *Welcome changing requirements, even late in development. Agile processes harness change for the customer's advantage*: Changes are not a devil but a natural state of software projects. It is not possible to prevent changes that are always unpredictable, therefore the development process has to accommodate and not fight them.

- *Business people and developers must work together daily throughout the project*: A close collaboration between the development team and the customer is a way to reduce the risk of a project since the correct interpretation of the customer needs is verified at every step. In this way, the rework caused by misunderstandings is reduced to the minimum and developers always know to proceed in the right way.

- *Deliver working software frequently, from a couple of weeks to a couple of months, with a preference to the shorter timescale*: Working software is the only valuable thing for the customer even if it is not complete. Shipping a few working functionalities very frequently and not just prototypes give the customer the possibility of using the product early. Moreover, it increases the visibility of the status of the project.

- *Build projects around motivated individuals*: AMs are not for everyone; skilled and motivated developers that are able to work in team are an essential factor for the success.

- *Give them the environment and support they need, and trust them to get the job done*: Managers should not interfere with the development team. Trust and support from the management is a good way to support a skilled and motivated team.

- *The most efficient and effective method of conveying information to and within a development team is face-to-face conversation*: Even if there are several high-tech ways of communicating, face-to-face communication is still the most effective preventing misunderstandings and shortening the time spent for exchanging information.

- *Working software is the primary measure of progress*: The only outcome important for the customer is working software. It does not matter if the team has produced wonderful design documents, but the product is not working or it does not satisfy the needs of the customer. The customer measure the progress of a project measuring the number of working functionalities delivered.

- *Agile processes promote sustainable development. The sponsors, developers, and users should be able to maintain a constant pace indefinitely*: Software development should be carried out through a constant and continuous collaboration among the stakeholders. Moreover, the effort of the development team should be constant in time, trying to avoid stressful periods that are not sustainable in the long term affecting the motivation and the productivity of the team.

- *Continuous attention to technical excellence and good design enhances agility*: Top developers produce top software. Top developers are able to create systems that can be enhanced and maintained minimizing the time and the effort required.
- *Simplicity—the art of maximizing the amount of work not done—is essential*: Identifying the code that is not required is a way to improve the efficiency of the development team. Simpler code is easier to write, understand, and maintain. Moreover, less code means less potential errors and tests.
- *The best architectures, requirements, and designs emerge from self-organizing teams*: The team is the only responsible for the entire product. There is no competition between teams that focus on specific activities (e.g., design and implementation). All the team members work to achieve a common goal, namely, satisfying the customer.
- *At regular intervals, the team reflects on how to become more effective, then tunes and adjusts its behavior accordingly*: The development process is not fixed. Teams have to continuously identify areas of improvement experimenting and evaluating new techniques.

The listed principles are implemented and stressed in different ways in the several AMs available. However, the focus on the customer needs and the continuous improvement are the main ones for all of them.

The ideas of the customer that drives the production and the continuous improvement of the process are not a novelty. These are the main concepts of the Lean Production (13, 22) and of the just-in-time production used at Toyota in 1960 for building cars. AMs are the implementation of these concepts in the software industry (15).

11.4. EXTREME PROGRAMMING (XP)

Probably, the most *well-heard-of* AM is eXtreme Programming, a.k.a. XP. At present, there are two versions of XP defined in the two editions of Beck's book (2, 4). However, in this chapter, we are going to consider only the first one since it is the most popular and accepted by the community. The second one is the most recent proposal by Kent Beck in which he proposes interesting modifications and enhancements. However, the community is still discussing it and it is not widely accepted yet. Moreover, the first version is simpler and it should be the starting point for people approaching AMs for the first time.

XP practices are defined as the description of a successful process followed by the C3 team (2) that developed the huge payroll system of Chrysler. The C3 team lead by Kent Beck was successful and delivered a working system after two years, while the previous team was not able to deliver anything in four years.

XP defines in details a sequence of development principles and practices. However, these are not defined directly, but they are derived from values and drivers that are the foundation of the methodology (Fig. 11.1).

The **values** of XP are the following:

- *Simplicity*: The system should be as simple as possible to satisfy the needs of the customer but not simpler. Implement the needed features, but do not include features to support future requirements that may not become real ones.

- *Communication*: Everything must improve communications between customers and developers, among developers, and between source code and its reader. Effective communication reduces misunderstandings and the need for spending time and effort for formal and written documentation.

- *Feedback*: At all levels, people should get very fast feedback on what they do. Customers, managers, and developers have to achieve a common understanding of the goal of the project and also about the current status of the project, what customers really need first and what are their priorities, and what developers can do and in what time. This is clearly strongly connected with communications. There should be immediate feedback also from the work people are doing, that is, from the code being produced. A substantial percentage of programming effort (about 50%) must be spent in automated test development. In this way, the quality of the developed system is reasonably high.

- *Courage*: Every stakeholder involved in the project should have the courage (and the right) to present his position on the project. Everyone should have the courage to be open and to let everyone inspect and also modify his work. Changes should not be viewed with terror, and developers should have the courage to find better solutions and to modify the code whenever needed and feasible. Using the right tools and a comprehensive test suite, it is possible to program and try new solutions without fear. This means that it is easy to test whether a modification introduces errors and it is easy to return to a previous working version, if needed.

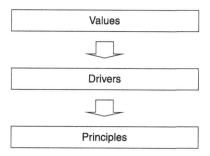

Figure 11.1. Values, drivers, and principles in XP.

The **drivers** of XP are the following:

- *Focus on Value*: Developers have to focus on what provides the most value to the customer. Priorities of the development are based on the priorities of the customer, not on technical issues that do not provide any value to the customer.
- *Constant Flow of Activities*: The development team has to work constantly, avoiding too much or too few workload.
- *No Defects*: Small and simple defects today may become large and difficult to manage bugs in the future. The team has to fix all the known defects and should verify that they are not coming back in future versions through automated testing.

The connections between the values and the drivers listed are shown in Fig. 11.2.

The **focus on value** is evident in the **simplicity**. The team develops only the features that are important for the customers. Such focus is also present in the **communication** with the customer for eliciting requirements and the related priorities. Moreover, **feedback** from the customer is the driver of the development, since he defines the priorities of what to add and/or improve in the product.

The **constant flow** is clear in **feedback**, where the developers ask the customers their priorities, and in the **courage**, where developers negotiate with the customers the amount of functionalities to deliver, without any fear from the customer side that developers "do not work enough."

The aim at the **absence of defect** requires **simplicity** of design, to avoid inserting defects, and **feedback** from tools and customers, to eliminate existing errors and detect nonconformance with the wishes of the customers. Moreover, **communication** among developers and **courage** to test the code under the most severe circumstances help very effectively to eliminate defects.

From the values and the drivers, XP defines a set of **practices**:

- *Planning Game*: Planning should be done together by developer, managers, and the customer. Together, these three stakeholders write user stories of the system; then the customer sets the priorities, the manager allocates resources, and the developers communicate what is likely to be feasible to do. The communication on plan should be kept honest and open.

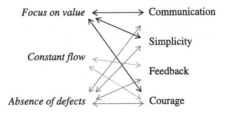

Figure 11.2. Connections among values and drivers in XP.

- *Short Releases*: The development of the system should proceed in small increments with frequent releases that the customer should use to provide useful
  feedback.
- *Metaphor*: The overall project team should use a jargon shared among developers, customers, and managers, so that developers could better understand the
  problem domain and customers could better appreciate developers' solutions.
  Such jargon could be built around an overall analogy of the system being built.
- *Simple Design*: The design should be kept simple and developed incrementally
  as the system evolves.
- *Test-Driven Development*: The test should be written together with the customer
  and before the actual code; they should also cover all the most relevant aspects of
  the system. In this way, they serve as a way to ensure that requirements are met
  and as a form of formal specification of the behavior of the system.
- *Refactoring*: The code should be constantly revisited and made simpler and
  more understandable, with a clear constraint that (a) such simplifications
  should be done test first, (b) the simplifications should be checked in only
  when passing all the existing and new tests, and (c) the simplifications should
  be done in pair.
- *Pair Programming*: Programmers should always work in pairs, where one stays
  at the keyboard and writes the code, while the other proposes ideas and verifies
  the code being written.
- *Collective Code Ownership*: Everyone in the team should have complete accessibility to any piece of code developed by anyone else in the team, and should be
  able to modify in and check in a new version of it, provided that it (a) proceeds
  test first, (b) checks in only a new version passing all the existing and new tests,
  and (c) works in pairs.
- *Continuous Integration*: The code should be integrated frequently, to ensure that
  all the pieces fit seamlessness together.
- *Forty-hour work week*: The project should proceed at a sustainable pace, along the
  lines of the constant flow advocated by lean management. Therefore, major efforts
  might be tolerable for a week or two per term, but overall the effort distribution
  should be flat and not exceed what is normally bearable: 40 hours per week.
- *On-Site Customer*: The customer and the developers should be easily accessible
  and, if possible, co-located. In this way, the customer would be ensured that the
  developers are working along their plan and the developers could receive fast
  feedback from the customer.
- *Coding Standards*: The code should be written in a style agreed upon by all the
  people in the team, to promote sharing and easy understanding. What standard to
  use is not so important, provided that it is reasonable and that it is accepted by
  everyone, but it is important to have one.

Drivers, values, and practices are deeply connected in XP. These connections are
showed in Table 11.1.

TABLE 11.1. Relations Among Drivers, Values, and Practices

	Drivers			Values			
	Focus on Value	Constant Flow	No Defects	Communication	Simplicity	Feedback	Courage
Planning game	✓	✓		✓		✓	✓
Short release	✓	✓		✓		✓	
Metaphor	✓			✓		✓	
Simple design	✓						
Testing			✓		✓	✓	✓
Refactoring		✓	✓		✓	✓	✓
Pair programming			✓	✓	✓	✓	
Collective code ownership	✓	✓	✓	✓		✓	✓
Continuous integration	✓	✓	✓			✓	✓
40 hours per week	✓			✓	✓	✓	✓
On-site customer	✓				✓	✓	
Coding standards	✓		✓				

11.4.1. Structure of XP Teams

The size and the structure of the team are very important for a successful implementation of XP. XP is designed to work with a small team (2–12 developers) located in the same room. Such small size and the co-location is of paramount importance for a correct implementation of some practices such as planning game, collective code ownership, customer on-site, and so on. If such requirements are not satisfied, there are other AMs that may help (i.e., SCRUM, Crystal, etc.).

The level of agility is often related to the size of the development team. Direct communication and limited documentation is possible only in small teams. On the contrary, when the team grows, the level of overhead grows as well. The overhead includes:

- Documentation
- Mediated communication (through a media such as paper)

To share knowledge and trace the status of the project, more documentation is required because direct, many-to-many interaction is not possible anymore (6). Moreover, the importance of the documentation increases and it becomes a way to improve knowledge sharing. In this case, the code itself is not enough and the direct communication between the development team and the customer is not possible due to the size of the team.

In XP teams there are three main components:

1. The customer
2. The developer
3. The manager

The customer is highly involved in the development process, and often he is a member of the development team. His presence is important in XP, since most of the communication is performed face-to-face and the requirements collection phase is spread across the entire project, not just at the beginning. Therefore, the development team often asks the customer to answer questions regarding requirements and check the correctness of the implementation.

The presence of the customer reduces the amount of documentation required to describe requirements in detail, and his direct contribution is a key factor for the success of the project. Moreover, the customer provides feedback to the developers to identify potential problems early in the development and avoid a major impact on project schedule.

The main activities of the customer are the following:

- Definition of the functionalities of the product
- Definition of the priorities for such functionalities
- Definition of acceptance tests (with the help of developers)

Developers in XP are not just the people in charge of the implementation of the product. They have to interact closely with the customer, providing working software and collecting valuable feedback. Therefore, they not only need to be good developers able to work in a team but also need to be able to communicate with the customer in his own language.

Developers have to provide working and high-quality software to the customer at every iteration and collect valuable feedback. This approach is valuable for both developers and customers. Developers can collect useful information to avoid the implementation of useless or wrong features that reduces the time spent in useful features; customers can test the product after a few weeks from the beginning of the project.

The main activities of the developer are as follows:

- Analysis, design, test, coding, and integration of the system.
- Estimation of the difficulty of the implementation of the requirements expressed by the customer.
- Working in pairs. Two programmers with one keyboard: one types, the other tells what to do.
- Sharing the code with all the other developers in the team.

In AMs, managers have to create and sustain an environment where it is possible to have a productive interaction between the development team and the customer. They can achieve this goal by identifying the best people to be included in the team, promoting collaboration, and negotiating contracts with the customer.

Usually, agile teams work with *variable scope–variable price* contracts rather than *fixed price–fixed scope* ones. This approach relies on the ability of the manager in the contracts definition to satisfy the customer and allow flexibility in the development process.

The main activities of the manager are as follows:

- Outline the contractual terms and negotiate with the customer the application of the agile practices.
- Help the customers and the developers to become one cohesive team.
- Facilitate customers and developers in doing their tasks.

A key factor for the success of an XP project is the commitment of the team members—not only the commitment of developers but also of the managers and of the customers. Managers have to support the development team and create the environment for a productive application of XP; customers have to be available to answer the questions coming from the development team and evaluate the proposed solutions.

11.4.2. Requirements Management in XP

Requirements are the base of all software products; and their elicitation, management, and understanding are very common problems for all development methodologies (17).

TABLE 11.2. Main Causes of Project Failure

Problem	%
Incomplete requirements	13.1
Low customer involvement	12.4
Lack of resources	10.6
Unrealistic expectations	9.9
Lack of management support	9.3
Changes in the requirements	8.7
Lack of planning	8.1
Useless requirements	7.5

According to a study of the Standish Group (18), five of the eight main factors for project failure deal with requirements (Table 11.2): incomplete requirements, low customer involvement, unrealistic expectations, changes in the requirements, and useless requirements.

In XP the requirements collection is not performed only at the beginning of the project, but this activity lasts for the entire development. In particular, the customer can change both the requirements and their priorities at every iteration of the project after evaluating the system shipped by the development team in the previous iteration. This continuous feedback is important to keep the project on track and deliver software that is really able to satisfy the needs of the customer.

XP acknowledges that requirements variability is a constant problem in nearly all software projects; therefore, the support to such changes is included in the process as a key strength (20). Moreover, XP does not try to forecast changes or future needs, it focuses only on the features for which the customer is paying. This approach avoids the development of a too general architecture that requires additional effort (2).

To improve the mutual understanding and the effectiveness of the requirements collection, XP teams use *user stories* and *metaphors*.

User stories are a description of the functional behaviour of the system. They are quite similar to use cases but they focus only on micro-functionalities; therefore a use case can be divided into several user stories. User stories are written in natural language by the customer with the help of the developers. Customers assign priorities to user stories, while developers estimate their difficulty and the effort needed for their implementation (story points).

Effective user stories should:

- Be understandable by both customer and developers
- Be written in natural language
- Be testable (and the test should be written by the customer with the help of the developers)
- Be independent from all the other stories to the largest possible degree (at least from the stories developed within the same iteration)
- Not exceed two weeks of work (typical length of XP iterations)

A typical user story is described in Fig. 11.3.

Developers estimate the effort required by a user story on the basis of their experience and on the basis of the ongoing project. Large user stories may require a deeper investigation to access their feasibility and the effort required. In these cases, developers implement *spike solutions*, which are a more accurate investigation and an experimental implementation of the skeleton of the solution to generate a more accurate estimate. The effort is specified in *story points* that have to be related to a specific amount of effort such as one day of a pair (developers always work in pairs!). If the story seems to require more than two weeks, the customer will be asked to split it.

Attached to every user story there is the *acceptance test* that specifies when the story is implemented correctly and the implementation is accepted by the customer.

Effective acceptance tests should:

- Verify that the stories are correctly implemented
- Be written by the customers after writing each individual user story
- Be at least one for each story
- Verify when it is possible to consider a story finished and start developing a new story

To write effective user stories, customer and developers should use *metaphors*. Metaphors are a kind of lingua franca that can be easily understood by both the customer

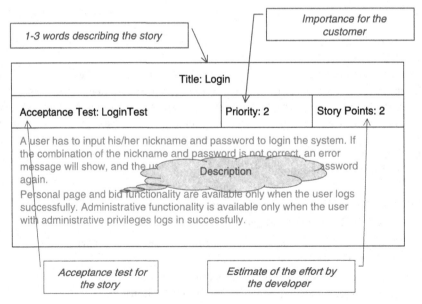

Figure 11.3. Structure of a user story.

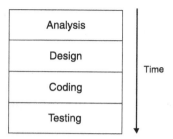

Figure 11.4. Waterfall process.

and the developers and should help them to communicate without using too much technical language that may generate misunderstandings if the application domain is not well known by the entire team.

11.4.3. Introduction to the XP Development Process

Traditional development processes such as the waterfall model (Fig. 11.4) identify phases of the development process (analysis, design, coding, testing) through which a product has to go. This rigid structure has been modified in different ways with other development processes such as the spiral model and several others.

XP organizes the development process in a radical different way (Fig. 11.5). The formal definition of phases is not present anymore, and the development process is organized in iterations in which developers have to produce something valuable for the customer. For every requirement identified through a user story, developers perform a little bit of analysis, a little bit of design, a little bit of testing, and a little bit of coding.

This process has some interesting points. Testing is performed before coding because XP uses the test-first approach (3): Tests are written before the code that satisfies them is written. It is not true that in XP there are no analysis and design. XP spreads the

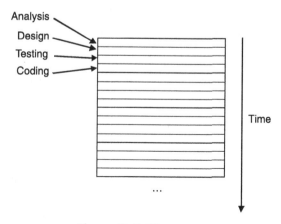

Figure 11.5. XP process.

analysis and design across the entire development process and does not concentrate them only at the beginning of the project. This approach allows developers to react quickly to the changes and reduce the waste of resources caused by the implementation of wrong requirements (2).

11.4.4. Comparing XP with other approaches

Table 11.3 compares some common approaches to software development of traditional software engineers, cowboy coders, and XP-ers.

11.4.5. Control Mechanisms in XP

Any kind of production process is regulated through some control mechanisms that define how to synchronize different activities to achieve a common goal.

There are two main ways to control a production process: exogenous and endogenous control. Exogenous control defines rules added to the process. This means that the process itself does not include such rules but they are added later to implement a control mechanism. On the contrary, endogenous control defines the control rules as part of the process. This means that the process has been designed so that control mechanisms are embedded in the process and it is not possible to separate them.

Traditional software engineering methods use mostly exogenous control. On the contrary, AMs take advantage of endogenous control. This means that several AM practices are designed to force developers to coordinate without asking them to do it explicitly, limiting the not directly productive activities needed only for coordination. Therefore, all the stakeholders can concentrate on their core business while problems are solved when they arise: The endogenous control prevents going ahead if a problem is not solved. Needless to say, this is a clear driver for quality: Anything that does not match the specified quality control cannot go ahead.

The Agile Manifesto includes endogenous control in all its principles. Endogenous control is much more effective than exogenous control; however, it may be hard to achieve. AMs try to obtain an adaptive development process whose control is built-in, rather than added later on the process. This approach is one of the tenets of Lean Management (22).

According to Malone and Crowston (12), the only way that two tasks can be dependent is via some kind of common resources. Consequently, there are three major kinds of dependencies among tasks:

- *Sequential Control*: It arises when a task creates a resource (output) that another task requires as an input (21). In this case there is a precedence dependency between the two tasks, requiring the correct execution order (11) (Fig. 11.6).
- *Shared Resource*: It arises whenever multiple tasks share some limited resources (12) (Fig. 11.7).
- *Common Output*: It occurs when two tasks contribute to create the same output. This dependency can have either positive or negative effects. In fact, if both tasks

TABLE 11.3. Comparing XP with Other Approaches

Traditional Software Engineer	Cowboy Coder	XP-er
"I need to have completed analysis and design before proceeding to code."	"I do **not** need **any** analysis and design."	"I do **not** need to have completed analysis and design before proceeding to code."
"I need to write **all the documentation in a complete and pervasive way** so that *people in the future will be able to understand what is in here*."	"I do **not** need **any** documentation."	"I need to write **the code** so that *people in the future will be able to understand what is in here*. I need to write **only** the documentation that is needed by people."
"**Especially** close to the deadline, I need to **work like crazy** to get the project done. Programming is **hard**."	"**Only** close to the deadline, I need to **work like crazy** to get the project done. Programming is **fun**."	"**Especially** close to the deadline, I need to **work no more than 40 hours a week** to get the project done, keeping a constant pace and a fresh mind. Programming is **fun**."
"The code is **mine** and **no one** is allowed to **touch** it!"	"The code is **mine** and **no one** is allowed to **touch** it!"	"The code is **of the team** and **everyone** is allowed to **modify it also extensively**, provided that the **tests keep running!**"
"**At the end** we will do integration. It **is going to be hard**, so we need to define precise interaction protocols, and to document them with maximal details."	"**At the end** we will do integration! No problem, **it's easy:** It will take 5."	"We need to integrate our system **at least daily**, so that **at the end** we **will not have any problem**."
"The customer should **only see working and cleaned-up versions of the product**. It is important to **balance the contact with the customer** so time is not wasted."	"If possible, the **customer should only see the final versions of the product**. It is important to **minimize the contact** with the customer so time is not wasted."	"The customer should (a) be **constantly exposed to the product being build** and to the **development team**, and, whenever possible, (b) **have a representative on site**."
"**If** it is **not broken, do not touch** it!"	"**Even if** it is **broken, do not touch** it! Try to **hide** it!"	"**Even if** it is **not broken**, constantly **refactor it! Use the test cases** to ensure that you do not introduce an undesired bug."

(Continued)

TABLE 11.3. *Continued*

Traditional Software Engineer	Cowboy Coder	XP-er
"Plan everything **well in advance** so that **there will be no need to change**! A change is a clear symptom of bad and/or not **sufficient** planning."	"**Do not plan** anything and **try not to change**! A change is a clear symptom of an **annoying** customer or manager."	"Plan everything **that you can reasonably foresee** and **get ready to change**! Changes occur **naturally** in software projects."
"Change is **evil**! **Fight** it!"	"Change is **evil**! **Fight** it!"	"Change is **human**! **Get ready to cope with** it!"

do exactly and unintentionally the same thing, it may result in a problem of duplication or waste of resources. Nevertheless, two tasks can affect different aspects of a common resource. This is the case of more actors that collaborate in order to achieve a common goal (Fig. 11.8).

The easiest coordination mechanism is the sequential one. In this case the activities are completely independent and the only relation is through the input and output documents. The shared resource coordination mechanism is more complex since activities have to define priorities for assigning the shared resources to the most important activity. The most difficult one is the coordination through common output. In this case, activities have to work together to produce the same output.

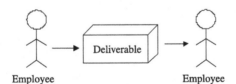

Figure 11.6. Sequential control.

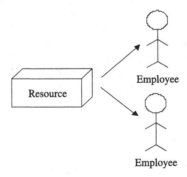

Figure 11.7. Shared resource.

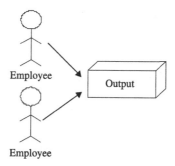

Figure 11.8. Common output.

Traditional software engineering techniques are mostly based on exogenous control and sequential coordination. On the contrary, AMs and XP in particular are based on endogenous control and common output coordination. Table 11.4 lists the control mechanisms used in the single XP practices.

In parallel to the control of processes, there is the organizational problem. Ouchi (14) has identified three major mechanisms, which depend on the ability to measure the output and the knowledge available on the processes (Fig. 11.9):

- *Behavioral*: Used when it is clear and transparent as to what operations are needed to produce the specified output. This is typical of clerical work.
- *Outcome*: Used when it is possible to measure the amount and/or the quality of the output. This is typical in simple professional or technological tasks, which might also be outsourced.
- *Clan*: Used when neither the process is clear nor the output is easy to measure. This is the typical situation in the most complex knowledge-based works, where the final evaluation of outcome of the work can be done only after a while.

TABLE 11.4. Coordination Mechanisms in XP

Practice	Control
Planning game	Endogenous
Short releases	Endogenous
Metaphor	Exogenous
Simple design	Exogenous
Test-driven development	Endogenous
Refactoring	Endogenous
Pair programming	Endogenous
Collective code ownership	Endogenous
Continuous integration	Endogenous
Forty-hour week	Exogenous
On-site customer	Exogenous
Coding standards	Exogenous

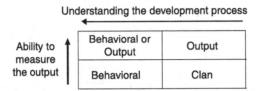

Figure 11.9. Organization and control types.

The understanding of the development process is higher in traditional, plan-based development techniques where there are formal definitions of tasks, procedures, and roles. For instance, in the waterfall model every phase of development has a very clear output and procedure to go from its input to its output (it is a different issue in which circumstances such approach is effective).

AMs acknowledge the difficulty in understanding the software development process and in measuring its output. Therefore, they prefer to oversee resources with a clan approach. This is clear in the Agile Manifesto, where "collaboration" is considered more important than "negotiation" and "interaction" is considered more important than "processes."

11.5. TOOLS SUPPORT FOR XP

There are several software tools to support XP development. However, many XP teams prefer low-tech and traditional tools such as paper, pencil, pin board, and face-to-face meetings.

For instance, in XP, user stories are written on small pieces of paper with the size of a postcard and hang on a pin board. The pin board is divided into three sections: user stories to be implemented, user stories under implementation, and user stories completed. This layout provides a visual representation of the project status.

Even if many XP teams do not use software tools, some of them are useful. Among these, there are standard applications not designed to support XP and ad hoc applications developed specifically to support it.

Among the general-purpose tools, there are:

- *UML Modeling Tools*: Such tools are used in two ways:
  1. to write a high-level description of the application;
  2. to reverse engineer the code to create documentation.
- *Requirements Negotiation Tools*: This kind of tools helps developers and customer to identify, prioritize, and manage requirements in different environments.
- *Instant Messaging Tools*: These tools are useful to keep in touch with the customer to discuss requirements when he is not on-site or to exchange information among developers when they cannot sit at the same desk.

- *Version Control Systems*: These tools help developers to trace changes in the code and retrieve a working version of the code in case a modification is not working properly.
- *Automated Testing Tools*: Continuous testing of the code is one of the key aspects of XP. Running automated unit and integration tests very frequently is of paramount importance to identify defects in the code as soon as they are introduced.

Among ad hoc applications, there are:

- *Project Management Tools*: Such tools focus on specific practices used in XP and helps to store and retrieve user stories in an electronic format, organize iterations, and so on.

11.6. CONCLUSIONS

AMs are the implementation of the basic concepts of the Lean Management in the software industry. The focus on the continuous improvement of the development process and on the customer satisfaction are two key components for their success. Such aspects are present in all the practices that developers apply every day.

The goal of AMs and XP in particular is to deliver high-quality software on time and on budget, focusing on what is valuable for the customer, creating a continuous feedback channel with him, and supporting changes that he may require. However, these methodologies do not pretend to be useful for any kind of software project and for any kind of organization. Like any other development techniques, AMs have specific areas in which they perform well and areas in which other techniques are better. Nevertheless, since these techniques are quite recent, the identification of such areas is still an ongoing activity.

REFERENCES

1. P. Abrahamsson, R. Salo, J. Ronkainen, and J. Warsta. *Agile Software Development Methods: Review and Analysis*. VTT Publications, Oulu, Finland, 2002.
2. K. Beck. *Extreme Programming Explained: Embrace Change*, Addison-Wesley, Reading, MA, 1999.
3. K. Beck. *Test Driven Development: By Example*, Addison-Wesley, Reading, MA, 2002.
4. K. Beck. *Extreme Programming Explained: Embrace Change*, second edition, Addison-Wesley, Reading, MA, 2004.
5. D. M. Berry. The inevitable pain of software development: Why there is no silver bullet. In *Proceedings of the 9th International Workshop on Radical Innovations of Software and System Engineering in the Future (RISSEF 2002)*, LNCS 2941, pages 50–74, 2004.
6. A. Cockburn. *Agile Software Development*, Addison-Wesley, Reading, MA, 2002.

7. D. Cohen, M. Lindvall, and P. Costa. *Agile Software Development*, DACS State-of-the-Art Report, available online at: http://www.dacs.dtic.mil/techs/agile/agile.pdf, 2003.

8. J. Highsmith. *Adaptive Software Development*. Dorset House Publishing, New York, 1996.

9. J. Highsmith. *Agile Software Development Ecosystem*. Addison-Wesley, Reading, MA, 2002.

10. J. Highsmith and A. Cockburn. Agile software development: The business of innovation. *IEEE Computer* 34(9):120–127, 2001.

11. T. W. Malone and K. Crowston. What is coordination theory and how can it help design cooperative work systems. In *Proceedings of the 1990 ACM Conference on Computer-Supported Cooperative Work,* pages 357–370, Los Angeles, 1990.

12. T. W. Malone and K. Crowston. The interdisciplinary theory of coordination. *ACM Computing Surveys* **26**(1):87–119, 1994.

13. T. Ohno. *Toyota Production System: Beyond Large-Scale Production*. Productivity Press, New York, 1988.

14. W. G. Ouchi. Markets, bureaucracies & clans. *Administrative Science Quarterly* **25**(1):129–141, 1980.

15. M. Poppendieck and T. Poppendieck. *Lean Software Development: An Agile Toolkit*. Addison-Wesley, Reading, MA, 2003.

16. K. Schwaber and M. Beedle. *Agile Software Development with Scrum*. Prentice-Hall PTR, Englewood Cliffs, NJ, 2001.

17. I. Sommerville and P. Sawyer. *Requirements Engineering—A Good Practice Guide*, John Wiley & Sons, New York, 2000.

18. Standish Group, CHAOS Report 1994, available online at: http://www.standishgroup.com/sample_research/chaos_1994_1.php

19. J. Stapleton. *DSDM—Dynamic System Development Method*, Addison-Wesley, Reading, MA, 1995.

20. J. E. Tomayko. Engineering of unstable requirements using agile methods. In *Proceedings of the International workshop on Time-Constrained Requirements Engineering (TCRE '02),* Essen, Germany, 2002, available at http://www.enel.ucalgary.ca/tcre02/

21. J. D. Thompson. *Organizations in Action: Social Science Bases of Administrative Theory*. McGraw-Hill, New York, 1967.

22. J. P. Womack, D. T. Jones. *Lean Thinking: Banish Waste and Create Wealth in Your Corporation*. Free Press, New York, 2003.

INDEX

Emerging Methods, Technologies, and Process Management in Software Engineering. Edited by
De Lucia, Ferrucci, Tortora, and Tucci
Copyright © 2008 John Wiley & Sons, Inc.

ABOUT THE AUTHORS AND THE EDITORS

Laura Bocchi is a research associate at the University of Leicester, United Kingdom, where she works on the Sensoria (Software Engineering for Service Overlay Computers) project. She received her Ph.D. in Computer Science from the University of Bologna, Italy. Her doctoral work concerned formal models for the orchestration of Web/Grid services, long-running transactions, and negotiation protocols.

Jan Bosch is currently a vice president of Engineering Process at Intuit, Inc. He was head of the Software and Application Technologies Laboratory at Nokia Research Center, Finland. Before joining Nokia, he headed the Software Engineering Research Group at the University of Groningen, The Netherlands, where he holds a professorship in software engineering. He received a Master of Science degree from the University of Twente, The Netherlands, and a Ph.D. from Lund University, Sweden. His research activities include software architecture design, software product families, software variability management, and component-oriented programming. He is the author of the book *Design and Use of Software Architectures: Adopting and Evolving a Product Line Approach*, editor of several other books and volumes, and author of a significant number of research articles. He has been guest editor for

Emerging Methods, Technologies, and Process Management in Software Engineering. Edited by
De Lucia, Ferrucci, Tortora, and Tucci
Copyright © 2008 John Wiley & Sons, Inc.

journal issues, chaired several conferences as general and program chair, served on many program committees, and organized numerous workshops.

Bernd Brügge is a professor of Computer Science and chairman of the Technical Committee for Applied Software Engineering at the University of Munich, Germany and adjunct associate professor in Computer Science at Carnegie Mellon University, Pittsburgh, Pennsylvania. Professor Brügge received a Master degree in 1982 and Ph.D. in 1985 from Carnegie Mellon, and received his diploma in 1978 from the University of Hamburg. He received the Herbert Simon Excellence in Teaching Award in Computer Science in 1995. He is the co-author of the book *Object-Oriented Software Engineering with UML, Design Patterns and Java*. His research interests include distributed software development, requirements engineering, software architectures for adaptive systems, agile software development processes, and problem-oriented software engineering education.

Paolo Ciancarini is a professor of Computer Science at the University of Bologna, Italy, where he teaches and researches software engineering topics. He received a Ph.D. in Computer Science from the University of Pisa in 1988. He is a Member of ACM, IEEE, AICA, ICGA (International Computer Games Association), and IFIP SG16 (Special Group on Entertainment Computing). His research interests include coordination models and agent-oriented languages, Web-based document management systems, and environments, methods, and tools for software engineering. He has been a visiting researcher at Yale University. He is author of more than 40 papers published in international journals and more than 100 papers published in proceedings of international conferences.

Andrea De Lucia received a Laurea degree in Computer Science from the University of Salerno, Italy, in 1991, a Master degree in Computer Science from the University of Durham, United Kingdom, in 1996, and a Ph.D. in Electronic Engineering and Computer Science from the University of Naples "Federico II," Italy in 1996. From 1996 to 2003, he was a faculty member of the Department of Engineering at the University of Sannio, Italy, where from 2001 to 2003 he was also a research leader of the Research Center on Software Technology. He is currently a full professor of Software Engineering in the Department of Mathematics and Computer Science at the University of Salerno, Italy, head of the Software Engineering Lab, and director of the International Summer School on Software Engineering. His research interests include software maintenance, reverse engineering, reengineering, global software engineering, traceability management, configuration management, document management, workflow management, web engineering, visual languages, and e-learning. Professor De Lucia has published more than 100 papers on these topics in international journals, books, and conference proceedings. He has edited international books and journals' special issues and serves on the organizing and program committees of several international conferences in the field of software engineering.

Michael Fischer received his Ph.D. in Computer Science from the Vienna University of Technology, Austria in 2007. He has contributed to various software projects since 1985. Beginning in 2002, he was a researcher for European research projects focusing on software evolution analysis for program families. In 2005, he joined the group of Professor Gall at the University of Zurich, Switzerland. Since October 2006, he has been a software engineer for the Swiss Seismological Service at the Swiss Federal Institute of Technology, Zurich. He contributes to projects such as seismicity analysis as part of the European NERIES project, earthquake early warning or alarm system. His research interests include software evolution, software architecture recovery, and model-driven architecture.

Filomena Ferrucci is an associate professor of Computer Science at the University of Salerno, Italy, where she teaches courses on software engineering and Web information systems. She was program co-chair of the 14th International Conference on Software Engineering and Knowledge Engineering and guest editor of the *International Journal of Software Engineering and Knowledge Engineering* special issue dedicated to a selection of the best papers of the conference. She has served as program co-chair of the 2nd, 3rd, and 4th sessions of the International Summer School on Software Engineering. She has served as program committee member for several international conferences. Her main research interests are software metrics for the effort estimation of OO systems and Web applications, software-development environments, visual languages, human–computer interaction, and e-learning. She is co-author of about 100 papers published in international journals, books, and proceedings of refereed international conferences.

Harald Gall is a professor of Software Engineering in the Department of Informatics, at the University of Zurich, Switzerland. He was associate professor at the Technical University of Vienna in the Distributed Systems Group (TUV), where he also received his Ph.D. and a Master degree in Informatics. His research interests are software engineering with focus on software evolution, software architectures, reengineering, program families, and distributed and mobile software engineering processes. He was program chair of ESEC-FSE 2005 (European Software Engineering Conference and ACM SIGSOFT Symposium on the Foundations of Software Engineering), IWPC 2005 (International Workshop on Program Comprehension), and IWPSE 2004 (International Workshop on Principles of Software Evolution).

Carlo Ghezzi is a professor and chair of Software Engineering in the Department of Electronics and Information of Polytechnica University of Milan, Italy, where he is the Rector's Delegate for Research. He is an ACM and IEEE Fellow. He was the recipient of the ACM SIGSOFT Distinguished Service Award 2006. He served as general and program chair of several conferences, such as the International Conference on Software Engineering (ICSE) and the European Software Engineering Conference (ESEC). He was the editor-in-chief of the *ACM Transactions on Software Engineering and Methodology* (TOSEM), 2000–2005. Ghezzi's research interests are software engineering and programming languages. He is currently interested in the theoretical, methodological, and technological issues involved in developing network-wide applications. He has published more than 150 papers and eight books.

Mehdi Jazayeri is the founding dean of the Faculty of Informatics and professor of Computer Science at the University of Lugano, Switzerland. He also holds the chair of

Distributed Systems at the Technical University of Vienna. He spent many years in software research and development at several Silicon Valley companies, including 10 years at Hewlett-Packard Laboratories in Palo Alto, California. His recent work has been concerned with component-based software engineering of distributed systems, particularly Web-based systems. He is a co-author of *Programming Language Concepts*, *Fundamentals of Software Engineering* and *Software Architecture for Product Families*. He is a Fellow of the IEEE and a member of ACM, Swiss, German, and Austrian computer societies.

Leonardo Mariani is a researcher at the University of Milan, Italy. He is interested in software engineering and particularly in software test and analysis. Before joining the Department of Informatics, Systems, and Communication, Dr. Mariani was a visiting scientist at the University of Paderborn. He holds a Laurea degree from the University of Camerino and a Ph.D. from the University of Milan. He is a Member of ACM and IEEE.

Cédric Mesnage received his Master's degree in Computer Science from the University of Caen, France, with specialization in Algorithmics and Information Modeling. His diploma thesis addressed visualization of software evolution artifacts. He is currently a Ph.D. student in Computer Science at the University of Lugano under the direction of Mehdi Jazayeri. He works for the Nepomuk European Project, where he focuses on the architecture of the social semantic desktop. His interests are the evolution of Web development, the semantic Web, collaborative tagging, social networks, and relations between computer science and social sciences.

Carlo Montangero is a professor of Informatics at the University of Pisa, Italy, where he teaches software engineering in the Department of Informatics. He contributed to the activities of the department, acting as chairman of the curriculum in computer science and as vice director. He spent a few years visiting research centers abroad, including Stanford University in Palo Alto, California and City University in London. His research interests are in programming languages, the modeling of software development process, and formal methods in software engineering. Currently, he is focusing on business process modeling and validation, in the context of service-oriented architectures (SOA), and UML model transformations to support user-friendly SOA verification.

Rocco Moretti received his Ph.D. in Computer Science from the University of Bologna, Italy. He is currently a research associate in the area of software engineering and service-oriented architectures in the Department of Computer Science at the University of Bologna.

Filippo Pacifici received his Bachelor of Science degree and Master degree in Computer Engineering from Polytechnic of Milan in 2003 and 2005, respectively and a Master degree in Computer Science from the University of Illinois, Chicago in 2006. He is now a Ph.D. student in the Department of Electronics and Information at Polytechnic of Milan. His research interest involves the application of software engineering methodologies to the development of pervasive and mobile computing systems. He is a student Member of IEEE.

Mauro Pezzè is a professor of Software Engineering at the University of Milan, Italy and visiting professor at the University of Lugano, Italy. He is interested in software engineering and in particular in software test and analysis. Before joining the Department of Informatics, Systems, and Communication at the University of Milan, Bicocca, Pezzè was associate professor at Polytechnic of Milan and visiting scientist at the University of California, Irvine and at the University of Edinburgh. Dr. Pezzè holds a Laurea degree from the University of Pisa and a Ph.D. from Polytechnical University of Milan. He is a Member of ACM and IEEE, where he served as executive chair of the Technical Committee on Complexity in Computing (TCCX).

Martin Pinzger is a senior research associate in the Software Engineering Group at the Department of Informatics, University of Zurich. He received his Ph.D. in Computer Science from the Vienna University of Technology, Austria in June 2005. His research interests are software engineering with a focus on software evolution analysis and software design and quality analysis.

Christian Prehofer is research team leader at Nokia Research Center. His research interests are self-organized and ubiquitous systems, as well as software architectures and software technologies for mobile communication systems. Before joining Nokia, he held different management and research positions in the mobile communication industry. He obtained his Ph.D. and his habilitation in Computer Science from the Technical University of Munich in 1995 and 2000. He is author of more than 80 publications and 12 granted patents, and he also serves on several program committees for conferences on networking and software technology.

Valentina Presutti is a research associate at the Laboratory for Applied Ontology, CNR, Rome. She received her Ph.D. in Computer Science from the University of Bologna, Italy. Her research interests include semantic Web technologies and software engineering, model-driven application for semantic Web, and ontology engineering.

Jeffrey Rose studied computer science at the University of Colorado in Boulder before moving to Switzerland to continue with a Ph.D. at the University of Lugano. He is interested in the democratization of information and the ongoing evolution of the Internet. His current area of research is in creating intelligent peer-to-peer networks that build connections between information and people.

Alberto Sillitti is an assistant professor at the Free University of Bolzano-Bozen, Italy. He received his Ph.D. in Electrical and Computer Engineering from the University of Genoa, Italy in 2005 and he is a professional engineer. His research interests include software engineering, component-based software engineering, integration and measurement of Web services, agile methods, and open source development. He is involved in several Italian and EU-funded projects in these areas.

Harry M. Sneed earned his Master of Information Science from the University of Maryland in 1969 and is highly respected as one of the leading technology and tool experts, specializing in supporting companies to carry their existing application to the next level of technology. He is presently with the Case Consult GmbH, Germany, where he is the technical director of Software Engineering Services. He has made numerous contributions to central areas of software engineering, such as maintenance, metrics, reengineering, program comprehension, and Web evolution and has served as general chair, program chair, steering committee member, and program committee member of the major conferences in these areas. He has written 15 books and more than 160 technical articles. He has personally developed more than 60 software tools and has taken part in more than 40 software projects. He now teaches at six universities: Passau, Regensburg, and Koblenz in Germany, Budapest and Szeged in Hungary, and Benevento in Italy.

Giancarlo Succi is a professor at the Free University of Bolzano-Bozen, Italy, where he directs the Center for Applied Software Engineering. Past positions include professor at the University of Alberta, Edmonton, Alberta, Canada, associate professor at the University of Calgary, Alberta and assistant professor at the University of Trento, Italy. He is a Fulbright Scholar. His research interests involve multiple areas of software engineering, including open source development, agile methodologies, experimental software engineering, software engineering over the Internet, software product lines and software reuse. He has written more than 150 papers published in international journals, books, and conferences, and is editor of four books. He is chair and co-chair of several international conferences and workshops, member of the editorial board of international journals, and leader of international research networks. Professor Succi is a consultant for several private and public organizations worldwide.

Genny Tortora is a full professor, since 1990, at the University of Salerno, Italy, where she teaches database systems and fundamentals of computer science. In 1998, she was a founding member of the Department of Mathematics and Computer Science, acting as chair until November 2000, when she became dean of the Faculty of Mathematical, Physical and Natural Sciences. Her research interests include software-development environments, visual languages, geographical information systems, and pictorial information systems. She is an author and co-author of several papers published in scientific journals, books, and proceedings of refereed conferences and is co-editor of two books. She is an associate editor and reviewer for international scientific journals. She has been program chair and a program committee member for a number of international conferences. From 1999 to 2003, she was a steering committee member of the IEEE Symposium on Human-Centric Computing Languages and Environments. She is a Senior Member of the IEEE Computer Society.

Maurizio Tucci received a Laurea degree in Computer Science from the University of Salerno, Italy in 1988. Since 1998, he has been a professor in Computer Science at the University of Salerno, teaching undergraduate courses on programming and graduate courses on interactive systems design. His research interests include formal models and development techniques for visual environments design and implementation, content-based indexing techniques for image database retrieval and tools for software engineering.

Jilles van Gurp is a research engineer at the Nokia Research Center in Helsinki, Finland, where he has been involved with research projects related to mobile services and search and is currently working on smart space application-related concepts. His research interests include object-oriented frameworks, software product lines, software variability management, software design erosion, and ubiquitous computing. Van Gurp received a Ph.D. from the University of Groningen, The Netherlands in 2003 and has published a wide range of articles related to these topics. Before joining Nokia in 2005, he was a release manager at GX Creative Online Development, which is a leading content management systems vendor in The Netherlands, and he was a researcher at the University of Groningen and the Blekinge Institute of Technology, Sweden.

Giuseppe Visaggio is a full professor of Software Engineering in the Department of Informatics at the University of Bari, Italy. His present scientific interests cover many areas of software engineering: software quality, empirical software engineering, software production and maintenance based on product lines, component and Web services, knowledge management, and experience factory. In these areas he has published international books and journal and conference papers. He is a member of many program committees of international conferences and is a reviewer for many software engineering journals in the fields of reverse engineering, software comprehension, software maintenance, and software engineering. Until 2003, he was a steering committee member of the International Conference on Software Maintenance (ICSM). He is part of the steering committee of IWPC, CSMR, and RCOST (Research Center on Software Technologies). He is a member of the International Software Engineering Research Network (ISERN), which includes many universities and industries throughout the world.

Timo Wolf is a research assistant at the Technical University of Munich, where he received his diploma in Computer Science in 2003. He is working on his Ph.D. covering the areas of requirements engineering, object-oriented design, tool support, and distributed development.

Printed in the United States
By Bookmasters